D0580781

B A B Y
Names

The
Complete Book Of

Names

Emily Qin

NEW HOLLAND

First published in 2013 by
New Holland Publishers
London • Sydney • Cape Town • Auckland
www.newhollandpublishers.com • www.newholland.com.au

Garfield House 86–88 Edgware Road London W2 2EA United Kingdom
1/66 Gibbes Street Chatswood NSW 2067 Australia
Wembley Square First Floor Solan Road Gardens Cape Town 8001 South Africa
218 Lake Road Northcote Auckland New Zealand

ISBN: 9781780092201

10 9 8 7 6 5 4 3 2 1

Publisher: Fiona Schultz
Senior editor: Simona Hill
Designer: Keisha Galbraith
Production director: Olga Dementiev
Printer: Toppan Leefung Printing Limited

10 9 8 7 6 5 4 3 2 1

Follow New Holland Publishers on
Facebook: www.facebook.com/NewHollandPublishers

Contents

Your name and you

'And ... you are?'

In this simple introduction to a stranger, the answer is your name. Your name, along with the smile on your face and the sound of your voice, becomes part of someone's first impression of you, even if it is likely to be forgotten, with great embarrassment, five minutes later.

Perhaps there won't be a face or a voice in the first impression. Maybe your name, centred and bold, appears as a first impression at the top of your CV.

So, what is your name to you?

Your name is seldom used by friends when they are talking to you, but will often be used when they are talking about you.

Your name is what some spammers may use in the subject line to convince you that they know you, and to offer a fake name in return to imply that you should know them.

A name is a representation of a person. It is a summary of all you know about a person. It is tempting to Google your own name, not just to see what the internet has recorded about you, but to stare at all those same-named doppelgängers in the world.

If you have unpleasant memories of a girl called Erika, meeting another Erika can prove painful, because it isn't always easy to dissect a name from a person. And, when Lula Mae wanted a fresh start in *Breakfast at Tiffany's*, she became a new person by becoming Holly.

Different people will call you different names. The variation symbolises the bond between you. Close friends tend to shorten first names or make up nicknames for each other. Politicians, with the rare mayoral exception, will be known to the public by their last names, or full names. But if your mother calls you by your full name, she is most likely not best pleased.

The act of giving a name symbolises the forming of a bond. That is why we give our anything from computers to pets names

We pass our surnames onto our children, and gift them with at least one other.

This book, I hope, will inspire you in the choosing of the gift.

The anatomy of a name

If a name is a representation, and the giving of a name is the forming of a bond, then what is a name before it is given? What are the names printed in this book, waiting to be owned?

To understand something, we can always try taking it apart before putting it all back together again. Let us take the name, then, and peel it down, layer by layer.

Sound

At the surface, just like any other word, a name is a collection of symbols that make up a sound. This, of course, gives us room to spell usual names in unusual ways. More importantly, sounds are not neutral. Which sounds more like an elegant type of bird carving: grolpurna or kib? Both are words with no meaning, but the collection of rounder sounds makes grolpurna a less likely candidate for something elegant. The shorter and sharper kib seems a better choice.

When it comes to names, we can ask very similar questions. Which sounds more like a tomboy: Matilda or Brooke?

Culture

Most names aren't simply a collection of sounds that exist in a vacuum. There are always associations with those who have owned the name and own it still, real and fictional.

For Matilda, we may associate the name with the genius girl created by Roald Dahl, or a slight variation in the girl from *Leon*. And for Brooke, maybe Brooke Shields springs to mind.

Our name associations and inclinations are also affected by fashion. William and George, for example, have been steady in their popularity. Macaulay is much more likely to be a boy who was born ten years ago than ten months ago. Rocco, on the other hand, is most likely to be younger than ten.

Additionally we may perceive Vladimir to be a boy of Russian descent, and Mohamed as one who is not, in the same way that Siobhan, on paper, appears to be an Irish girl, and Usha does not.

Meaning

For names such as Joy and Grace, the meaning is clear. However, for others, it can be bonus. Megan is a pearl, but Macy is a weapon. Eric is a ruler, and not the measuring kind, while Ethan is strong and enduring.

The hidden meaning of a name may not make as much difference to a person's day-to-day life as the sound of the name and how the name is embedded in culture, but it can be a buried treasure.

For and against unusual names

It's a delicate balance. A popular name, portrayed in a less flattering light, is a common name. After all, 14 per cent of all babies born in the UK in 2011 took on a name from the top 10 list. Yet an usual name takes a lot of character to pull off. Not many can live up to a name such as Sage Moonblood (courtesy of Sylvester Stallone and Sasha Czack) or Diva Muffin (thanks to Frank and Gail Zappa).

So what do we do? Well…

The joy of having a more common name is:
• Being just another Charlie in the class (in danger of being either renamed Charles or Charlie B for easier identification)
• Being able to buy one of those key rings with your name on it at a service station
• Being addressed by the right name in emails and on coffee cups (with a few exceptions of 'hi Carlie')

The fun of having a very unusual name is:
• You are the one and only Cairo in the whole school, and you are different, and special
• You are old friends with the following question: how comes you're Cairo?
• You are ready for stardom, because who needs a stage name when your real name is already that?
Some celebrities like giving their children unusual names, naming them after fruits, places and Superman, because they are special children. But back in the days, Robbie and Adele were never one-of-a-kind names. You don't have to have a name that no one else has to truly make a name your own.

Sound
Making up a new name
Not all names will have all three components of sound, culture and meaning. There will be names that are made-up, and, of course, this book won't contain those names. It can tell you what to avoid, and warn you that someone else has already been there, done that.

Girls' names with '-a' or '-ie / -y' endings, such as Olivia and Sophie, tend to sound pretty and feminine. Contrast this with names such as Scarlett and Madison. These sound bold and modern. By mixing the '-a' or '-ie/-y' ending with something short and sharp, you can form a name that is modern yet feminine, like Fifi or Lexa. Other feminine-sounding endings include '-ley/leah/leigh' and 'lyn'.

Looking at more traditional names can also help you find a name to twist and update into something new.

Ways of updating an existing name
The name Alivia appears in the list of already-in-use names in the UK, with a striking resemblance to the more traditional Olivia. Perhaps it references a character from Robert Jordan's *Wheel of Time* series, or perhaps it is an independent vowel swap to make a more familiar name new again. Similarly, it is possibly to swap the first consonant in the name. Both are commonly done with names for girls.

Culture
Popular names of 2011
The Office of National Statistics create a ranking of baby names from the analysis of registered births in England and Wales. Similarly, the General Register Office of Scotland and the Northern Ireland Statistics and Research Agency, create their own.

The top 10 ranking for 2011 show the latest available rankings.

GIRLS

Top 10 for England	Top 10 for Wales	Top 10 for Scotland	Top 10 for Northern Ireland
Amelia	Lily	Sophie	Sophie
Olivia	Amelia	Lily	Grace
Lily	Ava	Ava	Emily
Jessica	Ruby	Olivia	Sophia
Emily	Olivia	Emily	Lily
Sophie	Seren	Lucy	Lucy
Grace	Emily	Isla	Jessica
Ruby	Ella	Jessica	Chloe
Ava	Mia	Chloe	Eva
Isabella	Megan	Ellie	Olivia

Boys

Top 10 for England	Top 10 for Wales	Top 10 for Scotland	Top 10 for Northern Ireland
Harry	Oliver	Jack	Jack
Oliver	Jack	Lewis	James
Jack	Jacob	James	Matthew
Charlie	Riley	Logan	Ethan
Alfie	Ethan	Ethan	Daniel
Thomas	Alfie	Daniel	Harry
James	Harry	Ryan	Ryan
Jacob	Dylan	Alexander	Charlie
Joshua	Thomas	Harry	Conor
William	Charlie	Aaron	Thomas

Apart from paying attention to trends (to join in, to go against or to steer through a middle path), we will explore some other ways to find a fitting name.

Naming by the month of birth

Some people choose names to mark the time of birth, and although February won't make it onto a list of popular names, the months of April, May and June all have a fair share of girls named after them.

Looking at the mythology behind these months offer some alternatives.

January: named after Janus, the Roman god of sunsets and sunrises, of endings and beginnings
Other associated names: Jana, Dianus, Diana, Carmen (the feast day for the goddess Carmenta, of prophecy and childbirth, is in January)
February: named after the purification ritual Februa, linked to the Lupercalia festival
Other associated names: Lupa
March: named after Mars, the Roman god of war
Other associated names: Lucina (mother of Mars), Luna (a festival for the moon goddess falls at the end of March)
April: **may be named after Aphrilis, the month of Aphrodites**
Other associated names: Venus, Cybele (a festival for the Great Mother goddess falls in April)
May: named after Maia, the Roman goddess of spring and growth
Other associated names: Flora (the festival Floralia falls in May), Damara
June: named after the Roman goddess Juno
Other associated names: Regina, Flora (the festival Floralia falls in May)
July: named after Julius Caesar
Other associated names: Apollo (his games are held in July)
August: named after Augustus Caesar
Other associated names: Diana (her feast day falls on the August full moon)
September: named from the number seven
Other associated names: Latona (mother of Apollo is honoured this month)
October: (here's where it gets predictable) named from the number eight
November: named from the number nine
December: named from the number ten

Teresa / Terry (meaning 'late summer') is appropriate for children born in July and August.

Sadly, there are few names associated with the months in the latter part of the year, but there are also more subtle ways to name a child according to the month of birth.

Birthstones

Bearing your birthstone was thought to bring good luck to your life. As gemstones such as ruby and pearl already make good names, we can take inspiration from this and the symbolic meaning of each stone.

January: Garnet
February: Amethyst
March: Aquamarine
April: Diamond
May: Emerald
June: Pearl (purity, love)
July: Ruby
August: Peridot
September: Sapphire
October: Opal
November: Topaz
December: Turquoise

Interlude: these precious things…
Other gems to consider include:

Amber
Coral
Jade
Jasper

Birth flowers

Lily, Poppy, Daisy, Rose. These flower names have been gaining popularity over the past few years. Maybe it's because celebrities such as Beyoncé and Jay Z named their daughter Blue Ivy Carter. Perhaps it's the appearance of names such as Lily, Pansy and Lavender in the *Harry Potter* series, and Primrose and Rue in *The Hunger Games*.

Just like birthstones, there are birth flowers, and some make better names than others. They also have a deeper layer of meaning

January: Carnation: affection. Snowdrop: hope
February: Violet: faithfulness. Primrose: young love
March: Daffodil: respect, unrequited love
April: Sweet pea: happiness, goodbye. Daisy: innocence, loyalty
May: Lily-of-the-valley: sweetness, purity
June: Rose: love
July: Water lily: purity. Larkspur: joy
August: Poppy: remembrance, imagination. Gladiolus: generosity, love at first sight
September: Aster: love, trust. Morning glory: affection. Forget-me-not: true love, memories
October: Marigold: pain, grief. Calendula: joy
November: Chrysanthemum: happy, cheerful
December: Holly: good will, foresight. Narcissus: self-love

Although most flower names can be adapted into girls' names, only a common species of carnation, the Sweet William, is suitable for a boy.

Interlude: a rose by any other name...

Some others to consider?

Acacia: secret love, elegance
Ambrosia: reciprocated love
Angelica: inspiration
Azalea: take care
Bluebell: constant, humility
Buttercup: riches, cheerful
Camellia: admiration, perfection
Cherry blossom: gentleness, kindness
Clover: good luck
Dahlia: elegance
Daphne: glory
Freesia: trust
Fuchsia: good taste
Gillyflower: affection, beauty
Hazel: reconciliation
Heather: protection, luck
Iris: faith, wisdom

Ivy: fidelity, friendship
Jasmine: modesty, grace
Laurel: glory, ambition
Lavender: constancy, devotion
Lilac: first love
Lupine: always happy
Magnolia: sweetness, nobility
Olive: peace
Peach blossom: generosity, longevity
Rosemary: loyalty, remembrance
Tulip: caring, love
Veronica: faithful
Water willow: freedom
Zinnia: friendship, lasting love

Star signs and elements

Air signs

Names of wind and air: **Anil/Anila, Aura, Erion, Kari, Keanu, Rabi/Rabiah, Saba, Sefarina**

Aquarius
January 20–February 18

The water-carrier (and river-pourer)
River names: **Avon, Douglas, Jordan, Kelvin, Olsa, Reno, Rio, Sabrina, Tamina, Tina**

Gemini
May 2–June 20

The twins
Twin names: **Jacob, Kehinde, Linnea, Remus, Taiyewo/Taiyo, Tamsin, Thomas**

Libra
September 23–October 22

The scales (of balance and justice)
Balance names: **Adel, Adil/Adila, Artin, Dexter, Hamsa/Hamse, Harmony, Justin/Justine, Zed/Zedekiah**

Gemini   Libra   Aquarius

Earth signs

Names of land and earth: **Adam, Adana, Avani, Brent, Bryn, Demetrius, Gaia, Mahee/Mahi, Tierra**

Taurus
April 20–May 20

The bull
Bull names: **Bevis, Devine, Damona, Maha, Nandi, Oguzhan, Rohini**

Virgo
August 23–September 22

The virgin maiden
Pure names: **Adara, Afif, Agnes, Bianca, Catherine/Catlin, Cora, Kalifa, Katrina, Safi/Safia, Zaki/Zakiya**

Capricorn
December 22–January 19

The sea goat
Goat names: **Aja, Awa, Giles, Jael/Yael, Lamara/Lamarr, Marina, Marisa, Murphy**

Taurus   Virgo   Capricorn

Fire signs

Names of flame and fire: **Aden, Aidan, Blaise, Brenton, Keegan, Kenna/Kenneth, Mackenzie, Uri**

Ariel
March 21–April 19

The ram
Ram names: **Meesha, Rachel/Raquelle, Ray**

Leo
July 23–August 22

The Lion
Lion names: **Abbas, Aria, Ariel, Conlan, Dillon, Leandra, Leo/Leona, Saina, Usama**

Sagittarius
November 22–December 21

The archer
Archer names: **Arash, Fletcher, Gwendolen, Khamani, Kyler, Seth, Tejan**

Aries   Leo   Sagittarius

Water signs

Names of waves and water: **Brenna, Brooke, Irvin, Naida/Naia, Nix/Nixie, Tallulah, Trent, Yara**

Pisces
February 19–March 20

The fish
Fish names: **Braden, Dagan, Meera, Rudyard**

Cancer
June 21–July 22

The crab
Crab names: sadly, nothing to see here… but for gentle-meaning names, you can consider **Dalia, Gareth, Meegan**

Scorpio
October 23–November 21

The scorpion and the eagle
Eagle names: **Adler, Ari, Arnold, Joshan, Nasar, Peta**

Cancer   Scorpio   Pisces

Naming by the day of birth

Monday's child is fair of face... and can also be named after the moon: a nod to the special day of birth. Although the associated names are more limited than doing so by month, it can provide more inspiration for those born between October and December.

Monday: day of the Moon
Other associated names: Artemis, Badr/Bader, Celina/Selene/Selena, Chand, Chandra, Cynthia, Diana, Luciana, Luna, Mahina
Tuesday: day of Tiw, the Norse god of justice and combat
Other associated names: Tyr/Tyrell
Wednesday: day of Woden, or Odin, and previously day of Mercury, the Roman god of travel and trade
Other associated names: Hermia/Hermione, Sigmund
Thursday: day of Thor, the Norse god of thunder, and previously day of Jupiter, or Jove
Other associated names: Arthur, Jovan/Jove, Julia/Juliana/Juliette, Julian/Julius, Thorald, Thoreau, Tor, Tova, Tyra,
Friday: day of Frigg and Freya, Norse goddess and wife of Odin, and previously day of Venus, the Roman goddess of love
Other associated names: Freya, Venus
Saturday: day of Saturn
Other associated names: Kwame, Shani
Sunday: day of the Sun
Other associated names: Aodh/Aiden, Arun, Cymbeline, Dinesh, Elaine/Eleanor/Elena/Ellen, Idalia, Soleil

Name days
Many European countries celebrate name days in addition to birth dates, traditionally feast days for saints. You can find the dates to remember at the back of the book, with the grand list of names. These are included in the entries whenever the name has a corresponding name day.

High-flying names

In 2008, Professor Richard Wiseman (at the University of Hertfordshire) studied the perception of names in the Name Experiment for his book, *Quirkology*. It showed, among other things, that positive-sounding initials correlated with longer life, and that people had a strong perception of whether certain names are lucky, successful or attractive.

Names associated with royalty (which we shall explore in pages to follow) are perceived as more intelligent.

Those to score high in his study, in which more than 6000 people voted, include the following names:

Successful   Lucky

GIRLS	BOYS	GIRLS	BOYS
Elizabeth	James	Lucy	Jack
Caroline	Richard	Katie	Chris
Helen	Michael	Lisa	Ryan
Olivia	William	Sophie	Peter
Amanda	Andrew	Emma	James
Karen	Mark	Julie	Stephen
Sarah	Robert	Emily	Michael
Rachel	David	Heather	Lewis
Ann	John	Rachel	David
Laura	George	Grace	Ian

Attractive

GIRLS		BOYS	
Sophie	Sarah	Ryan	Lewis
Rachel	Grace	James	Andrew
Olivia	Emily	Jack	Mark
Karen	Amanda	Chris	David
Katie	Heather	Michael	Ian

Fit for royalty

There are only a certain number of names that are repeatedly associated with the English and British kings and queens. These are all names that follow a long tradition.

'Harry' has taken the top spot in England (and has made it to the top 10 in other parts of the UK), so we can also explore the variant forms of these other traditional names.

GIRLS

Anne (Annie, Nana, Nancy, Nina)

Catherine (Cat, Cathy, Cassie, Kit, Kitty)

Eleanor (Ella, Ellie, Nell, Nelly, Nora)

Elizabeth (Bettie, Beth, Betsy, Elise, Eliza, Elsie, Liz, Lizzie, Lisa, Lisbeth, Libby)

Isabella (Belle, Bella, Izzy)

Margaret (Daisy, Greta, Madge, Maggie, Maisy, Marge, Margery, Margo, Molly, Peggy, Rita)

Mary (Mae, Mimi, Molly, Polly)

Matilda (Mattie, Maud, Patty, Tilda, Tilly)

Philippa (Pippa)

Victoria (Vic, Vickie)

Also consider: Alexandra (Alex, Alexa, Ali, Elena, Lexie, Lisandra, Sandra, Sandy, Sasha), Caroline (Carrie, Carly, Carlotta, Carol, Karla, Lina), Charlotte (Carly, Charlie, Cheryl, Lola, Lotta, Lottie, Sherry), Sophia (Sonia)

BOYS

Albert (Al, Bert, Bertie)

Charles (Charlie, Chaz)

Edmund (Ed, Eddie, Ned, Ted, Teddy)

Edward (Ed, Eddie, Ned, Ted, Teddy)

George (Dod, Doddie, Georgie)

John (Jack)

Henry (Hal, Harry)

Richard (Dick, Rick, Rich, Richie)

Stephen (Steve, Stevie)

William (Bill, Billie, Will, Willie)

Also consider: Alfred (Alf, Alfie), Arthur (Art, Artie), Augustus (Gus, Gussie), David (Dave, Davie), Frederick (Fred, Freddie, Rick, Ricky), Louis (Lou, Louie)

Celebrities

This is a list of people who have made it, and the names that they carried into success. Naming a child after a celebrity is, perhaps, a tribute. It is also a way of wishing a child the same success. One thing to bear in mind though, is that it is very difficult to become the one: your child will be the so-and-so named after the so-and-so.

GIRLS

Audrey	Jean
Ava	Janet
Bette	Judy
Barbara	Lauren
Claudette	Lillian
Elizabeth	Mae
Gene	Marilyn
Ginger	Marlene
Gloria	Mary
Grace	Norma
Greta	Rita
Ingrid	Shirley
Katharine	Sophia
Joan	Vivien

BOYS

Burt	Laurence
Buster	Marlon
Cary	Orson
Charlton	Spencer
Clark	Tyrone
Fred	
Gary	
Gregory	
Henry	
Howard	
Humphrey	
James	
John	
Kirk	

The golden age of Hollywood
Greta? Garbo. Marlon? Brando. These names from Hollywood's bygone era have retained a certain glamour about them.

Most powerful celebrities of 2012

Fresh from the Forbes list of celebrity power ranking: these are a selection of the big names of 2012. And yes, Kanye, Beyoncé and Oprah made it too, though their names are rather unusual.

GIRLS		BOYS	
Adele	Katy	Alec	Rafael
Angelina	Kristen	Ashton	Roger
Britney	Julia	Ben	Ryan
Cameron	Rihanna	Brad	Seth
Charlize	Serena	David	Steven
Ellen	Sofia	Hugh	Tom
Eva	Taylor	Justin	Taylor
Jennifer		Leonardo	Tyler
Kim		Paul	

Other ways to name

Characters from games, books, comics, films and TV

Aerith, Eowyn and **Nyssa**: none of these are traditional names, yet all have been used, repeatedly, in the UK.

Place names

Persia, Texas and **Sicily**: whether it is the name of a country, a city, a village or a river, place names are now becoming the staple of people's names.

Surnames

Adison, Benton and **Brice**: surnames are constantly shifting into first name usage, particularly for boys.

For boys, footballers are also popular choices to be named after, whether it is from first names or surnames. **Beckham, Pele, Rivaldo, Ronaldo, Ronaldinho, Rooney, Zinedine, Zidane** and **Zico** all appear in the readily-used list of names for the UK.

Naming twins

It may be a tradition from the times of Romulus and Remus, the founders of Rome, but there is a tendency for twins to be given names starting with the same letter, ending in a rhyme, or both. Emma and Ella. Taylor and Tyler. Jayden and Jordan. Like being given matching clothes, sometimes twins are given matching names – except names stick around much longer.

There are also more subtle ways of linking the two names. Anagrams, for example. Diana and Nadia, Anita and Tania, Jason and Sonja, Eliott and Lottie: these are some that are less repetitive in terms of sound, unlike Dylan and Lynda, or Tina and Nita, which feel a bit more like tongue-twisters. If you choose to do this, please bear in mind that anagrams have been and still are inspirations for pseudonyms and pen names. Maybe Diana will one day be a name that Nadia wishes to claim.

Each twin is an individual, and being given a different-sounding name from the other can help others to remember that. Having said that, as the two will often be introduced together, their names should flow well together. Names with consecutive letters can work well, as can including one name with only one syllable. Just look at some famous duos: Ben and Jerry; Bonnie and Clyde. Names with some continuity of sound also go well together. This doesn't mean they have to alliterate or rhyme. They simply roll on, like Charlie and Lola.

If you do wish to connect the two names in some form, it's possible to choose names that both come from flower names, such as Lily and Rose; names that both come from Greek origins, such as Sebastian and Theo, or names that mean the same thing from two different roots, such as Olive and Zeta. It is also possible to choose names that mean similar things, like happy and lucky. We will explore these in the next section.

Meanings

Here you will find a selection of names with certain popular meanings buried within them. 'Happy, lucky and blessed', for example, will offer some names to choose from.

Happy, lucky and blessed

GIRLS

Aida Italian: happy
Alaia Basque: happy
Alisha/Aliza Hebrew: happiness, joy
Allegra Italian: happy, lively
Anoosha Arabic: delighted, happy
Bea/Beatrice Latin: blessed
Falisha Arabic: happiness
Felicia/Felicity Latin: happy, lucky
Hana Arabic: happiness
Hilary/Illaria Latin: cheerful, happy
Latisha Latin: happiness
Lowena Cornish: joy, bliss
Raima Arabic: happiness
Shriya Sanskrit: happiness, prosperity
Suranne Sanskrit: happiness, delight

BOYS

Asher/Osher Hebrew: happy, blessing
Ben/Benedict Latin: blessed
Bhavik Sanskrit: righteous, happy
Boruch Hebrew: blessed
Cai/Gaius possibly Latin: rejoice
Charalambos Greek: shine from happiness
Dhanyal Sanskrit: fortunate, healthy, rich, blessed
Dziugas Lithuanian: happy, jolly
Faustas Latin: favourable, fortunate, lucky
Felix Latin: happy, lucky
Harsh Hindi: cheerful, happy
Isaac Hebrew: he will laugh
Khuram Urdu: happy, prosperous
Mufaro Shona: happy, joyful man
Said Arabic: happy, lucky

Future, hope and dreams

GIRLS

Aislin Irish Gaelic: dream, vision
Amani Arabic: wishes, aspiration
Amila Arabic: hopeful
Ashia Arabic: life, hope
Dilek Turkish: wish, desire
Heela Pashto: hope, wish
Hulya Turkish: daydream
Maram Arabic: aspiration, wish, desire
Mona Arabic: wish, desire
Nadia/Nadine Greek: hope
Nisha Sanskrit: night, dream, vision
Roya Persian: dream, premonition
Sapna Sanskrit, Latvian and Lithuanian: dream
Tamana Arabic: to wish, to hope
Vilte Lithuanian: people of hope

BOYS

Amal Arabic: hope
Arman Persian: desire, longing
Ashish Sanskrit: blessing, prayer, wish
Bhavin Sanskrit: future
Exauce French: to fulfil a wish
Het Sanskrit: justification, purpose
Manas Sanskrit: intelligence, thought, desire
Murad Arabic: desire, wish, idea, purpose
Omed Persian: hope
Paras Sanskrit: beyond, in the future
Remel Hungarian: to hope
Renato Latin: reborn
Rohat Sanskrit: rising, ascending, growing
Umut Turkish: hope
William Old German: will, desire

Riches, prosperity and long life

GIRLS

Afia Arabic: healthy, beautiful
Aisha Arabic: vivacious, prosperous
Aishwarya Sanskrit: wealth
Ashira Hebrew: wealthy
Aysegul Turkish: prosperous rose, blooming rose
Ciana Irish Gaelic: long, enduring
Daria Persian: wealthy
Dhanya Sanskrit: fortunate, healthy, rich, blessed

Elodie Old German: other wealth
Eloise Germanic: healthy
Kulsuma Arabic: with chubby, rosy and healthy-looking cheeks
Prisca/Priscilla Latin: old, long lived
Riddhi Hindi: prosperity, wealth
Umaira Arabic: long life
Valentina/Valeria/Valerie Latin: healthy, strong

BOYS

Amir Arabic: full of life, prosperous
Ayush Sanskrit: long life
Darius Persian: wealthy
Dhanish Sanskrit: rich man, king of wealth
Ethan Hebrew: strong, long-lived
Feroz Persian: victorious, triumphant, prosperous
Iqbal Arabic: fortunate, prosperous, thriving
Khush Persian: happy, healthy, gentle, fair
Masud Arabic: happy, prosperous, fortunate

Otis/Otto Old German: riches, wealth
Rafferty Irish Gaelic: wielding prosperity
Siddharth/Siddhartha Sanskrit: successful, prosperous, achieving the goal
Valentine/Valentino Latin: strong, healthy
Yaser Arabic: prosperity, wealth
Yuvan Sanskrit: strong, beautiful, healthy

Kings, queens and noble ones

GIRLS

Adara Arabic: beautiful, noble, chaste

Adelaide Germanic: noble, kind

Alice Germanic: noble

Candace/Candice Cushitic: queen mother

Ethel Old English: noble

Freya Old Norse: noble lady

Maelys Breton: princess

Nabila Arabic: noble

Patricia Latin: patrician, noble

Raeesa Arabic: princess, noble lady

Saorla/Saorlaith Irish Gaelic: freeborn sovereign, noble woman

Sarah Hebrew: princess

Sharifa Arabic: noble, protector

Soraya Persian: princess

Talisa Spanish: noble

BOYS

Adel Persian: righteous, noble

Adonis Greek: lord

Albert Germanic: noble, bright, white

Alfonso Old German: noble and ready

Arthur Celtic: bear king

Aryan Sanskrit: worthy, noble, wise, polite

Cyril Greek: lord

Devraj Sanskrit: king of the gods

Frey Old Norse: lord

Gilbert Old German: noble, bright and famous youth

Karim Arabic: king, generous, noble

Mael Breton: prince

Patrick Latin: patrician, noble

Sultan Arabic: strength, authority

Tiarnan Irish Gaelic: lord, superior

Love, love, love

GIRLS

Adora Greek: gift, beloved
Alvina Arabic: loved one
Amanda Latin: worthy of love
Amee Old French: beloved
Amora Latin: love
Angharad Welsh: more love
Cara Italian: beloved
Carys Welsh: love

Davina Hebrew: beloved
Dilara Persian: beloved
Esma/Esme Old French: loved
Idil Turkish: pure and sincere love
Kerensa Cornish: love
Mabel Latin: worthy of love
Priya Sanskrit: beloved

BOYS

Aziz Arabic: cherished, beloved
Caner Turkish: loved from the heart
Carwyn Welsh: fair love
David Hebrew: beloved
Grady Irish Gaelic: beloved, distinguished
Habib Arabic: beloved, darling, sweetheart
Lennon Irish Gaelic: lover, sweatheart

Levin Old English: beloved friend
Mahbub Arabic: beloved, darling, friend
Milos Polish: love
Pranay Hindi: love
Prem Hindi: love
Priyan Sanskrit: beloved
Thando Ndebele: love
Zvi Hebrew: dear

Beauty, light and all things bright

GIRLS

Aliah Arabic: beautiful
Anwen Welsh: fair
Bella/Belle Latin: beautiful
Cadhla Irish Gaelic: beautiful
Callista Greek: most beautiful
Caoimhe Irish Gaelic: beautiful, gentle
Ceinwen Welsh: elegant and fair
Chandra Arabic: beautiful as the moon

Glenys Welsh: pure, fair, beautiful
Gwen Welsh: fair
Lamia Arabic: bright, shining, splendid
Nia Irish Gaelic: bright, radiant
Phoebe Greek: bright, shining, radiant
Shana Yiddish: beautiful, lovely
Zaina Arabic: beauty

BOYS

Bertan Turkish: beautiful, strong, like the dawn
Caoimhin Irish Gaelic: beautiful, gentle
Cemal Turkish: beautiful face
Dhaval Sanskrit: white, dazzling, handsome
Finan Irish Gaelic: fair
Findlay Irish Gaelic: fair warrior
Gwyn Welsh: fair
Iorwerth Old Welsh: beautiful lord, handsome lord

Jamil Arabic: beautiful
Khush Persian: happy, healthy, gentle, fair
Kunal Sanskrit: a type of bird with beautiful eyes
Mohan Sanskrit: handsome
Shakil Arabic: beautiful, handsome
Wyn Welsh: fair
Yuvan Sanskrit: strong, beautiful, healthy

Power, strength and putting up a fight

GIRLS

Abira Hebrew: strong, brave

Audrey Old English: noble strength

Aziza Arabic: strong, precious, respected, cherished

Bernadette Germanic: brave as a bear

Bree/Bridget Irish Gaelic: power, strength, force

Carolina/Caroline Old German: man, warrior

Charlotte Old German: man, warrior

Emery Germanic: universal power

Erica/Erika Old Norse: eternal ruler, ever powerful

Fianna Irish Gaelic: driving, pursuing, a term for warrior groups

Griselda Germanic: dark battle, stone, grey maiden warrior

Imara Swahili: strong

Nikita Greek: unconquerable

Silan Croatian: strong, powerful

Ulrika Germanic: power

BOYS

Arnold Old German: eagle ruler, eagle power

Balal Sanskrit: power

Conall Irish Gaelic: strong wolf

Eric Old Norse: eternal ruler, ever powerful

Ethan Hebrew: strong, long-lived

Gerard Old German: strong spear, brave spear

Kadir Arabic: powerful, able

Kendrick Old English: king's power

Montgomery Old German: power of man

Orry Old English: power of a wolf

Reginald Old Norse: power of council

Richard Old German: strong, brave king

Roderick Old German: fame and power

Savan Sanskrit: powerful

Vikram Sanskrit: prowess, power, step, stride

Wisdom and brains

GIRLS

Arifa Arabic: intelligent, full of knowledge

Arya Sanskrit: worthy, noble, wise, polite

Athena Greek: wise

Farzana Persian: wise, knowing

Kinza Arabic: intelligent

Mahera Arabic: expert, skilled

Manisha Sanskrit: idea, thought, wisdom

Minerva Latin: mindful, wise

Shannon Gaelic: wise one, little owl

Shruti Sanskrit: word, sound, listening, wisdom

Sophia/Sophie Greek: wisdom

Sufia Arabic: intellectual

Sunita Sanskrit: wisdom, prudence

Vidya Sanskrit: knowledge

Zakiya Arabic: bright, clever

BOYS

Alim Arabic: scholar

Arif Arabic: intelligent, full of knowledge

Berzan Kurdish: wise man

Eimantas Lithuanian: go smart, be clever, be intelligent

Farzan Persian: wise, learned

Hakim Arabic: doctor, philosopher, sage

Kavi Sanskrit: wise, intelligent

Labib Arabic: intelligent, wise, prudent

Manish Sanskrit: idea, thought, wisdom

Manu Sanskrit: wise, intelligent, prayer, mankind

Odin Old Norse: fury, frenzy, poetry, mind, inspiration

Przemyslaw Polish: clever, ingenious

Savio Italian: wise

Senan Old Gaelic: wise man

Shaikh Arabic: elder, wise man, chief

Naming checklist

While Sophie is a lovely name, naming a girl Sophie Annabelle Davies would give her the initials S.A.D. – not the best thing to do. And for a girl with the surname Windler, the name Sophie may result in her having a work email address of swindler.

So, here's a basic checklist for disaster prevention …

• Check if anyone well-known has the same name, and if so, make sure that it is fine for your child to carry that association with him/her. If in doubt, provide a more neutral middle name.
• Check all nicknames and diminutive forms of the first name and middle name, and combine it with your surname to make sure that these don't result in any rude or negative-sounding words. It might also be good to avoid puns.
• Check the initials. It doesn't need to be F.U.N., J.O.Y. or W.I.N, but try to avoid anything negative.
• Check the first letter of the first name, then the first letters of the first name and middle name, tacked onto the front and the back of the surname to make sure that you don't end up with something rude or negative here. These are likely to end up as computer log-ins.

Best of luck in trying to find the perfect name. We have provided a list of names that have actually been used in the U.K. without trudging too far back in history (Harthacnut might have been a king of England, but times have changed since then).

Changing names by deed poll

A name doesn't have to be for life. There's nothing stopping you from waking up tomorrow and asking everyone you know to abandon your current first name and call you 'Doctor' (apart from their cooperation).

But if you want a different name on your passport, you will need a deed poll.

A change of name deed isn't nearly as complicated as it sounds, and, although it is possible to pay for one, it is also possible to do it yourself for free, using the following format.

Change of name deed poll
Former name: [insert name to be changed]
Address of residence: [insert address]
I hereby relinquish all use of the former name in full [insert name to be changed], and have adopted for all purposes the name in full [insert new name].
Signed as deed by the above on [insert date] as [insert name to be changed and old signature] and [insert new name and new signature]
In the presence of [insert name, signature and address of 2 witnesses]

The grand list of names

Here you will find a list of names that have been recorded in the UK more times than you can count with one hand in a year, separated into Girls, Boys, and Girls and Boys. You will also find a list of less common names at the back.

Girls' names

a

Aabirah Sindhi: fleeting

Aadila *See* Adila

Aadya Sanskrit (from adya): primal one, the initial reality. One of the 108 names of the Hindu goddess Durga

Aaeesha *See* Aisha

Aafia *See* Afia

Aafreen Hindi: brave, worthy of praise

Aahana Sanskrit (from ahana): dawn

Aahna Sanskrit (from ahna): many days

Aaida *See* Aida

Aaila Turkish: beautiful, like the moon

Aaima Arabic: leader

Aaina Persian: mirror

Aaira Turkish: noble, honourable

Aaisha/Aaishah *See* Aisha

Aaiza *See* Aiza

Aakifah Arabic: devoted in the worship of Allah

Aaleyah/Aali/Aalia/Aaliah/Aaliya/Aaliyah/Aaliyha *See* Aliyah

Aamanee Arabic: good wish

Aamani Hindi: Vasanta (spring) season

Aamena/Aamina/Aamenah *See* Aminah

Aamilah Sindhi: good, righteous

Aamina/Aaminah Arabic: trustworthy. The name of Aminah bint Wahb, mother of prophet Muhammad

Aamira/Aamirah *See* Amira

Aamna/Aamnah *See* Amna

Aania *See* Ania

Aanisah *See* Anisa

Aanya *See* Anya

Aara Persian: adoring, adorable

Aaria *See* Aria

Aarifah *See* Arifa

Aariya *See* Aria

Aarna Sanskrit: river, wave

Aarti Sanskrit (from aratrika): light waved at night in front of an idol. A Hindu religious ritual

Aarushi *See* Arushi

Aarzoo Persian: wish, hope

Aasfa Arabic: guardian

Aashi *See* Ashi

Aashita Hindi: full of hope

Aashna Sanskrit: cloud, stone

Aashvi Sanskrit: horse, mare

Aasia *See* Asia

Aasira Arabic: bond. *See also* Ashira

Aasiya/Aasiyah *See* Asiya

Aaya/Aayah/Aayat *See* Ayah.
See also Aya

Aayushi *See* Ayushi

Aba *See* Yaa

Abbey A diminutive form of Abigail

Abbeygail *See* Abigail

Abbi/Abbie A diminutive form of Abigail

Abbiegail/Abbigail/Abbigale *See* Abigail

Abby A diminutive form of Abigail

Abbygail *See* Abigail

Abeeha *See* Abiha

Abeer Arabic: fragrance

Abeera/Abeerah Arabic: fragrance mix of rose and saffron

Abena/Abenaa Akan: born on Tuesday

Abhinaya Sanskrit (from abhinam): bend or turn towards. A term in Indian dance that means the art of expression

Abi A diminutive form of Abigail

Abia/Abiah Hebrew: great, god is my father

Abida/Abidah Arabic: worshipper of god

Abigael/Abigail/Abigaile/ Abigale/Abigayle Hebrew: father's joy, fountain of joy. One of the wives of David

Abiha Arabic: her father. The name given by the prophet Muhammad to his daughter Fatima az-Zahra

Abina *See* Abena

Abinaya *See* Abhinaya

Abiola Yoruba: born in honour

Abir/Abira Hebrew: strong, brave. Also creator god in Antioquia mythology

Abirami Sanskrit (from abhirama): pleasant, beautiful

Abisha Hebrew: gift of god

Abisola Yoruba: born to wealth

Abla *See* Abena

Abygail *See* Abigail

Acacia Greek: thorny tree (name from flowers and trees)

Acelya Turkish: a type of *Rhododendron* (name from flowers and trees)

Ada Hebrew: adorn, place an adornment on her. Also a diminutive form of Adelaide

Adaeze Igbo: princess

Adama/Adamma Igbo: beautiful

Adana/Adanna Hebrew: earth

Adara Arabic: beautiful, noble, chaste

Addie A diminutive form of Adelaide and Adeline

Ade *See* Aida

Adeela A diminutive form of Adelaide

Adeena *See* Adina

Adela A diminutive form of Adelaide

Adelaide Old German: noble, kind

Adele A diminutive form of Adelaide

Adelina/Adelinde/Adeline *See* Adelaide

Adelle A diminutive form of Adelaide

Adena *See* Adina

Adenike Yoruba: cherished crown

Adeola Yoruba: crown of honour

Aderinsola Yoruba: bringer of wealth

Adi/Adia *See* Ada

Adiba/Adibah Arabic: refined, well-mannered

Adila/Adilah Arabic: fair, just, righteous

Adina/Adinah Hebrew: noble, gentle. Also Amharic: she has saved

Aditi Sanskrit: boundless, entire, happy. A Hindu sky goddess and celestial mother

Adjoa *See* Adwoa

Adna Hebrew: happiness, pleasure, rejuvenation

Adora Greek: gift, beloved

Adria/Adriana/Adrianna/ Adrianne/Adrienne Latin: from Hadria, a city in Italy

Adrija Sanskrit: red chalk, produced from stones, found in the moutains

Adwoa/Adzo Akan: born on a Monday

Aeeda *See* Aida

Aela Breton: rampart

Aemilia *See* Emily

Aeris/Aerith *See* Eris and Iris. Also the name of Aerith Gainsborough from *Final Fantasy VII* (name created to sound similar to Earth)

Aeryn *See* Erin

Aesha *See* Aisha

Afarin Persian: praise

Afeefah *See* Afifa

Afi *See* Afua

Afia Arabic: healthy, beautiful. *See also* Afua

Afifa/Afifah Arabic: chaste

Afiya/Afiyah Arabic: good health

Afizah Arabic: guardian. Also from Hafiz, ones who know the Qur'an by heart

Afnaan/Afnan Arabic: branches. A surname mentioned in the Qur'an

Afra Arabic: earth coloured, pale red (colour name). *See also* Aphra

Afrah Arabic: happiness

Afreen Arabic: beautiful. Also Persian: lucky

Afrin *See* Afreen. Also a city in Syria (geographical name)

Afsa/Afsar Persian: crown

Afsana Persian: myth

Afsha/Afshan Persian: scattered, sprinkled

Afsheen Arabic: shine like a star

Afua Akan: born on a Friday

Agata/Agatha Greek: good

Agnes/Agnesa/Agnieszka Ancient Greek (from agnós): pure, chaste

Ahana Sanskrit: dawn

Ahlaam/Ahlam Arabic: imaginative, witty, pleasant dream

Aicha *See* Aisha

Aida/Aída/Aidah/Aide/Aidee
Arabic: returning, helper. Also
Italian: happy
Aideen *See* Etain
Aiesha *See* Aisha
Aila/Ailah *See* Ayla. Also a
village in Estonia (geographical
name)
Ailee/Aileen/Aileigh/Ailey *See*
Evelyn
Ailidh/Ailie Gaellic: light
Ailis/Ailish *See* Alice
Ailsa Old Norse: island of Alfsigr
Also an island in Scotland
(geographical name)
Aima/Aime/Aimee/Aimi/Aimie
See Amy
Aina Finnish: always. Also Japanese:
various, including enduring love.
See also Aaina, Aine and Anna
Aine Irish Gaelic (from áine):
splendour, glory, fame. Also the
name of the Irish goddess of
summer and sun
Aini Arabic: beginning, spring
Aira Greek: darnel. Also the name
of hair grass (name from flowers
and trees). Also a city in Japan
(geographical name)
Aisha/A'isha/Aishah Arabic:
vivacious, prosperous. The name
of Aisha bint Abu Bakr, one of
prophet Muhammad's wives
Aishani A name for the Hindu
goddess Durga
Aishat/Aishia *See* Aisha

Aishling *See* Aisling
Aishwarya Sanskrit (from aizvarya):
wealth
Aisla A diminutive form of Aisling
See also Isla
Aislin/Aisling/Aislinn Irish Gaelic
(from aislinge): dream, vision. Also
a type of Irish poem
Aisosa Benin: god is the highest
Aiste Irish Gaelic: special quality,
peculiar
Aisyah *See* Aisha
Aiva *See* Ava
Aiya A diminutive form of Aiyana
Aiyana/Aiyanna Native American:
always in bloom
Aiyla *See* Ayla
Aiysha *See* Aisha
Aiza Arabic: noble. Also Basque
Spanish: rock, cliff
Aja Hindi: goat. *See also* Asia
Ajda *See* Aida
Aji Swahili: swift. Also Japanese:
the prince of the historical Ryukyu
Kingdom. Also the name of a
river in India and a river in Iran
(geographical name). *See also* Ajia
Ajia Arabic: wonderful
Ajoba *See* Adwoa
Ajuni Punjabi: June, without birth
or beginning
Ajwa Arabic: date fruit. Also a dam
in India
Akasha Sanskrit: sky
Akeelah *See* Akilah
Akifah Arabic: devoted

Akilah Arabic: reasonable, intelligent

Aklima Urdu: first step

Akosua Akan: born on a Sunday

Aksa/Aksah Arabic: furthest mosque. Also the name of a mosque in Jerusalem (geographical name)

Akshara/Akshaya Sanskrit (from aksara): letter, syllable

Also Hindi (from akṣaya): everlasting. A name of Brahma, the Hindu creator god

Akshita Sanskrit: water, undecaying, unchanging

Akua/Akuba Akan: born on a Wednesday

Ala A diminutive form of Alice. *See also* Ella

Alaia Arabic: sublime
Also Basque: happy

Alaina *See* Alanna
See also Helen

Alana/Alanah/Alani/Alanis/ Alanna/Alannah Germanic: precious

Alanta *See* Atlanta. Also a town in Lithuania (geographical name)

Alanya Germanic: precious. Also a city in Turkey (geographical name)

Alara Turkish: red decoration

Alarna *See* Alanna

Alaska Aleut: mainland. The name of the US state (geographical name)

Alaw Welsh: melody, water lily (name from flowers and trees)

Alaya/Alayah *See* Alaia

Alayna *See* Alanna

Alba Latin: white. Also Scottish Gaelic: Scotland (geographical name)

Albany Latin: from Alba. Also various place names (geographical name)

Alberta Germanic: noble, bright, white

Alea/Aleah *See* Alia

Aleasha/Alecia *See* Alice

Aleeha *See* Alia

Aleema/Aleemah Arabic: exhalted

Aleen/Aleena Arabic: beautiful

Aleesa/Aleesha *See* Alice

Aleeya/Aleeyah *See* Alia

Aleeza/Aleezah/Aleezay *See* Alice

Aleigha *See* Alia

Aleisha *See* Alice

Alejandra *See* Alexandra

Aleksa A diminutive form of Alexandra

Aleksandra *See* Alexandra

Alena *See* Helen

Alesha/Aleshia/Alesia/Alessa *See* Alice

Alessandra *See* Alexandra

Alessia *See* Alice

Alethea Greek: truth

Alev Turkish: flame

Alex/Alexa A diminutive form of Alexandra

Alexandra/Alexandrea/

Alexandria Greek: defender of men

Alexcia/Alexi/Alexia/Alexus Greek: to help. *See also* Girls and Boys: Alexi

Aleya/Aleyah *See* Alia

Aleyna *See* Alana

Aleysha *See* Alice

Alia/Aliah Arabic: beautiful. *See also* Aliyah and Alya

Aliana A blend of Alia and Anna

Alica/Alice/Alicia/Alicja/Aliesha Germanic: noble

Aliha *See* Alia

Alika Igbo: most beautiful. *See also* Alice

Alima/Alimah Arabic: wise

Alina/Aline Greek: light

Aliona *See* Helen

Alis/Alisa/Aliscia/Alise/Alisha/Alishah Hebrew: happiness, joy *See also* Alica

Alishba/Alishbah Arabic: innocent, pretty

Alishia/Alishya/Alisia/Alison/Alissa/Alissia *See* Alice

Alivia *See also* Olivia

Alix Germanic: noble. Also a diminutive form of Alexandra

Alixandra *See* Alexandra

Aliya/Aliyah Hebrew: rising, exalted

Aliye Turkish: exalted

Aliysha *See* Alica

Aliyyah *See* Aliya

Aliza/Alizah *See* Alisha

Alla *See* Ella

Allana/Allanah/Allannah *See* Alana

Allegra Italian: happy, lively

Allicia *See* Alice

Allie A diminutive form of various names, including Aliza and Alice

Allisha/Allison/Allissa *See* Alice

Alliyah *See* Aliya

Allysha/Allyson/Allyssa *See* Alice

Alma Latin: nourishing, soul

Almaas/Almas Arabic: diamond

Almira Arabic: princess

Althea Greek: healer

Alveena/Alvina Arabic: loved one

Alya Arabic: sky, heaven

Alyce/Alycia/Alyesha/Alys/Alysa/Alyse/Alysha/Alyshia/Alysia/Alyson/Alyssa/Alyssia/Alyx *See* Alice

Ama Akan: born on a Saturnday

Amaal Arabic: hope. *See also* Girls and Boys: Amal

Amaani *See* Amani

Amaara/Amaarah *See* Amara

Amaia Basque: end, resolution

Amaira *See* Ameera

Amaiya/Amaiyah *See* Amaia

Amala Sanskrit: stainless, pure, shining, white

Amalia German: work, industrious Also Hebrew: work of god

Amelia/Amalie/Amalya *See* Amalia

Amana/Amanah Arabic: trust

Amanda Latin: worthy of love

Amandine *See* Amanda

Amanpreet Punjabi: love of peace (Sikh name)

Amany *See* Amani

Amara Latin: everlasting. Also Igbo: grace. Also Amharic: paradise

Amarachi/Amarachukwu Igbo: god's grace

Amarah *See* Amara

Amariah Hebrew: god has said

Amaris Greek: to sparkle, from Amaryllis (name from flowers and trees)

Amarni *See* Amani

Amarpreet Punjabi: immortal love (Sikh name)

Amatullah Arabic: servant of Islam

Amaya/Amayah Sanskrit: free from deceit. Also Native American: beloved daughter. *See also* Amaia

Amba/Ambar Arabic: perfume

Amber (colour name, gemstone name, name from an English word)

Amberleigh A blend of Amber and Leigh

Amberley A combined name of Amber and Kimberly

Ambia A town in the US (geographical name). *See also* Amber

Ambika Sanskrit: mother, good woman, harvest. One of the names of the Hindu goddess Parvati

Ambra *See* Amber

Ambreen/Ambrin Arabic: sky

Ambrosia Greek: food and drink of the gods. *See also* Amrita

Amealia *See* Amelia

Amee Old French: beloved

Ameena/Ameenah Arabic: faithful. *See also* Amina

Ameera/Ameerah *See* Amira

Ameilia *See* Amelia

Ameera/Ameira Arabic: princess

Amel *See* Amal

Amelia/Ameliah/Amelie/ Amelija/Ameliya/Amelle/ Amellia/Amelya Germanic: industrious

Amena *See* Amina

Amera/Amerie *See* Emery

Amethyst (gemstone name, name from an English word)

Amey *See* Amee

Ami/Amia/Amiah *See* Amee

Amie/Amiee *See* Amee

Amiera *See* Ameera and Amira

Amii *See* Amee

Amiira *See* Ameera and Amira

Amila/Amilah Arabic: hopeful

Amilia/Amilie *See* Amelia

Amima Arabic: full, complete

Amina/Aminah/Aminat/Aminata Arabic: safe, secure, protected. The name of Aminah bint Wahb, mother of prophet Muhammad. *See also* Ameena

Amira/Amirah Arabic: adundant treasure. *See also* Ameera

Amisha Sanskrit: gift, beautiful. Also a blend of Ami and Misha

Amity (name from an English

word)

Amiya/Amiyah *See* Ameya

Amma *See* Ama

Ammaarah/Ammara/Ammarah
Arabic: tolerant. *See also* Amara

Ammie *See* Amee

Amna/Amnah Arabic: peace,
beautiful

Amneet *See* Avneeet

Amora Latin (from amor): love

Amour French: love

Amra Arabic: crown. Also Irish
Gaelic (from amrae): wonderful.
See also Girls and Boys: Amran

Amreen Arabic: sky

Amreet/Amreeta/Amrita Sanskrit
(from amrta): immortality, the
nectar that grants immortality.
Also the holy water used in Amrit
Sanskar, a baptism ceremony in
Sikhism. *See also* Ambrosia. *See
also* Girls and Boys: Amrit

Amtul Unknown, possibly from
Amtullah (Arabic: servant of
Allah)

Amy/Amye *See* Amee

Amylee/Amyleigh A blend of Amy
and Lee/Leigh

Amyra *See* Ameera and Amira

An/Ana *See* Ann

Anaaya *See* Anaya

**Anabel/Anabela/Anabella/
Anabelle** A blend of Anna and
Belle. Also possibly from Amabel.
See Mabel.

Anabia Arabic: door of paradise

Anagha Sanskrit: without sin

Anah Hebrew: answer

Anahita The name of Aredvi Sura
Anahita, an Iranian goddess of the
waters, associated with healing and
wisdom

Anaia/Anaiah *See* Anaya

Anais *See* Anne

Anaiya/Anaiyah *See* Anaya

Analeigh A blend of Anna and
Leigh

Analiese/Analise A blend of Anna
and Elise

Anam Arabic: blessings of god

Anamaria A blend of Anna and
Maria

Anamika Sanskrit and Hindi: ring
finger

Ananya Sanskrit: unique,
unswerving

Anashe Shona: with god

**Anastacia/Anastasia/Anastasija/
Anastazja** Greek: resurrection

Anaum Arabic: blessings of Allah

Anaya/Anayah Hebrew: god
answers

Andie A diminutive form of Andrea

Andra/Andreea/Andreia/Andreja
Greek: man. *See also* Girls and
Boys: Andrea

Andriana *See* Adriana

Andzelika *See* Angela

Aneeka *See* Aneeqa

Aneela Persian: innocent girl

Aneeqa Arabic: beautiful

Aneesa/Aneesah/Aneesha *See*

Anisa

Aneira Welsh (possibly from eira): snow

Aneka A diminutive form of Anna

Anesha Greek: pure

Aneta A diminutive form of Anna

Aneya *See* Anya

Anfal Arabic: the spoils of war, named after the eighth chapter of the Qur'an

Angela Greek: messenger of god

Angelica/Angelika/Angelina/ Angeline/Angelique *See* Angela

Angharad Welsh: more love. The name of Angharad Golden-Hand, the love of Peredur, a young knight at King Arthur's court from Welsh mythology

Angie A diminutive form of Angela and Angelica

Ani/Ania/Aniah A diminutive form of Anna

Aniela *See* Angela

Anika A diminutive form of Anna

Anila Sanskrit: wind, air. A Hindu god of the wind

Anina A diminutive form of Anna

Aniqa/Aniqah Arabic: elegant, smart

Anisa/Anisah Arabic (from anees): close friend, companion, friendly, kind

Anise (name from flowers and trees, name from an English word)

Anisha/Anishka *See* Agnes

Anissa Greek: pure, holy

Anita Sanskrit: taken, brought near, implying leader

Aniya/Aniyah *See* Anya

Anja *See* Anna

Anjalee/Anjali A blend of Anja and Lee

Anjana The mother of the Hindu god Hanuman. Also a type of fairy from Cantabrian mythology who are beautiful and do good deeds

Anjelica *See* Angela

Anjolaoluwa Yoruba: enjoying god's blessings

Anjum/Anjuma Arabic: star

Ankita Sanskrit (from agkita): marked, with auspicious marks

Ann/Anna Hebrew: favoured by god

Annabel/Annabell/Annabella/ Annabelle A combined name of Anna and Belle, meaning lovable

Annalee/Annaleigh A combined name of Anna and variations of Leigh

Annaleise/Annalese/Annaliese/ Annalisa/Annalise/Annalyse A combined name of Anna and variations of Lisa

Annam *See* Anam

Annamaria/Annamarie A blend of Anna and Maria

Annastasia *See* Anastasia

Annaya/Annayah *See* Anaya

Anne *See* Ann

Anneka A diminutive form of Anna

Anneli/Annelie A blend of Anne

and Ellie

Anneliese/Annelise A blend of Anne and Elise

Annemarie A blend of Anne and Marie

Annest *See* Agnes

Annette/Anni/Annia A diminutive form of Anna

Annice *See* Agnes

Annie/Annika A diminutive form of Anna

Annis *See* Agnes

Annisa *See* Agnes and Anisa

Anniyah *See* Anya

Annmarie A blend of Ann and Marie

Annum *See* Anam

Annya *See* Anya

Anoosh/Anoosha Arabic: delighted, happy

Anouk/Anousha/Anoushka/ Anouska *See* Ann and Anoosh

Ansa Finnish (from ansio): virtue. Also the name of a Hindu sun god

Anshika Hindi: small particle

Anthea Greek: blossom. A name for the Greek goddess Hera

Anthonia *See* Antonia

Antigone Greek: against birth. The daughter of Oedipus from Greek mythology

Antoinette/Antonella/Antonia/ Antonina Latin: from the Antonius family, most notably that of Marcus Antonius

Anum *See* Anam

Anuoluwapo Yoruba: the mercy of god is great

Anureet Unknown

Anusha/Anushka Hindi: morning star

Anvi Unknown, possibly Sanskrit: to follow, to be guided

Anwen Welsh (from gwyn): fair

Anya Arabic: woman with large eyes. Also a diminuitive form of Anna

Aoibh/Aoibhe/Aoibheann/ Aoibhin/Aoibhinn/Aoife Scottish Gaelic (from aoibhinn): cheerful

Aphra Hebrew: young deer

Apollonia Greek: named after the Greek god Apollo

April/Apryl (name from an English word)

Aqeela/Aqeelah Arabic: the best. *See also* Akilah

Aqsa *See* Aksa

Araba *See* Abena

Arabella/Arabelle Latin: answered prayer. *See also* Annabel

Aramide Yoruba: my people have arrived

Araminta Unknown, possibly created by William Congreve for *The Old Bachelor*

Araya Armenian (from arkṣay): king

Archana Sanskrit: honouring, praising. A Hindu ritual for guidance and blessing

Arden Celtic: high (shifted from surname usage)

Areeba/Areebah *See* Ariba

Areej Arabic: fragrance, aroma

Areena Arabic: bird song. *See also* Girls and Boys: Areen

Areesa/Areesha *See* Arisa

Arella The nickname of the character Angela Roth from the *DC Universe*. *See also* Aurelia

Arfa Arabic: exalted, high

Ariadna/Ariadne Greek: holy. The daughter of King Minos in Greek mythology who helped Theseus escape the Minotaur's labyrinth

Ariah Hebrew: lioness. Also Italian: air, a song accompanying a solo voice in the musical terms. *See also* Girls and Boys: Aria

Ariam Amharic: heaven

Ariana/Ariane/Arianna/ Arianne Greek: an area in ancient Afghanistan. *See also* Girls and Boys: Arian

Arianwen Welsh: pale silver

Ariba/Aribah Arabic: wise

Ariela/Ariella/Arielle Hebrew: lion of god. *See also* Girls and Boys: Ariel

Arifa/Arifah Arabic (from aref): intelligent, full of knowledge

Arij *See* Areej

Arina *See* Areena

Arisa/Arisha/Arissa *See* Irina

Ariya/Ariyah *See* Ariah

Ariyana *See* Ariana

Arla/Arlaith *See* Orlaith

Aroob/Arooj Persian: wife who loves her husband

Aroosa Arabic: bride

Aroosh/Aroush Arabic: angel of heaven

Arrabella *See* Arabella

Arshiya Persian: throne. Also possible Sanskrit (from arghya): honey. *See also* Girls and Boys: Arshia

Arshpreet Punjabi: love of the sky (Sikh name)

Artemis Greek: bear. The Greek goddess of hunting, wild animals and the moon

Arub Arabic: loving to her husband

Arusa Sanskrit: red, day, sun

Arushi Sanskrit: red mare, dawn

Arwa/Arwaa Arabic: satisfied, goat or dear

Arwen *See* Awen. Also Tolkien's Sindarin: noble maiden, the name of Arwen Undómiel

Aryana/Aryanna *See* Ariana

Arzoo/Arzu Persian: desire

Aseel/Asel Arabic: smooth, pure, noble

Ashalina Arabic: sweet, shy

Ashani Sanskrit (from azani): thunderbolt

Ashante/Ashanti A region of Akanland where the Ashante people live (geographical name). Also the name of the singer Ashanti

Asheka Unknown, possibly Sanskrit (from aseka): sprinkling, watering

Asherah Hebrew: a Semetic fertility goddess

Ashi Dzongkha: princess, lady. Also Avestan: attained

Ashia Arabic: life, hope. *See also* Aisha

Ashira Hebrew: wealthy. *See* Asherah

Ashlea/Ashleen/Ashli/Ashlie Old English (aesc and leah): ash clearing (shifted from surname usage). *See also* Girls and Boys: Ashley

Ashlin/Ashling/Ashlyn/Ashlynn *See* Ashli and Aisling

Ashna *See* Aashna

Ashpreet Punjabi: love of ash (Sikh name)

Ashvika Sanskrit (from azvika): little mare

Ashwini Sanskrit (from azvini): the stars that form the head of Aries. Also from Ashvin, the seventh month of the Hindu calendar

Asia/Asiah Greek: sunrise (geographical name)

Asiya/Asiyah Arabic: nurse. The name of Asiya bint Muzahim, the pious wife of Fir'awn

Asli Arabic: pure, original

Asma/Asmaa Arabic: exalted, sublime

Asmin *See* Jamine

Asmita/Asmitha Sanskrit (from asmita): pride

Asra Arabic: travel by night

Assia *See* Asia

Aston Old English: east town (geographical name, shifted from surname usage)

Astra Greek: star

Astrid Old Norse: beautiful god

Asya A diminutive form of Anastasia. Also a form of the Turkish name Asiye (unknown, possibly Turkish: rebel)

Atalanta Greek: equal in weight. The name of a huntress from Greek mythology

Atene *See* Athena

Athalia Hebrew: god is exalted. The queen consort to King Jehoram

Athea Irish Gaelic: mountain ford. The name of a village in Ireland (geographical name)

Athena/Athene/Athina Greek: wise. The Greek goddess of wisdom and war

Atia *See* Atiya

Atifa Arabic: compassion, sympathy

Atika Arabic: generous

Atiya/Atiyah/Atiyyah Arabic: gift

Atlanta The capital of the state of Georgia in the US (geographical name)

Attiya *See* Atiya

Aubree French: ruler of elves. *See also* Girls and Boys: Aubrey

Audrey Old English: noble strength

Augusta/Auguste Latin: great

Aukse Lithuanian: golden

Aura Latin: wind. The goddess of

wind in Roman mythology

Aurelia/Aurelie Latin: golden

Aurora Latin: dawn. The goddess of dawn in Roman mythology

Austeja Lithuanian: bee goddess in Lithuanian mythology

Autumn (name from an English word)

Ava Persian: pleasant sound, music. *See also* Eve

Avaani *See* Avani

Avah *See* Ava

Avalon Welsh (from afal): apple. The name of the mythical island where King Arthur is taken to recover from his fight against Mordred

Avani Sanskrit: ground, earth

Avia *See* Abia

Aviana Unknown, possibly Latin (from avis): bird

Avie A diminutive form of Avigail

Avigail *See* Abigail

Avital Hebrew: night dew is my father. Also from Abital, the fifth wife of King David

Aviva Hebrew: spring

Avleen Punjabi: unknown, possibly engrossed in god (Sikh name)

Avneet Punjabi: unknown, possibly always of god (Sikh name). Also possibly from Avner (Hebrew: father of light)

Avni Turkish: unknown, possibly helper. *See also* Avani

Avril *See* April

Awa *See* Eve

Awel Welsh: breeze

Awen Welsh: poetic inspiration, muse

Awo *See* Ama

Aya German: sword. Also Hebrew: bird, flying. Also Japanese: various, including colours, truth, order, writing. *See also* Ayaat

Ayaan/Ayaana *See* Ayanna

Ayaat/Ayah Arabic: evidence, sign, a term for verses in the Qur'an. *See also* Aya

Ayala Hebrew: deer

Ayan Arabic: lucky

Ayana Oromia: beautiful flower. *See also* Ayanna

Ayanda Yoruba: growing family

Ayanna Swahili: beautiful flower

Ayasha Cheyenne: little one. *See also* Aisha

Ayat *See* Ayaat

Ayda *See* Aida

Ayeda/Ayeeda *See* Aida

Ayeesha/Ayeisha/Ayesha/ Ayeshah/Ayeshia/Ayisha/ Ayishah *See* Aisha

Ayla Hebrew: oak tree (name from flowers and trees). *See also* Ayala

Aylin Turkish: halo around the moon

Aylish/Aylisha *See* Alice

Ayra Arabic: respectable

Ayse *See* Aisha

Aysegul Turkish (from Ayse and Gul): prosperous rose, blooming rose

Aysha/Ayshah/Aysia *See* Aisha

Ayushi Sanskrit (from ayus): long life

Ayva *See* Ava

Ayza *See* Aiza

Azaria Hebrew: god has helped

Aziza/Azizah Arabic (from azza): strong, precious, respected, cherished

Azka Arabic: generous

Azra/Azraa Arabic: maiden

Azuba/Azubah Hebrew: assisted

Azura Spanish: sky blue (colour name)

Azure (name from an English word). *See also* Azura

b

Bahar/Bahara Persian: spring

Bahja Arabic: splendour

Bakhtawar Arabic: lucky

Balqis *See* Bilqis

Bana Hindi: descendants of King Banasur

Banita Hindi: woman

Banu Persian: lady, princess, sister

Barbara/Barbora Greek: foreign

Bareerah Arabic: pious

Basma/Basmah Arabic: smile

Batool Arabic: true worshipper

Batoul/Batul Arabic: pure, chaste

Batsheva Hebrew: daughter of the oath. The mother of Solomon from the Old Testament

Bayan Arabic: eloquent

Baylea/Baylie Old English: bailiff (shifted from surname usage). *See also* Girls and Boys: Bailey

Bea/Beata A diminutive form of Beatrice

Beatrice/Beatrix/Beatriz Latin: blessed

Beaux *See* Bella. *See also* Girls and Boys: Beau

Bebe A diminutive form of Beatrice. Also French: baby (term of endearment)

Beca/Becca/Becci/Becki/Beckie/Becky A diminutive form of Rebecca

Begum Persian: queen

Bejna The name of a river in Romania (geographical name)

Bela Czech: white

Belicia *See* Isabel

Belinay/Belinda A blend of Bella and Linda

Bella/Belle Latin: beautiful

Benedicta/Benedicte/Benita Latin: blessed

Berenice Greek: bring victory

Berfin *See* Parveen

Berivan Kurdish: milk maid

Bernadette Germanic: brave as a bear

Bernice *See* Berenice

Berrie/Berry Old English: berry

Bertha Germanic: bright one

Beryl Greek: precious blue-green stone (gemstone name)

Bess/Bessie A diminutive form of Elizabeth

Betania See Bethaney

Beth/Bethan A diminutive form of Elizabeth

Bethaney/Bethani/Bethanie/ Bethannie/Bethany Hebrew: house of figs, home town of Lazarus (geographical name)

Bethel Hebrew: house of god, a city mentioned in the Bible

Bethen/Betheny See Bethany

Bethia A diminutive form of Elizabeth

Bethlehem Hebrew: house of meat, birthplace of Jesus (geographical name)

Bethney See Bethaney

Beti A diminutive form of Elizabeth

Betsan Hebrew: god is a vow

Betsey/Betsi/Betsie/Betsy/Bettie/ Bettina/Betty A diminutive form of Elizabeth

Betul/Betula/Betulah Hebrew: maiden

Beulah Hebrew: married

Beverley/Beverly Old English: beaver stream (shifted from surname usage)

Beyonce From the name of Beyoncé Knowles, taken from Beyincé, her mother's maiden name

Beyza Persian: bright, shining. Also Turkish: very white. Also a city in Iran (geographical name)

Bhakti Sanskrit: faithful, devotion, attachment. A term showing the love for god in Hinduism

Bhavika Sanskrit: future

Bhavini Sanskrit: noble and beautiful woman

Bhavisha See Bhavika

Bhavneet Unknown, possibly Punjabi: always with Shiva

Bhumi/Bhumika From Bhūmi, the Hindu goddess that represents earth

Bianca/Bianka Latin: white

Biba Punjabi: sweet little girl (term of endearment)

Bibi Persian: noble woman

Bijal Gujarati: lightning

Billi Used as a feminine form of William

Billiejo A blend of Billie and Jo

Bilqis The name of the Queen of Sheba

Binta Mandinka: with god

Bintou Mandinka: daughter of

Bisma/Bismah Unknown, possibly from bismillah (Arabic: in the name of god) or Basima (Arabic: smiling)

Blaithin Irish Gaelic (from bláth): flower

Blanca/Blanche/Blanka See Bianca

BlathnaidIrish Gaelic (from bláth): flower. A woman who loved Cú Chulainn in Irish Gaelic mythology

Bleona Albanian, unknown, possibly a shifted version of Blerina (from blerim): verdure, greenery, or a modernised and shifted variant of Leona. The name of Bleona Qereti, an Albanian singer and entertainer

Blerta Albanian (from blertë): green

Blimi Unknown, possibly from Bellami (Old French: beautiful friend)

Bliss (name from an English word)

Blossom (name from an English word)

Bluebell (name from flowers and trees, name from an English word)

Bluebelle A blend of Blue and Belle. *See also* Bluebell

Blythe (name from an English word). *See also* Bliss

Bonita Spanish: pretty

Bonnie/Bonny Scots expression: pretty. Also known in the context of the duo Bonnie and Clyde

Boo (term of endearment). From beau, meaning beautiful and boyfriend, but now also covers close family members

Bow (name from an English word)

Bracha Hebrew (from berakhah): blessing, recited at various points, including over food

Bradie From the Brádaigh family (Scottish Gaelic, from bradach: pilfering; shifted from surname usage)

Brandi/Brandy (name from an English word)

Branwen Welsh (from bran and gwyn): fair crow. The name of Branwen, sister of Brân the Blessed, King of Britain, who is badly treated by her husband, the King of Ireland, causing Brân to attack Ireland

Brea/Breagha Scottish Gaelic (from brèagha): lovely, good looking

Breanna/Breanne *See* Briana

Bree Irish Gaelic (from bríg): power, strength, force. *See also* Bridget

Breeze (name from an English word)

Brenda/Brenna Old Norse: sword

Bria A diminutive form of Brianna

Briana/Brianna/Briannah/Brianne Unknown, possibly Celtic: hill, high, exalted

Briar (name from flowers and trees, name from an English word)

Bridey A diminutive form of Bridget

Bridget/Bridgette Irish Gaelic (from bríg): power, strength, force. *See also* Bree

Bridie A diminutive form of Bridget

Brielle A diminutive form of Gabrielle. Also a town in the Netherlands (geographical name)

Brigid/Brigitte *See* Bridget

Brihanna *See* Briana

Briony *See* Bryony

Britani/Britany/Britnee/Britney/Brittaney/Brittani/Brittanie/

Brittany/Britteny/Brittney From Brittany (geographical name)

Brocha *See* Bracha

Brogen/Broghan From the O'Brogan family (shifted from surname usage). *See also* Girls and Boys: Brogan

Brona/Bronach/Bronagh Irish Gaelic (from brón): sadness, sorrow

Bronia A diminutive form of Bronwen

Bronte From the Bronte family, most notably that of Anne, Emily, and Charlotte Brontë (shifted from surname usage)

Bronwen/Bronwyn Welsh Gaelic (from bron and gwyn): fair breasted

Bronya Russian (from bronâ): armour

Brooklynn/Brooklynne Named after an area in New York (geographical name). *See also* Girls and Boys: Brooke and Brooklyn

Bruna Old German: brown

Bryana/Bryanna *See* Briana

Bryany (name from flowers and trees, name from an English word)

Brydie A diminutive form of Bridget

Bryher *See* Briar

Bryoney/Bryoni/Bryonie/ Bryonny/Bryony *See* Bryany

Buse Turkish: kiss

Bushra/Busra Arabic: good news

C

Cacey *See* Casi

Cadee A diminutive form of Catherine

Cadence (name from an English word)

Cadey A diminutive form of Catherine

Cadhla Irish Gaelic: beautiful

Cadi/Cadie/Cady A diminutive form of Catherine

Caela/Caelyn *See* Cayla

Cagla Turkish: almonds

Caia A diminutive form of Catrina

Caileigh/Cailey *See* Kayla

Cailin/Cailyn Irish Gaelic (from cailín): girl, maid. *See also* Colleen

Caira *See* Cara and Ciara

Caisey *See* Casi

Cait/Caitie A diminutive form of Catherine

Caitilin/Caitlain/Caitlan/ Caitland/Caitlen/Caitlin/ Caitlyn/Caitlynn/Caitriona *See* Catherine

Caleigh/Caley *See* Caileigh

Cali A diminutive form of Catherine

Calista *See* Callista

Calla A diminutive form of Catherine

Calleigh *See* Caileigh

Calli/Callia/Callie A diminutive

form of Catherine

Calliope Greek: beautiful voice. The muse of epic poetry from Greek mythology

Callista Greek: most beautiful

Calypso Greek: to conceal. The sea nymph who enchants Odysseus and keeps him on her island for many years during his journey home to his wife in Ithica

Camara Bantu: teacher

Camelia/Camellia (name from flowers and trees, name from an English word)

Camila/Camilla/Camille Latin: from the Camillus family (Latin: in religious services). *See also* Camellia

Camryn Scottish Gaelic (from cam and sròn): crooked nose (shifted from surname usage). *See also* Girls and Boys: Cameron

Canan Turkish: beloved

Candace/Candice Cushitic: queen mother. The title for queens of the Kush empire in modern day Sudan

Candy (name from an English word)

Cansu Turkish: water of life

Caoife *See* Aoife

Caoimhe Irish Gaelic (from caomh): beautiful, gentle

Caprice Italian (from capriccio): following your fancy, the term for a lively piece of music with free form and an improvised feel

Cara/Caragh Italian: beloved. Also Manx: songster

Carenza *See* Kerenza

Carey/Cari From the Ciardha family (Irish Gaelic, from ciar: black) Cariad. Welsh: darling

Carina *See* Cara

Caris/Cariss/Carissa *See* Carys

Carla A diminutive form of Charlotte

Carlee/Carleigh A blend of Carla and Lee/Leigh

Carlene/Carley/Carli/Carlie A diminutive form of Charlotte

Carlota/Carlotta *See* Charlotte

Carly A diminutive form of Charlotte

Carmel/Carmela/Carmella Hebrew: god's vineyard. The Virgin Mary is known as Our Lady of Mount Carmel

Carmen Latin: song, tune. *See also* Carmel

Carol A diminutive form of Caroline

Carolanne A blend of Carol and Anne

Carole A diminutive form of Caroline

Carolina/Caroline/Carolyn Old German: man, warrior. *See also* Charlotte

Carragh *See* Cara

Carrera An Italian surname from Venice (shifted from surname usage)

Carrie A diminutive form of Caroline

Carrigan Irish Gaelic: little rock

Carris *See* Carys

Caryl A diminutive form of Caroline

Carys Welsh: love

Casi/Casie From the Irish surname Cathasach (Irish Gaelic, from cathaisech: watchful, vigilant). *See also* Girls and Boys: Casey

Cassandra Greek: to shine upon men. The Trojan princess during the Trojan War who was given the gift of prophecy, but upon spurning the god Apollo, was cursed so that no one would believe her prophecies

Cassey *See* Casi

Cassia/Cassie Latin: empty. Also a diminutive form of Cassandra and Cassiopeia

Cassiopeia Greek: cassia juice. The mother of Andromeda in Greek mythology, who was punished by the god Poseidon for being boastful about her beauty, tied to a chair and turned into a constellation

Catalina/Catarina *See* Catherine

Cate A diminutive form of Catherine

Catelin/Catelyn/Caterina *See* Catherine

Catharine/Catherine/Cathrine/ Cathryn Greek: pure

Cathy/Catie A diminutive form of Catherine

Catrin/Catrina/Catriona *See* Catherine

Caydee A diminutive form of Catherine

Caydence *See* Cadence

Cayla From Caoilainn (Irish Gaelic, from cáel and finn): slim and beautiful

Caylee/Cayleigh A blend of Cay, a diminutive form of Catherine, and Lee/Leigh

Ceara *See* Ciara

Cece A diminutive form of Cecilia

Cecelia/Cecile/Cecilia/Cecilie/ Cecily Latin: way of the blind

Ceilidh Scottish Gaelic: companion, gathering including folk music and dancing

Ceinwen Welsh (from cain and gwyn): elegant and fair

Ceira *See* Ciara

Celeste/Celestine Latin: heavenly

Celia Latin (from caelum): heaven. Also a diminutive form of Cecilia

Celina/Celine From the Caelius family, Latin (from caelum): heaven. *See also* Selena

Cemile Turkish: kindness

Ceren Turkish: young gazelle

Cerian/Ceridwen Unknown, possibly Welsh (gwyn): fair

Ceridwen is an enchantress from Welsh mythology who swallows her servant Gwion Bach and causes his rebirth as the poet Taliesin

Ceris/Cerise French: cherry (name from flowers and trees)

Ceryn A diminutive form of Ceridwen

Cerys *See* Carys and Ceris

Ceyda Turkish: beautiful long neck

Ceylan Turkish: gazelle

Ceylin Turkish: door to heaven

Chahat Hindi: love and affection

Chana/Chanae *See* Hanna

Chanay Unknown, possibly Old French: wood grove (shifted from surname usage)

Chandni Arabic: moonlight

Chandra Arabic: beautiful as the moon

Chanel/Chanell/Chanelle French: pipe (shifted from surname usage). The surname of Coco Chanel

Chani A diminutive form of Chaniya

Chanice/Chaniece/Chanise A shifted version of Janise. *See also* Jane

Chaniya Swahili: wealthy

Channel/Channelle *See* Chanel

Channon *See* Shanon

Chantae/Chantai *See* Chantay

Chantal From the place Chantal (French: stony)

Chantay/Chante French: sing

Chantel/Chantell/Chantelle *See* Chantal

Chardonay/Chardonnay (name from flowers and trees, name from an English word)

Charelle *See* Cheryl

Charis Greek: grace, kindness

Charisma (name from an English word)

Charissa/Charisse *See* Charis

Charity (name from an English word)

Charla/Charlea/Charlee A diminutive form of Charlotte

Charleen/Charleigh/Charlene/ Charlette/Charlize *See* Charlotte

Charlotte Old German: man, warrior. *See also* Caroline

Charmaine Unknown, possibly from English: charm

Charnelle *See* Chanel

Charvi Sanskrit (from carvi): beautiful woman

Chava Hebrew: living being

Chavi Sanskrit: beauty, splendour, ray of light

Chaya Hebrew: life

Chelcie/Chelsea/Chelsee/ Chelsey/Chelsi/Chelsie/Chelsy Old English: landing place of chalk

Chelsea comes from the name of the district in London (geographical name)

Chenai *See* Chennai

Chenelle *See* Chanel

Chenice *See* Chanice

Chenille *See* Chanel

Chenise *See* Chanice

Chennai A city in India (geographical name)

Cher French: dear, precious.

Also a diminutive form of Cheryl

Cherelle *See* Cheryl

Cheri *See* Cherie

Cherice *See* Cerise

Cherie French: dear, precious, darling. *See also* Cherrie and Sherry

Cherise *See* Cerise

Cherish (name from an English word)

Cherisse *See* Cerise

Cherrelle *See* Cheryl

Cherrie/Cherry (name from an English word)

Cheryl A blend of Cherrie and Beryl

Chevonne *See* Siobhan

Cheyanne/Cheyenne/Cheyne Dakota: unintelligible speakers

Chiamaka Igbo: god is beautiful

Chiana *See* Cheyenne

Chiara An Italian variant of Claire. *See also* Ciara

Chidinma Igbo: god is good

Chiedza Shona: light

Chimamanda Igbo: god will never fail

China (geographical name)

Chinenye *See* Cheyenne

Chioma Igbo: good god, good luck

Chizara/Chizaram Igbo: god answered me

Chloe/Chloie Greek: green shoot

Chole Greek: flowering

Chrissie/Christa A diminutive form of Christina

Christabel/Christabelle Latin: beautiful Christian

Christal *See* Crystal

Christelle Latin: follower of Christ. *See also* Christina

Christiana/Christiane/ Christianna *See* Christina

Christina/Christine Latin: follower for Christ

Chrystal *See* Crystal

Chyanne *See* Cheyenne

Chyna/Chynna *See* China

Ciana/Cianna Irish Gaelic (from cían): long, enduring

Ciara Scottish Gaelic (from ciaradh): darkening, twilight. Also Irish Gaelic (from cíar): dark, murky, black. *See also* Sierra

Ciarrai *See* Kerrie

Cicely (name from flowers and trees, name from an English word)

Cienna *See* Sienna

Ciera *See* Ciara

Cindy A diminutive form of Cynthia

Cira *See* Ciara

Clair/Claira/Claire/Clara/Clare/ Clarice/Clarissa/Clarisse Latin: bright, clear, famous

Claudia Latin: from the Roman family name of Claudius

Clea A diminutive form of Cleopatra

Clemence/Clemency/ Clementina/Clementine Latin: merciful, gentle

Cleo A diminutive form of Cleopatra

Cleopatra Greek: glory to the father. The name of the famous Egyptian queen

Clio A diminutive form of Cleopatra

Cliodhna/Cliona The queen of the Banshees from Irish mythology

Clodagh The name of a river in Ireland (geographical name)

Cloe *See* Chloe

Clover (name from flowers and trees, name from an English word)

Coco The nickname of Gabrielle Bonheur Chanel, better known as Coco Chanel

Colbie/Colby Old Norse: dark town (shifted from surname usage)

Coleen An American variant of Cailin

Colette A diminutive form of Nicolette

Colleen An American variant of Cailin

Collette A diminutive form of Nicolette

Comfort (name from an English word)

Connie A diminutive form of Constance

Constance (name from an English word)

Cora *See* Corrina

Coral (name from an English word)

Coralie *See* Coral

Cordelia The name of the youngest daughter in Shakespeare's *King Lear*

Corey/Cori/Corie/Corin A diminutive form of Corrina. *See also* Girls and Boys: Kori

Corina/Corinna/Corinne *See* Corrina

Cornelia Latin (from cornu): horn, symbolising strength and courage

Corrie/Corrin A diminutive form of Corrina

Corrina/Corrine/Corrinne Greek: maiden

Cortney *See* Courtnay

Cory A diminutive form of Corrina. *See also* Girls and Boys: Kori

Cosima Greek: order, decency

Courtenay/Courteney/Courtnay/ Courtnie Old French: pug nose. *See also* Girls and Boys: Courtney

Cressida Greek: golden. Also the name of the girl from Chaucer's *Troilus and Criseyde*

Cristal *See* Crystal

Cristiana/Cristina *See* Christina

Crystal Old English: clear mineral

Cyan (name from an English word)

Cydnee/Cydney *See* Sydnee

Cynthia Greek: from Mount Cynthus. A name for the Greek moon and hunting goddess Artemis

Cyra The name of an Irish saint

d

Daania/Daanya/Daena *See* Daina and Diana

Dagmara Old Norse: maid of the day

Dahlia (name from flowers and trees, name from an English word)

Daiana *See* Daina and Diana

Daina Lithuanian: song

Daisey *See* Daisy

Daisha *See* Aisha

Daisi/Daisie/Daisy/Daizy Old English: day's eye (name from flowers and trees)

Dalia *See* Daliah

Dalila *See* Delilah

Damaris Greek (from damalis): calf. The wife of Dionysius the Areopagite

Damini Hindi: stroke of lightning

Damla Turkish: water drop

Dana/Danae/Danah Old English (from Dene): Danish, from Denmark. Arabic: perfect pearl

Daneen Arabic: princess

Dania A diminutive form of Daniela

Danica Latin: from Denmark

Daniela/Daniele/Daniella/ Danielle Hebrew: god is my judge

Danika *See* Danica

Danisha A blend of Dani and the feminine -sha ending

Danita/Daniya/Daniyah A diminutive form of Daniela

Danna/Danni *See* Dana

Danniella/Dannielle *See* Daniela

Dannii *See* Dana

Danya/Danyelle *See* Daniela

Daphne Greek: laurel (name from flowers and trees). A nymph pursued by Apollo in Greek mythology

Darby Old English: from Derby, village of deer (geographical name)

Darcee/Darci/Darcie Old English: from Arcy in France (shifted from surname usage). *See also* Girls and Boys: Darcey

Dareen *See* Daria, Darina and Darleen

Daria/Darian/Darija Persian: wealthy. Also Arabic: to learn

Darina Irish: from the Dáirine tribe, or descendants of Dáire, notably Dáire Doimthech, High King of Ireland. Also Slovak (from dar): gift

Darion *See* Daria

Darla A diminutive form of Darleen

Darleen/Darlene English: darling

Darya Persian: sea. *See also* Daria

Daryl Old French: dear little one

Dasha *See* Dorothy

Dasia *See* Daisy. *See also* Dorothy

Daveena/Davida/Davina/Davinia Hebrew: beloved

Dawn Old English: become day

Daya Sanskrit: compassion. An

important concept in Sikhism

Dayana Sanskrit: flight of a bird. *See also* Deanna

Dayna *See* Daina

Dea Latin: goddess

Deana/Deanna Old English: valley *See also* Diana. *See also* Girls and Boys: Deanne

Dearbhail/Dearbhaile Irish Gaelic (from der and Fál): daughter of Ireland

Dearbhla Irish Gaelic (from der and fili): daughter of a poet, Seer. *See also* Dearbhail

Debbie A diminutive form of Deborah

Debora/Deborah/Debra Hebrew: bee. The name of a prophetess in the Bible

Dee A diminutive form of Cordelia or Deanna

Deema *See* Dima

Deena/Deenah Arabic: obediance. *See also* Daina and Deana

Deepa Punjabi: light, lamp (Sikh name)

Deepali Sanskrit (from dipali): row of lamps

Deepika Sanskrit (from dipika): light

Deeya *See* Diya

Defne Turkish: laurel. *See also* Daphne

Deimante Lithuanian (from deimantas): diamond (gemstone name)

Deirbhile *See* Dearbhla

Deja French: already

Dekota *See* Dakota

Delaney Old French: from the alder grove (shifted from surname usage)

Delia Greek: from Delos, which was the birth place of the Greek goddess Artemis

Delicia Latin: delight

Delilah Hebrew: she who weakens. The name is derived from the story of Samson and Delilah, in which Delilah cuts off Samson's hair, effectively severing his oath to god, weakening him and betraying him to his enemies

Delina *See* Adeline

Delisha *See* Delicia

Della A diminutive form of Adeline

Delphi Greek: dolphin. The name of the Greek city where Apollo slew the python, and where the Delphic oracle was based. Also diminutive form of Delphine

Delphine Greek: from Delphi

Delta Greek: the fourth letter in the alphabet

Delyth Welsh (from del): pretty

Demelza The name of a hamlet in Cornwall (geographical name)

Demetra Greek: related to the Greek goddess of harvest, Demeter

Demi/Demie/Demii A diminutive form of Demetra

Demilee A blend of Demi and Lee

Demileigh A blend of Demi and

Leigh

Demmi A diminutive form of Demetra

Dena Native American: valley. *See also* Deanna

Deni A diminutive form of Denise

Denisa/Denise French: Dionysius. Named after Saint Denis rather than the Greek god of wine, Dionysus

Deniz Turkish: sea

Denni A diminutive form of Denise

Deonne *See* Dionne

Derryn *See* Deryn

Dervla *See* Dearbhla

Derya Turkish: ocean

Deryn Welsh (from aderyn): bird

Desire/Desiree (name from an English word)

Destina/Destinee/Destiney/Destini (name from an English word). *See also* Girls and Boys: Destiny

Devika Sanskrit: goddess, divine

Devina *See* Davina

Devorah *See* Deborah

Deya *See* Diya

Dhanvi Telugu: fine, good. Also related to Dhanvanti (Telagu: wealthy)

Dhanya Sanskrit (from dhanya): fortunate, healthy, rich, blessed

Dhara Sanskrit: blade, current. The name of a Hindu god who represents the earth

Dharma Sanskrit: nature, natural order. A central concept in both Hinduism and Buddhism

Dhiya *See* Diya

Dhriti Sanskrit: courage, will, resolution

Dhruvi Sanskrit: firm, fixed

Dhyana Sanskrit: meditation. *See also* Diana

Dia *See* Ziya

Diana/Diane/Dianne Latin: divine. The name of the Roman goddess of the moon and the hunt. *See also* Artemis

Dila A diminutive form of Dilara

Dilara Persian: beloved

Dilek Turkish: wish, desire

Dilly A diminutive form of Dilys

Dilpreet Punjabi: pleasing the heart (Sikh name)

Dilys Welsh: certain, genuine

Dima Arabic: gentle storm

Dimple (name from an English word). Old English: small pools

Dina/Dinah Sanskrit: day. Also Hebrew: judged

Dione Greek: mother of Aphrodite, the Greek goddess of love and beauty

Dionne Greek: follower of Dionysus, the Greek god of wine

Dior French: of gold (made more well-known by the French brand Christian Dior). Also Tolkien's Doriathrin: descendant (the name of Dior Eluchíl)

Disha Hindi: direction

Diva Italian: goddess

Divina Latin: of god, divine

Divya Sanskrit: wonderful, magical, divine

Dixie English: Southern US states (geographical name)

Diya Arabic: light. Also Sanskrit: gift

Diyana Persian: honesty

Dolce/Dolcie Italian: sweet

Dollie/Dolly English: doll (term of endearment). A diminutive form of Dorothy

Dolores Latin: sorrowful (from the Virgin Mary of Sorrows)

Dominica/Dominika/ Dominique/Dominyka Latin: belonging to god. Also from the Commonwealth of Dominica (geographical name)

Dona *See* Donna

Donia From Donalda (Celtic: ruler of the world)

Donika *See* Danica and Donna

Donna Italian: lady

Donya *See* Donia

Dora *See* Doreen

Dorcas Greek: Tabitha, meaning gazelle

Doreen/Dorina Green: gift

Doris Greek: Dorian woman. Also a sea nymph from Greek mythology

Dorota/Dorothea/Dorothy Greek: god's gift

Dottie/Dotty A diminutive form of Dorothy

Dounia *See* Dunya

Dua/Duaa/Duha Arabic: pray

Dulcie *See* Dulce

Dunya Arabic: world, earth

Duygu Turkish: emotions, feelings

Eabha *See* Eva

Eadaoin *See* Etain

Eadie A diminutive form of Eadaoin

Easha *See* Esha

Eavi *See* Eva

Ebany *See* Ebony

Ebba German: wild boar

Eboney/Eboni/Ebonie/Ebonnie/ Ebony English: black wood from the ebony tree (name from flowers and trees, colour name)

Ebru Turkish: paper marbling

Ebunoluwa Yoruba: god's gift

Ece Turkish: queen

Ecem Turkish: my queen

Echo Greek: reflection of sound

Ecrin French (from écrin): jewellery box

Eda Turkish: well-mannered. Also a diminutive form of Edith. *See also* Hedda

Ede/Edee *See* Eda

Edel Old German: noble

Edie *See* Eda

Edith Old English: rich and blessed war

Edlyn *See* Adelaide

Edna Hebrew: pleasure

Edona Unknown, possibly from Edana, from Etain. Also possibly from Edoni, a Thracian tribe mentioned in Greek mythology

Edwina Old English: rich friend, blessed friend

Eemaan/Eeman *See* Imaani

Eesha *See* Esha

Eevie/Efa *See* Eva

Effie/Effy A diminutive form of Euphemia

Efie/Efua *See* Afua

Ehlana *See* Helen

Eibhlin The Irish form of Avelina (Germanic: desired)

Eila A diminutive form of Eileen

Eileen *See* Evelyn

Eilidh *See* Helen

Eilis/Eilish A diminutive form of Elizabeth

Eiliyah *See* Elija and Aliya

Eimaan *See* Imaani

Eimear/Eimer/Eimhear *See* Emer

Eira Arabic: snow

Eireann *See* Eirian

Eirene *See* Irene

Eirian *See* Arian

Eirini *See* Irene

Eirinn *See* Erin

Eirlys Welsh: snowdrop (name from flowers and trees)

Eisha Hebrew: woman. *See also* Aisha

Eithne Irish Gaelic (from etne): kernel, nut. A variation on Ethniu,

the daughter of King Balor from Irish mythology

Ejo *See* Adwoa

Ekam Sanskrit: single, one

Ekamjot Punjabi: light of god (Sikh name)

Ekampreet Punjabi: love of god (Sikh name)

Ekaterina *See* Catherine

Ekta Sanskrit (from ekata): unity, oneness

Ekuwa *See* Akua

Ela *See* Ella

Elain Welsh: fawn. *See also* Helen

Elaina/Elaine/Elan/Elana/Elani *See* Helen

Elanor/Elanur *See* Eleanor

Elara A princess who bore Zeus a son, so one of Jupiter's moons is named after her

Elayna *See* Helen

Elcie A diminutive form of Elizabeth

Elda *See* Hilda

Eldana Unknown

Eleana *See* Helen and Eleanor

Eleanor/Eleanora/Eleanore Old French: from the name of Eleanor of Aquitaine, queen of Henry II

Eleasha *See* Elisa

Electra Greek: shining, bright. Also the heroine from the Greek tragedies who plotted with her brother to kill her mother in order to avenge her father, which caused the Electra complex to be named after her

Eleena *See* Helen

Eleesha/Eleeza/Eleisha *See* Elisa

Elektra *See* Electra

Elen/Elena/Elene/Eleni *See* Helen

Elenor *See* Eleanor

Elenya *See* Helen

Eleonora/Eleonore *See* Eleanor

Eleora *See* Eliora

Eleri Unknown, of Welsh origins

Elese *See* Elisa

Elesha *See* Elisa

Elexa/Elexis *See* Alexia

Elfie Unknown, possibly from Ailbhe (Irish Gaelic, from albho: white)

Eliana/Eliane/Elianna/Elianne Unknown, possibly Latin (from helios): sun

Elicia *See* Alicia. Also a diminutive form of Elizabeth

Eliesha *See* Elisa

Elif Turkish: slender

Elija Hebrew: my god is Jehovah. A prophet from the Book of Kings. *See also* Girls and Boys: Elijah

Elika A diminutive form of Elikapeka, a Haiwaiian form of Elizabeth

Elim A place mentioned in Exodus, where the Israelites camped

Elin/Elina *See* Helen

Elinor/Elinore *See* Eleanor

Eliora Hebrew: my god is my light

Elisa Hebrew: my god is salvation. The name of a prophet who

could work wonders, including the ressurection of a child. Also a diminutive form of Elizabeth. *See also* Girls and Boys: Elisha

Elisabeth/Elisabetta *See* Elizabeth

Elise A diminutive form of Elizabeth

Elisheva *See* Elizabeth

Elishia/Elisia/Eliska/Elissa/ Elisse/Elissia *See* Elisa

Elivia *See* Olivia

Eliya/Eliyah *See* Elija

Eliz A diminutive form of Elizabeth

Eliza *See* Elisa

Elizabet/Elizabete/Elizabeth Hebrew: god's promise

Elizah *See* Elisa

Elizaveta *See* Elizabeth

Elize *See* Elisa

Elke/Elkie From Elkanah (Hebrew: god has purchased)

Ella/Ellah German: complete. *See also* Alia

Ellamae/Ellamay A blend of Ella and Mae/May

Ellana *See* Helen

Ellanor *See* Eleanor

Ellarose A blend of Ella and Rose

Elle French: she. Also a diminutive form of Eleanor

Elleanor *See* Eleanor

Ellee Also a diminutive form of Eleanor

Elleigh A blend of Elle and Leigh

Ellemay A blend of Elle and May

Ellen/Ellena *See* Helen

Ellenor *See* Eleanor

Ellese/Ellesha/Ellesse *See* Elisa

Elley/Elli/Ellia A diminutive form of Elizabeth

Elliana/Ellianna *See* Helen

Ellice/Ellicia/Ellie A diminutive form of Elizabeth

Elliemae/Elliemay A blend of Ellie and Mae/May

Elliesha *See* Elisa

Ellinor *See* Eleanor

Ellisa/Ellise/Ellisha/Ellisia/ Ellissa/Ellissia *See* Elisa

Elliw Welsh: colour

Elloise *See* Eloise

Ellora *See* Eliora

Ellouise *See* Eloise

Ellsie/Elly A diminutive form of Elizabeth

Ellyn *See* Helen

Ellys/Ellyse/Ellysia A diminutive form of Elizabeth

Elma A diminutive form of Wilhelmina

Elodie Old German: other wealth

Eloisa/Eloise Germanic: healthy

Elona *See* Helen

Elora *See* Eliora

Elouisa/Elouise *See* Eloise

Elowen Cornish: elm tree (name from flowers and trees)

Elsa A diminutive form of Elizabeth

Elsbeth *See* Elizabeth

Elsi/Elsie A diminutive form of Elizabeth

Elspeth *See* Elizabeth

Eluned Welsh: image, idol

Elva/Elvie *See* Elfie

Elvira Old German: all truth

Elyse A diminutive form of Elizabeth

Elysha/Elyshia *See* Elisa

Elysia/Elyssa/Elysse/Elyssia/ Elyza/Elze A diminutive form of Elizabeth

Ema *See* Emma

Eman *See* Imaani

Emanuela Hebrew: god is with us

Ember (name from an English word). *See also* Amber

Emel Turkish: desire

Emelia/Emelie/Emeline/Emelye *See* Emily

Emer Wife of Cú Chulainn from Irish mythology

Emerald (gemstone name, name form an English word)

Emery Germanic: universal power

Emi/Emie A diminutive form of Emily

Emile/Emilee *See* Emily

Emileigh A blend of Emily and Leigh

Emiley/Emili/Emilia/Emiliana/ Emilie/Emilija/Emillia/Emillie/ Emilly/Emily Latin: rival

Emina/Emine Turkish: trustworthy

Emma Germanic: universal

Emmaleigh A blend of Emma and Leigh

Emmanuela/Emmanuella/ Emmanuelle *See* Emanuela

Emme A diminutive form of Emma and Emily

Emmelia/Emmeline See Emily

Emmi/Emmie A diminutive form of Emma and Emily

Emmily See Emily

Emmy/Emy A diminutive form of Emma and Emily

Ena Hebrew: renew. Also from Eithne (Irish Gaelic: kernel)

Enaya/Enayah See Inaaya and Inaya

Enfys Welsh: rainbow

Enid Welsh (from enaid): life, soul

Enlli An old name for Bardsey Island in Wales

Enna See Ena

Enola Native American: solitary

Enrika Old German: home ruler

Enya See Ena

Eowyn Old English (from eoh and wynn): horse joy. The name that Tolkien created for Éowyn of Rohan

Era Albanian: wind

Eram See Erum

Eri A diminutive form of Erinn

Erica/Erika Old Norse (from ei and ríkr): eternal ruler, ever powerful

Erina/Erinn Gaelic: Ireland. See also Girls and Boys: Erin

Erisa Greek: strife. See also Girls and Boys: Eris

Erona Unknown, possibly from Verona

Errin See Erina

Erum Arabic: heaven

Erykah See Erika

Eryn/Erynn See Erin

Erza Unknown, possibly from Erzya, a language from the Republic of Mordovia. See also Ezri

Esha Sanskrit: desire

Eshaal/Eshal Arabic: flower of paradise Eshani. Arabic: in god's grace

Esi See Akosua

Esma/Esmae/Esmai/Esmay/ Esme/Esmee Old French: loved. Also a diminutive form of Esmeralda

Esmeralda/Esmerelda Spanish: emerald (gemstone name, colour name). Also a county in the US (geographical name)

Esmie See Esme

Esra See Ezri

Essie/Esta A diminutive form of Estella

Estela/Estella/Estelle See Stella

Ester/Estera/Esther Persian: star. Also the name of the Jewish queen in the Book of Esther

Esyllt See Isolde. Also an Irish princess in the Arthurian legend

Etain/Etaine An Irish sun goddess. Also a heroine from Irish mythology, Tochmarc Etaine

Etana Hebrew: long lived

Ethel/Etholle Old English: noble

Etienne See Etain. See also Stephanie

Etta/Ettie/Etty A diminutive form

of Henrietta

Eugenia/Eugenie Greek: well born

Eunice Greek: good victory

Euphemia Greek: speak well

Eva Hebew: to live (the name of the first woman from the Bible). *See also* Aoife

Evalina/Evalyn/Evalynn *See* Evelyn

Evana Hebrew: Jehovahis gracious. *See also* Girls and Boys: Evan

Evangelina/Evangeline Greek: good news. Latin: gospel

Evanna *See* Evana

Eve/Evee/Eveie *See* Eva

Evelina/Eveline/Evelyn/Evelyne/ Evelynn/Evelynne/Everlyn Old French: hazelnut (shifted from the surname Aveline)

Evey/Evi/Evie/Eviee *See* Eva

Evita *See* Eva

Evlyn *See* Evelyn

Evonne/Evony *See* Yvonne

Evy/Ewa *See* Eva

Ewelina *See* Evelyn

Eylul Turkish: September

Ezgi Turkish: melody

Ezmae/Ezmai/Ezmay A blend of Esme and May

Ezme/Ezmee *See* Esme

Ezri Hebrew: help. *See also* Girls and Boys: Ezra

Ezzah Hindi: respect

f

Faaiza/Faaizah *See* Faiza

Faatima/Faatimah *See* Fatima

Fabbiha *See* Fabiha

Fabia/Fabiana/Fabienne Latin: bean (name from flowers and trees)

Fabiha Urdu: gifted

Faduma/Fadumo *See* Fatima

Fae *See* Faye

Faheema/Faheemah/Fahema/ Fahima/Fahimah Arabic: intelligent. *See also* Fatima

Fahmida Arabic: intelligent and wise

Faigy Yiddish: bird, fig

Faisa *See* Faiza

Faith (name from an English word)

Faiza/Faizah Arabic: victorious

Fajar/Fajr Arabic: dawn, beginning

Falak/Falaq Arabic: sky, celestial sphere

Falisha Arabic: happiness

Fallon Irish Gaelic: from the Ó Fallamháin clan (shifted from surname usage). Also a city in the US (geographical name)

Fantasia Greek: to imagine

Farah Arabic: joy

Fardowsa Arabic: paradise

Fareedah/Fareeha Arabic: cheerful, happy

Farha/Farhana/Farhat/Farheen/ Farhia/Farhiya Arabic: happiness,

delight
Faria/Fariah Arabic: towering,
slender
Farida/Faridah Arabic: unique
Fariha/Farihah/Fariya Arabic:
happy, glad
Farjana *See* Farzana
Farrah Arabic: joy. Also Persian:
divine glory
Farren Old English: iron grey
(colour name, shifted from
surname usage)
Farwa Arabic: fur
Faryal/Faryl Arabic: name
Farzana Persian: wise, knowing
Fateha *See* Fatiha
Fatema/Fatemah/Fathema *See*
Fatima
Fathia Arabic: continuous victory
Fathima *See* Fatima
Fatiha Arabic: opening
Fatim/Fatima/Fatimah/Fatma
Arabic: one who weans a baby.
Also the name of Fatima bint
Muhammad, daughter of the
prophet Muhammad.
Fatmata Arabic: captivating. *See also*
Fatima
Fatos Albanian: bold, daring. *See
also* Fatou
Fatou Arabic: abstaining
Fatoumata/Fatoumatta/Fatuma
See Fatmata
Favour (name from an English
word). Latin: goodwill
Fawzia/Fawziyah Sindhi: successful

Fay/Faye Old English: fairy
Fayth *See* Faith
Fazeela/Fazila Arabic: excellent,
outstanding
Fearn/Fearne Old English:
navigating a boat (shifted from
surname usage). Also Irish Gaelic
(from fern/fernóc): alder tree.
See also Fern
Federica *See* Frederica
Feigy *See* Faigy
Felicia/Felicity Latin: happy, lucky
Fenella A Manx variant of
Fionnuala
Fern (name from an English word,
name from flowers and trees)
Fernanda Germanic: adventurous
Ferne *See* Fern
Ffion Welsh: red flowers, foxglove
(name from flowers and trees)
Fflur Welsh: flowers
Fia A feminine form of Fiachna
(Irish Gaelic: from fiach, raven, a
king in Irish mythology)
Fiadh Irish Gaelic (from fiad):
various, including lord, respect and
wild
Fianna Irish Gaelic (from fian):
driving, pursuing, a term for
warrior groups mostly made up of
young men and women of noble
birth
Fifi A diminutive form of Fiona
and Josephine
Filipa/Filippa *See* Philippa
Filsan Cushitic: good age, mature of

her age

Filza Arabic: rose from heaven

Finlay/Finley Scottish Gaelic (from fionn and laoch): fair warrior

Finn Irish Gaelic: bright, white

Finola *See* Fionnuala

Finty From a diminutive form of the boy's name Finnian, used by Finty Williams (Tara Cressida Frances Williams), the daughter of Judi Dench

Fiona/Fionn *See* Finn

Fionnuala Irish Gaelic: fair shouldered (the daughter of Lir from Irish mythology)

Fiorella Italian: little flower

Firdaus/Firdaws/Firdous Arabic: the highest level of paradise

Fiyinfoluwa Yoruba: glory to god

Fiza/Fizah/Fizza/Fizzah Arabic: open hearted. Also Persian: water running on land

Fjolla Albanian: snowflake

Flavia Latin: golden, blonde

Fleur French: flower

Flo A diminutive form of Flora

Flora Latin: flower

Florence *See* Florentina. Also the name of the city in Italy (geographical name)

Florentina Latin: in bloom

Florie/Florrie A diminutive form of Florentina

Folasade/Folashade Yoruba: honour bestows a crown

Forida *See* Freda

Fozia Arabic: successful

Frances/Francesca/Franceska/ Francessca/Franchesca/ Francheska Latin (from Franciscus): from France

Francine French: French

Francisca *See* Francesca

Frankee A diminutive form of Francesca. *See also* Girls and Boys: Frankie

Fraya/Frayah/Frayer *See* Freya

Freda Germanic: peaceful. Also Yiddish: joy

Frederica Germanic: peaceful ruler

Freeda *See* Freda

Freia/Freja/Freya/Freyah/Freyja Old Norse: noble lady. The Norse goddess of love and beauty

Frida/Frieda *See* Freda

Fruma Yiddish: pious

g

Gabija Lithanian: goddess of fire and hearth in Lithuanian mythology

Gabriela/Gabriella/Gabrielle Hebrew: warrior of god, strength of god. *See also* Girls and Boys: Gabriel

Gaby A diminutive form of Gabrielle

Gagandeep Punjabi: lamp of the sky (Sikh name)

Gaia Greek: earth (the Greek goddess of the earth)

Gail A diminutive form of Abigail

Gala Greek: calm

Gamze Turkish: dimple

Gauri Sanskrit: fair

Gayle A diminutive form of Abigail

Gaynor See Guinevere

Geena A diminutive form of Georgina and Regina

Geet Hindi: song

Gemma Italian: gemstone

Genesis Greek: birth

Geneva Germanic: juniper tree. Also the city in Switzerland (geographical name)

Genevieve Latin: kin and wife

Genna A diminutive form of Jennifer

Georga/George/Georgea/ Georgette/Georgi Greek: farm worked

Georgia The name of the country (geographical name). See also Georga

Georgiana/Georgianna/Georgie/ Georgina See Georga

Geraldine Germanic: ruler of the spear

Gerda Old Norse: shelter. Also Cornish: fame

Geri A diminutive form of Geraldine

Germaine Latin (from germanus): brother, sibling

Gertrude Germanic: spear, strength

Gia A diminutive form of Giovanna

Giada See Jada

Gianna A diminutive form of Giovanna

Gift/Gifty (name from an English word)

Gigi A diminutive form of Georgine and Virginie

Gila From Gili (Hebrew: my joy)

Gillian See Juliana

Gina A diminutive form of Georgina and Regina

Ginevra See Guinevere

Ginny A diminutive form of Ginevra and Virginia

Gintare Lithanian: amber (gemstone name)

Giorgia See Georgia

Giovanna See Joanna

Gisele/Giselle Germanic: pledge

Gittel Yiddish: good

Gitty A diminutive form of Gittel

Giulia See Julia

Giuseppina See Josephine

Gizem Turkish: mystery

Gladys Unknown, possible Welsh (from gwlad): land, realm

Glenys Welsh (from glân): pure, fair, beautiful

Glesni Welsh: blueness

Gloria Latin: glory

Glory (name from an English word)

Glynis Welsh (from glyn): valley, glen. See also Glenys

Goda A diminutive form of Godiva

Godiva Old English: gift of god

Golda Yiddish: gold

Gozde Turkish: favourite

Grace/Gracey/Graci/Gracia/ Gracie/Gracy (name from an English word)

Grainne Irish Gaelic: grain. A daughter of the High King who runs away with Diarmaid despite being engaged to Fionn, Diarmaid's much older lord

Grayce *See* Grace

Grazina Lithuanian: beautiful

Gresa Unknown, possibly French (from grés): sandstone

Greta/Gretchen/Gretel A diminutive form of Margaret

Griselda Germanic: dark battle, stone, grey maiden warrior

Guinevere Welsh (from gwyn and hwyfar): fair hwyfar, where hwyfar is of uncertain origins. Also the queen in Arthurian legends. *See also* Jennifer

Gul Persian: flower, rose

Gulcan Kurdish: unknown, possibly from the words for 'life' and 'rose', implying as delicate as a rose

Guneet Punjabi: virtuous, glorious (Sikh name)

Gurkiran Punjabi: ray of the Guru (Sikh name)

Gurleen Punjabi: engrossed in the Guru (Sikh name)

Gurneet Punjabi: always with the Guru (Sikh name)

Gurnoor Punjabi: divine light of the Guru (Sikh name)

Gurpreet Punjabi: love for the Guru (Sikh name)

Gursharan Punjabi: shelter in the Guru (Sikh name)

Gursimran Punjabi: remembering the Guru (Sikh name)

Guste A diminutive form of Auguste

Gwen Welsh (from gwyn): fair. Also a diminutive form of Gweyneth

Gwenan *See* Gwen

Gwendolen/Gwendoline/ Gwendolyn Welsh (from gwyn and dolen): fair ring or bow

Gwenllian Welsh (from gwyn and llin): white flax

Gwennan/Gwenno *See* Gwen

Gwyneth Welsh (from gwyn): fair

Gypsie/Gypsy (name from an English word)

h

Ha Vietnamese: river, ocean

Haadiya/Haadiyah Arabic: leader, guide to righteousness

Haafizah Arabic: good memory, knows the Qur'an off by heart

Haajarah/Haajirah/Haajra *See* Hagar

Haania *See* Haniya

Habeeba/Habeebah/Habiba/ Habibah Arabic (from habib):

beloved, darling, sweetheart

Hadassa/Hadassah Hebrew: myrtle tree (name from flowers and trees)

Haddy A diminutive form of Harriet

Hadeel Arabic: cooing of a pigeon

Hadia *See* Hadya

Hadiqa Arabic: garden

Hadiya/Hadiyah *See* Haadiya

Hadya Arabic: gifts

Haf Welsh: summer

Hafiza/Hafizah Arabic: guardian, protector

Hafsa/Hafsah/Hafza Arabic: cub. The name of Hafsa bint Umar, one of prophet Muhammad's wives

Hagar Hebrew: unknown, possibly to do with uncertainty. The first wife of Abraham

Haidee Greek: modest

Haifa Arabic: slender, beautiful

Hailee/Hailey/Hailie/Haillie *See* Hayley

Haiqa Arabic: true believer

Haja/Hajar/Hajara/Hajer/ Hajera/Hajira/Hajirah/Hajra/ Hajrah *See* Hagar

Hala Arabic: halo around the moon

Haleema/Haleemah *See* Halima

Haleena *See* Halina and Helena

Haleigh *See* Hayley

Halema *See* Halima

Haley/Hali *See* Hayley

Halima/Halimah Arabic: patient, tolerant. The name of Halima Al-Sadiyah, prophet Muhammad's wet nurse

Halina Greek: calm

Halle Old Norse: rock. Also German: hall

Hallie/Halley/Hally *See* Hayley

Hamda/Hamdi Arabic: praise of god

Hameeda/Hameedah/Hameida/ Hamida/Hamidah Arabic: giving thanks

Hamima Arabic: dear friend

Hamna/Hamnah/Hammanah The name of Hammanah bint Jahsh, a wife of the prophet Muhammad's

Han Hebrew: god is gracious. Also Chinese: various, including cold

Hana/Hanaa Arabic: happiness. Also Japanese: flower. Also Korean: one. Also Chinese: various. *See also* Hannah and Henna

Hanaan Arabic: compassion, love

Hanah *See* Hannah

Hanasa *See* Hansa

Haneefa/Haneefah *See* Hanifa

Haneen Arabic: longing, desire

Hanfa The name of Ismael's wife from Egypt who bore him twelve sons

Hania/Haniah *See* Haniya

Hanifa/Hanifah Arabic: true believer, one true faith

Haniya/Haniyah Arabic: pleasant, happy

Hanna/Hannah Hebrew: favour, gracious, god has favoured me

Hansa Hindi: swan

Hansika Hindi: small swan

Hanya *See* Haniya

Hareem Arabic: walls of the house

Hargun Punjabi: many godly merits (Sikh name)

Harini Sanskrit: beautiful like deer. One of the 108 names of Laksmi, the Hindu goddess wealth and beauty

Harisa Sanskrit: joy

Harkiran Punjabi: ray of god's light (Sikh name)

Harleen Punjabi: engrossed in god (Sikh name)

Harmoni/Harmonie/Harmony (name from an English word)

Harneet Punjabi: always with god (Sikh name)

Harrie A diminutive form of Harriet

Harriet/Harriett/Harriette/Harriot Germanic: ruler of the home

Harshini *See* Hasini

Harshita Sanskrit (from harsita): charmed, happy

Harsimran Punjabi: remembering god (Sikh name)

Harveen Hindi: close to god

Haseena *See* Hasina

Hasiba Arabic: noble

Hasina Hindi: beautiful

Hasini Sanskrit (from hasin): bright, smiling, laughing

Hasna Arabic: beautiful

Hastee/Hasti Farsi: existence

Hatice Turkish: Khadija (name of Khadija bint Khuwaylid, the first wife of prophet Muhammad)

Hattie/Hatty A diminutive form of Harriet

Hava Hebrew: life. *See also* Eve

Havana Spanish: Capital city of Cuba (geographical name)

Haven/Havin Old English: safe place

Hawa/Hawaa/Hawwa/Hawwaa/Haya/Hayat *See* Hava

Haydee *See* Haidee

Hayden Germanic: heathen

Haylee/Hayleigh/Hayley/Haylie Old English: meadow, hay clearing. Also Old Norse: hero

Hazal/Hazel Old English: hazel tree (name from flowers and trees)

Hazera/Hazira *See* Hajira. Also a town in India (geographical name)

Heather Old English: heather plant (name from flowers and trees)

Heaven/Heavenly Old English: home of god, sky

Heba/Hebe Greek: goddess of youth (daughter of Zeus and Hera from Greek mythology). Also a type of flowering plant from New Zealand (name from flowers and trees)

Hedda A diminutive form of Hedwig (Germanic: battle, war)

Heela Pashto: hope, wish

Heena *See* Henna

Heer Hindi: diamond (gemstone name)

Heidi A diminutive form of Adelaide

Helaina/Helana/Helayna *See* Helen

Heledd A Welsh princess from Canu Heledd

Heleena/Helen/Helena/Helene/ Helin/Helina Greek: torch, light. Also Amharic: conscious

Heloise *See* Eloise

Hema Sanskrit: gold

Hemali Sanskrit (from hemala): goldsmith, chameleon

Hena/Henna/Hennah Arabic: thorny tree (name from flowers and trees). Also *See* Hanna

Henny A diminutive form of Henrietta

Henrietta *See* Harriet

Hephzibah/Hepzibah Hebrew: my delight is in her

Hera Greek: queen (the queen of gods in Greek mythology)

Hermela A blend of Hermione and Ella

Hermione Greek: messenger (feminine form of Hermes, the Greek messenger god)

Hero (name from an English word) Greek: of superhuman strength *See also* Hera

Hertha Old English: Earth

Hessa A diminutive form of Helene Also an island in Norway

(geographical names)

Hester/Hesther Greek: star

Hetal Sanskrit (from hrdayalu): warm, loving

Hettie/Hetty A diminutive form of Hester

Hetvi Hindi: love

Hiba/Hibah/Hibaq/Hibba/ Hibbah/Hibo Arabic: gift, gift from god

Hidaya/Hidayah Arabic: guidance from god. Also Swahili: beautiful

Hifsa/Hifza Arabic: protecting angel

Hijab Arabic: veil

Hilal Arabic: crescent

Hilary Latin: cheerful, happy

Hilda Germanic: warrior woman

Hillary *See* Hilary

Himani Sanskrit: a mass of snow

Hina *See* Hena. Also Japanese: various, including sun-plant. Also a moon goddess from Polynesian mythology

Hind/Hinda/Hindy Hebrew: doe

Hinna *See* Hena

Hira/Hirah/Hiral/Hirra Sanskrit (from hira): diamond

Hiya Hindi (from hrdaya): heart

Hiyam Arabic: love

Hoda Arabic: grateful

Hodan Cushitic: do well

Holley/Holli/Hollie/Holly (name from flowers and trees, name from an English word)

Holy (name from an English word.

See also Holly

Honey (name from an English word, term of endearment)

Honeysuckle (name from flowers and trees, name from an English word)

Honie *See* Honey

Hoor/Hoorain/Hooria/Hooriya Arabic: women with beautiful eyes, women of heaven

Hosana/Hosanna/Hosna Greek: prayer of salvation

Huda Arabic: guidance

Hui Chinese: various, including grey, wisdom and bright

Hulya Turkish: daydream

Huma Persian: griffin-like mythological bird

Humaira/Humairaa/Humairah/ Humayra/Humayrah/Humera/ Humerah Arabic: reddish. Also the nickname of the prophet Muhammad's first wife, Aisha. *See also* Aisha

Humma/Humna *See* Huma

Hunni/Hunnie *See* Honey

Huriya/Hurriya Arabic: freedom, liberty

Husna/Husnaa/Husnah Arabic: most pious

i

Ianthe Greek: purple flower (name from flowers and trees). Also the name of several figures in Greek mythology, including a sea nymph

Iara Tupí: water lady (a water goddess from Brazilian mythology)

Iba Arabic: pride

Ibtisam Arabic: smile

Ida Sanskrit: praise, speech. The founder of the Lunar Dynasty in Hindu mythology whose gender changes every month, sometimes seen as the goddess of speech, and is also known as Ila. *See also* Aida

Idil Turkish: pure and sincere love

Idman Somali: permitted

Ieeda *See* Aida

Iesha *See* Aisha

Ieta *See* Aida

Ieva *See* Eva

Ifeoma Igbo: good, beautiful thing

Iffah/Iffat Arabic: purity, modesty, chastity

Ifra/Ifrah Arabic: sublimity

Ifza *See* Hifza

Iga A diminutive form of Jadwiga, a variant of Hedwig

Ijeoma Igbo: safe journey

Ikhlas Arabic: sincerity, honesty, fidelity

Ikhra/Ikra/Ikrah Arabic: mental or physical force

Ikran Unknown, possibly from Ikram. Also James Cameron's Na'vi: Pandora's mountain banshees used by hunters seen in *Avatar*

Ila The founder of the Lunar Dynasty in Hindu mythology whose gender changes every month, is sometimes seen as the goddess of speech, and is also known as Ida

Ilana Hebrew: tree

Ilaria *See* Hillary

Ilayda Turkish: water fairy

Ilhaam Arabic: intuition, inspiration

Iliana *See* Helen

Ilma Finnish: air

Ilona *See* Helen and Ilana

Ilsa/Ilse A diminutive form of Elizabeth

Ilyana *See* Helen

Imaani Arabic: faith. *See also* Girls and Boys: Imaan

Imama Arabic: leader

Imana *See* Imaani. Also a creator god in Banyarwanda mythology

Imane *See* Imaani

Imara Swahili: strong. Also a village in Estonia (geographical name)

Imarni *See* Imaani

Imelda Germanic: the entire battle

Immogen/Imogen/Imogene Irish Gaelic (from ingen): maiden

Ina *See* Ena. *See also* Inna

Inaaya/Inaayah Arabic: gift of god *See also* Inaya

Inara Arabic: sent from heaven. Also a goddess of wild animals from Hittite mythology

Inas Arabic: friendly

Inaya/Inayah Arabic: loving, caring, gift of care

Inca *See* Inga. Also the name of the Inca empire (geographical name)

Inda/Indea/Indee *See* India

Inderpreet Punjabi: love for god (Sikh name)

India/Indiah Old English: India (geographical name)

Indiana/Indianna Latin: from India. Also a state in the US (geographical name)

Indira Sanskrit: beauty, splendour. One of the 108 names of Laksmi, the Hindu goddess of wealth and beauty

Indiya *See* India

Indra Sanskrit: drops of rain, lord of the sky and atmosphere. The name of the Hindu god of war and thunderstorms

Indya *See* India

Ines/Inez *See* Agnes

Inga/Inge/Inger Old Norse: guarded by Ing, the god who fathered the lines of Swedish and Norwegian kings

Ingrid Old Norse: Ing's beauty

Inka *See* Inca

Inna Russian: strong water

Innaya/Innayah *See* Inaya

Innes Celtic: one choice. *See also* Agnes

Insha Arabic: creation

Intisar Arabic: victory, triumph, singing

Ioana *See* Joanna

Iola/Iona/Ione/Ionie Greek: violet

Ipek Turkish: silk

Iqra/Iqraa/Iqrah Arabic: study, read

Iram/Irem The city with lofty pillars is mentioned in the Qur'an as a beautiful place smote by god because of corruption among the rulers

Irena/Irene/Irina Greek: peace (the goddess of peace in Greek mythology)

Iris Greek: rainbow (the rainbow goddess in Greek mythology). Also the name of the flower (name from flowers and trees). Also the violet-purple colour (colour name). Also the name of the waterfall, Iris Falls, in the US

Irmak Turkish: river

Irram *See* Iram

Irsa/Irsah Arabic: rainbow

Irum *See* Iram

Isabel/Isabela/Isabell/Isabella/Isabelle *See* Elizabeth

Isadora *See* Isidora

Isatou A Gambian name, possibly shifted from Aisha, which means 'living one'. *See also* Aisha

Isbah Arabic: light

Isha/Ishaa Arabic: night prayer

Ishaal Arabic: flower of heaven

Ishah *See* Isha

Ishana/Ishani Sanskrit (from izana): ruling, lord. One of the names of the Hindu god Shiva

Ishbel *See* Isabel

Ishika Sanskrit (from isika): painter's brush

Ishita Sanskrit (from izita): supremacy, superiority

Ishmeet Punjabi: beloved friend of god (Sikh name)

Ishrat Arabic: enjoyment, delight

Isidora/Isidore Greek: gift of Isis

Isis The Egyptian goddess of the throne

Isla/Islay Old French: island. Also the name of a Scottish Gaelic island in the Inner Hebrides (geographical name)

Isma/Ismah Arabic: safeguarding

Ismahan Unknown, possibly from Asmahan (Persian: seeker of excellence). *See also* Isma

Ismat Arabic: pious

Ismay *See* Esme

Isobel/Isobell/Isobella/Isobelle *See* Elizabeth

Isolde Old German: ice battle

Isra/Israa Arabic: journey by night

Issabella/Issabelle *See* Elizabeth

Issey A diminutive form of Isabelle. Also used as a Japanese name, usually for boys, with various meanings including one life and one policy

Issra *See* Isra

Italia Italian: Italy (geographical name)

Iulia *See* Julia

Iva A diminutive form of Ivana

Ivana/Ivanna *See* Joanna

Ivie/Ivy (name from flowers and trees, name from an English word)

Iyana *See* Aiyana

Iyanuoluwa Yoruba: god's wonder is great

Iyeeda *See* Aida

Iyesha *See* Aisha

Iyla/Iylah *See* Isla

Izabel/Izabela/Izabell/Izabella/ Izabelle *See* Elizabeth

Izel Turkish: one who will leave a mark

Izma Arabic: high, exalter

Izobel/Izobella/Izobelle *See* Elizabeth

Izza A diminutive form of Isabella. *See also* Izzah

Izzabella/Izzabelle *See* Elizabeth

Izzah Arabic: honour

Izzie/Izzy A diminutive form of Isabella

Jacie A diminutive form of Jacqueline

Jacinda/Jacinta Greek: purple, hyacinth flower (name from flowers and trees)

Jacqueline Hebrew: on the heel, to follow behind

Jacqui A diminutive form of Jacqueline

Jada From the word 'jade'. Also Hebrew: he knows. *See also* Girls and Boys: Jade

Jadene From the word 'jade' with an added feminine ending

Jadesola Yoruba: arrive into wealth

Jadie/Jadine *See* Jadene

Jadzia *See* Hedwig

Jaeda *See* Jada

Jael Hebrew: mountain goat

Jagoda Slavic: strawberry

Jahnavi A name of the sacred River Ganges, from the name of the sage Jahnu who drank up the river and let it back out through a slit in his knee

Jahzara Ethiopian name, possibly shifted from Sarah: blessed princess

Jaia *See* Jaya

Jaida/Jaide *See* Jada

Jaimee Hebrew: on the heel, to follow behind. A Scottish variant of James, now used as a name for girls as well

Jaimini Gujarati: victory

Jaina *See* Jane

Jainaba Unknown. A Wolof name, popular in Senegal

Jaipreet Punjabi: love of victory (Sikh name)

Jaiya *See* Jaya

Jaiyana Arabic: strength

Jakia A diminutive form of Jacqueline

Jameela/Jameelah/Jamelia *See*

Jamila

Jami *See* Jaimee

Jamieleigh A blend of Jamie and Leigh. *See also* Girls and Boys: Jamielee

Jamila/Jamilah/Jamilla Arabic: beautiful

Jamima *See* Jemima

Jana Hebrew: god is gracious

Janae/Janai *See* Jane

Janani Hindi: mother

Janay/Janaya *See* Jane

Jane A variant of Joanne

Janelle Hebrew: god is gracious

Janet/Janey/Janice/Janie *See* Jane

Janina/Janine *See* Jeanne

Janki Hindi: daughter of a Janaka, a title given to the kings of Videha, (now in modern day Nepal)

Janna/Jannah/Jannat/Jannath Arabic: garden, paradise

Jannatul From Jannatul Mualla, the burial grounds for prophet Muhammad's ancestors and wives

Janvi *See* Jahnavi

Japji Punjabi: chant of the soul (Sikh name). The universal song composed by the Sikh founder Guru Nanak Dev

Jaskiran Punjabi: ray of light from god's glory (Sikh name)

Jasleen Punjabi: engrossed in god's glory (Sikh name)

Jasmeen *See* Jasmin

Jasmin/Jasmina/Jasminder/Jasmine/Jasmyn (name from flowers and trees, name from an English word)

Jasneet Punjabi: always in god's glory (Sikh name)

Javairia/Javaria/Javeria Arabic: mysterious

Javine The name of a god of grains from Lithuanian mythology

Jaweria *See* Javairia

Jaya/Jayah Sanskrit: victorious, conquering
One of the 108 names of the invincible Hindu goddess Durga. *See also* Jay

Jaycie A blend of two letters from the alphabet. *See also* Girls and Boys: Jaycee

Jayda/Jayde/Jaydene *See* Jada

Jayla/Jaylah From the letter 'J'. *See also* Girls and Boys: Jay

Jayleigh A blend of Jay and Leigh

Jayme/Jaymee/Jaymie *See* Jaimee

Jayna/Jayne *See* Jane

Jazmin/Jazmine/Jazmyn *See* Jasmin

Jazz (name from an English word)

Jazzmin/Jazzmine *See* Jasmin

Jeana/Jeanette/Jeanie/Jeanne/Jeannie A variant of Jane, therefore also from the same root as Joanna

Jeevika Hindi: water

Jeeya *See* Jiya

Jelena A Serbian variant of Helena

Jema *See* Gemma

Jemila *See* Jamila

Jemima/Jemimah Hebrew: warm, affectionate. One of the three daughters of Job

Jemma *See* Gemma

Jena/Jenae/Jenai A diminutive form of Jennifer

Jenan Arabic: paradise

Jenaya *See* Jane

Jenelle *See* Janelle

Jenessa A blend of Jennifer and Vanessa

Jenifer *See* Jennifer

Jenika/Jenisha A blend of Jenni and feminine endings

Jenna A diminutive form of Jennifer

Jennah Arabic: paradise

Jenni/Jennie A diminutive form of Jennifer

Jennifer Cornish: white, fair and smooth. *See also* Guinevere

Jenny A diminutive form of Jennifer

Jeorgia *See* Georgia

Jeri A diminutive form of Geraldine

Jersey From the island near Normandy (geographical name)

Jerusha Hebrew: possession The mother of Jotham

Jesamine *See* Jasmin

Jessamy *See* Jasmin

Jesica/Jesika *See* Jessica

Jeslyn *See* Joscelyn

Jessamy Old English: jasmine (name from flowers and trees)

Jessi A diminutive form of Jessica. *See also* Boys and Girls: Jesse

Jessica/Jessicca Hebrew: with foresight

Jessika *See* Jessica

Jeyda *See* Jada

Jhanvi *See* Jahnavi

Jihan Arabic: heavenly place

Jill A diminutive form of Gillian

Jillian *See* Gillian

Jilly A diminutive form of Gillian

Jinan Arabic: garden, paradise

Jiya Sanskrit (from jiva): chord of life, soul, existence

Joan/Joana *See* Joanna

Joanie A diminutive form of Joan

Joanna/Joanne Hebrew: Jehovah is gracious

Jocasta The mother of Oedipus in Greek mythology, who also married him and bore him four children

Jochebed Hebrew: Jehovah is glory. The mother of Moses

Jodie A variant of Judy. *See also* Girls and Boys: Jodi

Joella/Joelle Hebrew: Jehovah is god

Joely *See* Joley

Johanna *See* Joanna

Johara/Johura From Jawharah (Arabic: jewel)

Jolee *See* Joley

Joleen/Jolene A blend of Joley and a feminine ending

Joley/Jolie French: pretty

Jonelle A variant of Joanna

Joni A diminutive form of Joanne

Jood A diminutive form of Judith

Jordaine/Jordana/Jordane/ Jordann/Jordanna/Jordanne Hebrew: flowing down. Named after the River Jordan (geographical name). *See also* Girls and Boys: Jordan

Jorgia/Jorja *See* Georga

Joscelyn/Joselyn Old French: From the tribe of the Gauts. *See also* Girls and Boys: Jocelyn

Josephina/Josephine Hebrew: Jehovah will increase

Josiane A French diminutive form of Josephine

Josie A diminutive form of Josephine

Josslyn *See* Joscelyn

Jovana A Serbian variant of Joanna

Jovie A diminutive form of Jovana

Joyce Latin: lord. Also from the word 'joy'

Joycelyn *See* Joscelyn

Juanita A Spanish variant of Joanna

Judith Hebrew: praised. In the Book of Judith, she uses her charm to get close to Holofernes and ultimately cut off his head

Judy A diminutive form of Judith

Judyta A Polish variant of Judith

Juhi Sanskrit (from yuthi): jasmine (name from flowers and trees)

Julia Latin: devoted to Jove

Juliana/Julianna/Julianne Latin: of Julia. *See* Julia

Julie *See* Julia

Julienne *See* Juliana

Juliet/Juliette/Julita A diminutive form of Julia

Jumaimah One of prophet Muhammad's female companions

Jumana/Jumanah Arabic: pearl

June (name from an English word)

Juniper (name from flowers and trees, name from an English word)

Juno Latin: younger. The Roman goddess who is the wife of Jupiter

Justina/Justine/Justyna Latin: just

Juwairia/Juwairiyah/Juwairiyyah/ Juwariah/Juwariyah/Juwayriya/ Juwayriyah The name of Juwayriyya bint al-Harith, one of prophet Muhammad's wives

Jyoti Sanskrit (from jyotis): divine light, light of freedom, bliss or victory

k

Kaavya Sanskrit: poem, sonnet. *See also* Girls and Boys: Kavya

Kacee A blend of two letters from the alphabet

Kacia A diminutive form of Katherine

Kacie/Kacy A diminutive form of Katherine. *See also* Kacee

Kadee A blend of two letters from the alphabet

Kadence *See* Cadence

Kader Arabic: powerful. Also

Turkish: destiny. Also Cornish: pretty

Kadey/Kadi/Kadie A diminutive form of Cadence. *See also* Kadee

Kadija *See* Khadija

Kady *See* Kadey

Kaela/Kaelyn A blend of Kae, a diminutive form of Katherine, and a feminine ending

Kahlan/Kahlen Unknown, possibly created by Terry Goodkind for *The Sword of Truth* series, when naming Kahlan Amnell

Kaia *See* Kaja

Kaidy *See* Kadey

Kaila/Kailah/Kailey/Kailyn A blend of Kai, a diminutive form of Katherine, and a feminine ending

Kainaat/Kainat Arabic: universe

Kaira/Kairi/Kaisha A blend of Kai, a diminutive form of Katherine, and a feminine ending

Kaitlan/Kaitland/Kaitlen/ Kaitlin/Kaitlyn/Kaitlynn *See* Catherine

Kaiyah A blend of Kai, a diminutive form of Katherine, and a feminine ending. *See also* Girls and Boys: Kaiya

Kaja Old Norse: hen. Also a diminutive form of Katarina. *See also* Girls and Boys: Kaiya

Kajal/Kajol Sanskrit: kohl

Kala Sanskrit: virtue

Kaleigh/Kaley A blend of Ka-, a diminutive form of Katherine, and a feminine ending

Kali Arabic: bud, flower. Also Sanskrit: the black one, beyond time. The name of the Hindu goddess of change

Kalia/Kalila/Kalina/Kalise/ Kalisha/Kaliyah A blend of Ka-, a diminutive form of Katherine, and a feminine ending

Kalli/Kallie/Kally A diminutive form of Caroline

Kamara A blend of Ka-, a diminutive form of Katherine, and a feminine ending. Also possibly from Kamala (Sanskrit: lotus)

Kamila/Kamilah/Kamile/Kamilla Arabic: perfect, complete, genuine

Kamiyah Sanskrit (from kamaya): from love

Kamryn *See* Camryn

Kandice *See* Candice

Kani A diminutive form of Kanishka

Kanisha Unknown, possibly a variant of Kanishka

Kanishka The name of Kanishka the Great, emperor of Kushan, and a Buddhist

Kanwal Arabic: water lily

Kara/Karah *See* Cara

Kardelen Turkish: snowdrop (name from flowers and trees)

Kareema/Kareemah *See* Karima

Kareena *See* Cara

Karen *See* Catherine

Karena *See* Cara

Karenza *See* Kerensa
Kari A diminutive form of Caroline
Karima/Karimah Arabic: king, generous, noble
Karin *See* Catherine
Karina *See* Cara
Karis *See* Carys
Karishma/Karisma Ancient Greek (from khárisma): favour, gift. *See also* Charisma
Kariss *See* Carys
Karissa *See* Charis
Karla/Karleigh/Karley/Karli/ Karlie/Karly A diminutive form of Charlotte
Karma The Buddhist and Hindu concept of the cause-and-effect cycle, and of rebirth
Karman *See* Carmen
Karmel *See* Carmel
Karmen *See* Carmen
Karolina *See* Carolina
Karrie A diminutve form of Karoline
Karris *See* Carys
Karyn *See* Caroline
Karys *See* Carys
Kasha A diminutive form of Katherine
Kashaf Arabic: unveiling. A Sufi concept to do with the truth in the heart
Kashish Arabic: attraction
Kashvi Sanskrit: beautiful, shining
Kasia/Kasie A diminutive form of Karoline and Kassandra

Kassandra *See* Cassandra
Kassia A diminutive form of Karoline and Kassandra
Kassidy Irish Gaelic: curly haired (shifted from surname usage). *See also* Girls and Boys: Cassidy
Kassie A diminutive form of Karoline and Kassandra
Katalina *See* Catherine
Katana Japanese: knife. The sword used by samurai warriors
Katarina/Katarzyna *See* Catherine
Kate A diminutive form of Catherine
Katelan/Kateland/Katelin/ Katelyn/Katelynn/Katerina *See* Catherine
Katey A diminutive form of Catherine
Katharina/Katharine/Katherine/ Katheryn/Kathleen/Kathrine/ Kathryn/Kathryne *See* Catherine
Kathy/Kati/Katia/Katie/Katja A diminutive form of Catherine
Katlin/Katlyn A blend of Kate, a diminutive form of Catherine, and Lynne
Katrin/Katrina/Katriona *See* Catherine
Katy/Katya A diminutive form of Catherine
Kauthar *See* Kawsar
Kavita/Kaviya Sanskrit: poetry
Kawsar/Kawthar Arabic: abundance, plenty. The name of the 108th chapter of the Qur'an,

named from al-Kawthar, the river
in paradise

Kay A diminutive form of Katherine

Kayah *See* Kaja

**Kayce/Kaycee/Kaycey/Kayci/
Kaycie** *See* Kacie

Kaydee *See* Kadee

Kaydence *See* Cadence

Kaydi/Kaydie *See* Kadie

Kaye *See* Kay

Kayla/Kaylah A blend of Kay, a
diminutive form of Katherine, and
a feminine ending. *See also* Cayla

**Kaylea/Kaylee/Kayleigh/Kayley/
Kayli/Kaylie/Kayliegh** A blend
of Kay, a diminutive form of
Katherine, and a feminine ending.
Also an anglicised variant of
Ceilidh

Kaylin/Kaylyn A blend of Kay, a
diminutive form of Katherine, and
a feminine ending. *See also* Cailin

Kaynat *See* Kainat

Kaysey *See* Casi

Kaysha A diminutive form of
Katherine

Kaysie *See* Casi

Kaytie A diminutive form of
Katherine

Kaytlin/Kaytlyn *See* Catherine

Kazia A diminutive form of
Karoline and Kassandra

KC A blend of two letters of the
alphabet. *See also* Casi

Ke Chinese: various, including jade.
Also Haitian Creole: heart

Kea/Keah Hawaiian: white.
Also the name of several places,
including a town in Cornwall
(geographical name). Also the
name of a type of parrot from
New Zealand

Kealeigh/Kealey/Kealy A blend of
Kea and a feminine ending

Keana/Keanna Unknown, possibly
a feminine variant of Keane, from
Ò'Calthán (shifted from surname
usage)

Keara *See* Ciara

Keavey/Keavie/Keavy An
anglicised variant of Caoimhe

Keedie Unknown. The name of
Keedie Babb, a soprano who was
named after Kiki Dee

Keela An anglicised variant of
Cadhla

Keeleigh/Keeley/Keelie/Keely
A blend of Kea and a feminine
ending. Also An anglicised variant
of Ceilidh

Keera *See* Ciara

Keerat Punjabi: sing god's glory
(Sikh name)

Keerthana Sanskrit (from kirtana):
celebrating, praising

Keesha *See* Kezia

Keeva/Keevah An anglicised
variant of Caoimhe

Keia *See* Kea and Keya

Keianna *See* Kiyana

Keighley A blend of Kea and a
feminine ending

Keila/Keilah *See* Keela

Keileigh/Keiley A blend of Kea and a feminine ending. Also an anglicised variant of Ceilidh

Keira *See* Ciara

Keisha *See* Kezia

Keita A Latvian variant of Kate

Kejsi An Albanian variant of Kelci

Kelcey/Kelci/Kelcie/Kelcy *See* Kelsea

Keleigh A blend of Kea and a feminine ending. Also an anglicised variant of Ceilidh

Kelis/Kelise/Kelisha A blend of Kea and a feminine ending. *See also* Kelley

Kelley/Kelli/Kellie/Kellis Irish Gaelic (from ceallach): bright headed. *See also* Girls and Boys: Kelly

Kelsea/Kelsi/Kelsie/Kelsy Old English (from cēol and sie): victorious ship. *See also* Girls and Boys: Kelsey

Kemi A town in Finland (geographical name)

Kenadie *See* Kennady

Kenaya Unknown, possibly a variant of Kenya

Kendell Old English (from Kent and dæl): valley of Kent shifted from surname usage). *See also* Girls and Boys: Kendal

Kendra Unknown, possibly a blend of Kenna and Sandra

Kenisha/Kenna An anglicised variant of Cinaed, Irish Gaelic: born of fire. Also an anglicised variant of Cainnech, Irish Gaelic: handsome

Kennady/Kennedi/Kennedy From Ó Ceannéidigh, Irish Gaelic (from ceann and éidigh): ugly head (shifted from surname usage)

Kensa *See* Kenza

Kensey *See* Kenna

Kenya Kikuyu (from kere and nyaga): white mountain. The name of the country (geographical name)

Kenza Arabic: treasure

Keona Hawaiian: the attractive one, the beautiful one

Kera *See* Ciara and Keran

Keran/Keren Hindi: beam, ray, light, spark. *See also* Girls and Boys: Kiran

Kerensa/Kerenza Cornish: love

Keri/Keris/Kerri *See* Kerrie

Kerrianne A blend of Kerrie and Ann

Kerrie/Kerris Irish Gaelic: Ciar's people. *See also* Girls and Boys: Kerry

Kerryanne A blend of Kerrie and Ann

Kerryn *See* Ciara and Keran

Kerstin *See* Christina

Keryn *See* Ciara and Keran

Kerys *See* Kerrie

Kesha/Keshia/Kesia/Ketsia *See* Kezia

Keturah Hebrew: incense. A wife of

Abraham

Kevser The Turkish name of a river in paradise

Keya From Khyah, a type of in Nepalese folklore, where white Khyah bring good luck

Keyanna *See* Kiyana

Keyla *See* Keela

Keyleigh A blend of Key and a feminine ending. Also an anglicised variant of Ceilidh

Keyshia/Kezia/Keziah/Kezzia Hebrew: cassia tree (name from flowers and trees)

Khadeeja/Khadeejah/Khadeja/ Khadija/Khadijah/Khadiza The name of Khadija bint Khuwaylid, the first of prophet Muhammad's wives

Khadra Arabic: green

Khaira/Khairah Arabic: the best, good, virtuous

Khaleesi The title of Daenerys Targaryen in George R. R. Martin's *A Song of Ice and Fire* series, where it is a Dothraki title for the wives of their warlords

Khalia A diminutive form of Khalida, Arabic (from khalada): eternal, lasting forever

Khalisa/Khalisah Arabic: pure, clear, real

Khansa Arabic: pug-nosed

Kharis A diminutive form of Karisma

Khatija Arabic (from khadija):

premature child. The name of Khadija bint Khuwaylid, the first wife of prophet Muhammad

Khawla Arabic: female deer

Khia *See* Kiyah

Khianna *See* Kiyana

Khiara/Khira *See* Ciara

Khloe *See* Chloe

Khushi Hindi (from khaushi): happy, joyful, jubilant

Khyra *See* Ciara

Kiana/Kianna/Kiannah/Kianne *See* Kiyana

Kiara/Kiarah/Kiarna/Kiarra *See* Chiara

Kiaya *See* Kaja

Kieara/Kiera/Kierah/Kierra *See* Ciara

Kiersten A Danish variant of Christina

Kiesha *See* Kezia

Kiki A diminutive form of various names, including Kadence, Karen and Kamila. Also the name of the young witch from Studio Ghibli's *Kiki's Delivery Service*

Kimaya *See* Kimia

Kimberley/Kimberly Old English: royal forest field. A South African place name (geographical name, shifted from surname usage)

Kimia Persian (from kimiya): alchemy

Kimora Unknown, possibly a modernised and shifted variant of Kimberley. The name of the model

Kimora Lee Simmons

Kimran Unknown, possibly a modernised and shifted variant of Kimberley or Keran

Kinga A Hungarian variant of Kunigunde, Old German: brave war. Hungarian name day for Kinga: 24th July

Kinza Arabic: intelligent

Kiona See Keona

Kira/Kirah See Ciara and Keran

Kirandeep Punjabi: lamp of bright light (Sikh name)

Kiranjeet Punjabi: one who wins the ray of light (Sikh name)

Kiranjit Punjabi: victorious through the ray of light (Sikh name)

Kiranpreet Punjabi: love of the ray of light (Sikh name)

Kirbie Old English (from kirk): church (shifted from surname usage)

Kiren See Keran

Kiri Japanese: mist, fog

Kirpa Punjabi: mercy, blessing (Sikh name)

Kirra See Kira

Kirsten A Danish and Norwegian variant of Christina

Kirsti/Kirstie/Kirstin/Kirsty/ Kirstyn A diminutive form of Kirsten

Kisha See Kezia

Kisi See Akosua

Kitana Unknown, possibly a blend of Kit and Anna. Also possibly a modernised and shifted variant of Katana. A character from *Mortal Kombat*

Kittie/Kitty A diminutive form of Katherine

Kiyah/Kiyana/Kiyanna Hindi (from kiyana): raise up

Kiyra See Ciara and Keran

Kizzie/Kizzy A diminutive form of Kezia

Klara See Clara

Klaudia See Claudia

Klea A diminutive form of Cleopatra

Kloe See Chloe

Komal Hindi: delicate, fine, soft, smooth

Konnie A diminutive form of Constance

Kora/Koren See Corrina

Kornelia A Polish variant of Cornelia

Kornelija A Lithuanian variant of Cornelia

Kotryna A Lithuanian variant of Katherine

Kourtney See Courtnay

Kowsar A Somalian variant of Kawthar

Krisha Unknown, possibly a modernised and shifted variant of Trisha

Krishma See Karishma

Krista A diminutive form of Kristina

Kristal See Crystal

Kristi A diminutive form of Christina

Kristiana A Latvian variant of Christina

Kristie A diminutive form of Christina

Kristin A Scandinavian variant of Christina

Kristina/Kristine A German, Scandinavian and Russian variant of Christina

Kristy A diminutive form of Christina

Kristyna A Czech variant of Christina

Kritika Sanskrit (from krtika): adopted as a daughter. A star cluster that corresponds to the Pleiades, named after the six sisters who brought up the Hindu god Murugan

Kriya Sanskrit: acting, performing, undertaking, religious action, ceremony

Krupa Sanskrit (from krpa): grace, compassion, loving kindness

Krystal See Crystal

Krystina See Christina

Krystle See Crystal

Krystyna See Christina

Ksenia A Polish variant of Xenia

Ksenija A Croatian, Latvian, Macedonian and Slovenian variant of Xenia. Latvian name day for Ksenija: 24th January

Kubra Arabic: major, great, elder

Kukuw See Akua

Kulsoom/Kulsum/Kulsuma Arabic: with chubby, rosy and healthy-looking cheeks

Kumba Kikongo: roar. Also a city in Cameroon (geographical name)

Kundai Shona: success

Kushi See Khushi

Kyana/Kyanna/Kyanne See Kiana

Kyara See Chiara

Kyesha See Kaisha

Kyia See Kaja

Kyla/Kylah Scottish Gaelic: narrow, strait (shifted from surname usage)

Kylie Unknown, possibly Noongar: curved stick, boomerang. The name became widely used in New Zealand and Australia, and may have gained popularity because of the singer Kylie Minogue

Kymberley/Kymberly See Kimberley

Kyna Unknown, possibly from Kina (Hawaiian: China, or Hawaiian variant of Dinah)

Kyra/Kyrah See Ciara

Kyrie Greek: lord. Kýrie, eléison, meaning 'Lord, have mercy', is a Christian prayer that is traditionally used as choral text

l

LA Named after the city Los

Angeles (Spanish: the angels; geographical name)

Laaiba/Laaibah *See* Laiba

Labiba/Labibah Arabic: intelligent, wise, prudent

Lace/Lacee/Lacey *See* Laci

Laceymay A blend of Lacey and May

Laci/Lacie/Lacy Old English: di Laci, from Lassy, a place in Normandy (shifted from surname usage). Also connected to the word lace

Ladan Persian: flower

Lady (name from an English word)

Laetitia *See* Latisha

Laiba/Laibah The name of a hoor, a beautiful woman in paradise

Laicee/Laicey *See* Laci

Laila/Lailah *See* Layla

Laina/Lainey/Lainie A diminutive form of Elaine/Elaina

Laiqah Arabic: elegant, deserving, worthy

Lakeisha A blend of La and Keisha

Laken From the word 'lake'

Lakisha *See* Lakeisha

Lakshmi The name of the Hindu goddess of beauty, wealth and fortune

Lalita Sanskrit: playful, charming

Lama Arabic: beautiful lips that look naturally lined

Lamara Arabic: liquid gold Also Old French: from the sea *See also* Girls and Boys: Lamar

Lamees *See* Lamis

Lamia Arabic: bright, shining, splendid. Also the name of a Libyan queen from Greek mythology who ate children. Also siren-like women in Basque mythology who live in rivers and have duck feet

Lamis Arabic: tender girl

Lamisa Arabic: soft to touch

Lamorna The name of a Cornish village, mentioned in a folk song of the same name

Lamya *See* Lamia

Lana/Lanah/Laney A diminutive form of Elaine/Elaina

Lani Hawaiian: heaven Also a diminutive form of Elaine. *See also* Nalani

Lanie/Lanya A diminutive form of Elaine

Laoise *See* Louise

Lara/Larah A diminutive form of Larisa

Laraib Arabic: truth

Larisa/Larissa Greek: citadel. One of the biggest citys in Greece, and the birthplace of Achilles in Greek mythology

Larna *See* Lara and Lana

Lashay From La Shay, Shay (Irish Gaelic: admirable or hawk-like)

Latasha *See* Latisha

Lataya From La Taya. *See* Taya

Latesha *See* Latisha

Latia A diminutive form of Latisha

Latifa/Latifah Arabic: gentle, kind, charming, sweet

Latisha Latin: happiness

Latoya A diminutive form of Victoria. This version was made popular by La Toya Jackson

Laura Latin: laurel (name from flowers and trees)

Lauran *See* Lauren

Laurel/Laurelle (name from flowers and trees, name from an English word)

Lauren Latin: from Laurentum, an ancient Roman city, or crowned with laurel

Laurissa A blend of Laura and Larisa

Lauryn *See* Lauren

Lavanya Sanskrit: beauty, grace

Lavin/Lavina/Lavinia The daughter of King Latinus in Roman mythology, whose hair catches fire at the alter while she remains unharmed – a good omen

Laya Arabic: twist

Layaan Arabic: soft

Layah *See* Laya

Layal Arabic: night

Layan *See* Layaan

Layba *See* Laiba

Laycee/Laycie *See* Laci

Layla/Laylah Arabic: of the night

Layna/Laynie A diminutive form of Elaine/Elaina

Le Chinese, various, including happy and laughing

Lea/Leah/Leaha Hebrew: weary

Leala *See* Layla

Leana A blend of Lee and Anna/Anne

Leandra Greek: lion of a man

Leann/Leanna/Leanne A blend of Lee and Anna/Anne

Leasha A diminutive form of Alicia

Leeann/Leeanne A blend of Lee and Anna/Anne

Leela *See* Layla

Leen/Leena A diminutive form of Elaine/Elaina

Leeya *See* Leiah

Leeza A diminutive form of Elisa and Elizabeth

Leia *See* Leah

Leiah/Leigha Old English: clearing. *See also* Lea

Leighann/Leighanne A blend of Leigh and Ann/Anne

Leighla/Leila/Leilah *See* Layla

Leilani Hawaiian: heavenly flowers

Leisha A diminutive form of Alicia

Leja *See* Leiah

Lela *See* Layla

Lema Arabic: eye

Lena/Lene A diminutive form of Elaine/Elaina

Leni/Lenka A diminutive form of Helena and Magdelena

Leola/Leona/Leoni/Leonie/Leonna/Leonnie Greek: lion

Leonor/Leonora A diminutive form of Eleonor/Eleonora

Leora *See* Leona

Leshay From Le Shay, Shay
(Hebrew: gift)

Lesley Scottish Gaelic (from leas
and celyn): garden of holly (shifted
from surname usage)

Letia A diminutive form of Latisha

Leticia/Letisha/Letitia *See* Latisha

**Lexi/Lexia/Lexie/Lexii/Lexine/
Lexis/Lexxi/Lexxie/Lexy** A
diminutive form of Alexandria,
Alexi or Alexia

Leya/Leyah *See* Leiah

Leyla/Leylah *See* Layla

Leyna A diminutive form of Elaina

Lia *See* Leiah

Liaba *See* Laiba

Liah *See* Leiah

Liana/Liane/Lianna/Lianne A
diminutive form of Juliana and
Liliana

Liara *See* Liora

Liarna *See* Liana and Liora

Liba *See* Laiba

Libbi/Libbie/Libby A diminutive
form of Liberty

Liberty (name from an English
word)

Libi A diminutive form of Liberty

Licia A diminutive form of Alicia

Lidia/Lidya *See* Lydia

Liepa Lithuanian: linden tree

Lila Sanskrit: play, amuse

Lilac (colour name, name from an
English word)

Lilah *See* Lila

Lilee/Lili/Lilia/Lilian/Liliana/

Lilianna/Lilie/Lilien *See* Lily

Lilith Hebrew: of the night. In
mythology, she is the first wife of
Adam, and is created at the same
time as Adam, but not from one of
his ribs, unlike Eve

**Liliya/Lilja/Lilla/Lillee/Lilley/
Lilli/Lillia/Lilliah/Lillian/
Lilliana/Lillianna/Lillie** *See* Lily

Lillith *See* Lilith

Lilly/Lillya *See* Lily

Lillyann/Lillyanna A blend of Lilly
and Ann/Anna

Lillybelle A blend of Lilly and Belle

Lillymae/Lillymay A blend of Lilly
and Mae/May

Lillyrose A blend of Lilly and Rose

Lilou A blend of Lily and Lou

Lily/Lilya (name from flowers and
trees, name from an English word)

**Lilyana/Lilyann/Lilyanna/
Lilyanne** A blend of Lily and
Ana/Ann/Anna/Anne

Lilybelle A blend of Lily and Belle

Lilyella A blend of Lily and Ella

Lilymae/Lilymay A blend of Lily
and Mae/May

Lilyrose A blend of Lily and Rose

Lima The capital of Peru
(geographical name)

Lin Chinese: various, including
forest and beautiful jade

Lina Arabic: gentle, soft, tender

Linda Old German: soft, elegant,
tender. Also Spanish: beautiful.
Also Ndebele: guard

Lindsay/Lindsey Old English: from Lincoln island (shifted from surname usage)

Linnea Swedish: twinflower (name from flowers and trees)

Linsey/Linzi *See* Lindsay

Liora Hebrew: my light

Lisa A diminutive form of Elisa and Elizabeth

Lisamarie A blend of Lisa and Marie. This version was made popular by Lisa Marie Presley

Lisha A diminutive form of Alicia

Lita A diminutive form of Lillita

Liv/Livi/Livia/Livie/Livvi/ Livvie/Livvy/Livy Old Norse: protection, or life. Also a diminutive form of Olivia

Liwia Also a diminutive form of Olivia

Liya/Liyah *See* Leiah

Liyana A diminutive form of Juliana and Liliana

Liyba *See* Laiba

Liz A diminutive form of Elizabeth

Liza Arabic: dedicated to Allah. Also a diminutive form of Elizabeth

Lizzie/Lizzy A diminutive form of Elizabeth

Lleucu *See* Lucia

Llinos Welsh: greenfinch

Llio A diminutive form of Gwenllian

Lohan From the Leoghain family (shifted from surname usage).

Also possibly related to Logan (Scottish Gaelic: little hollow)

Lois Greek: better. *See also* Louise

Lola/Lolah A diminutive form of Dolores

Lolita *See* Dolores. Also the titular character from the novel by Vladimir Nabokov

Lollie A diminutive form of Dolores

Lona A moon goddess in Hawaiian mythology

Lora Manx: sufficient. *See also* Laura

Loran *See* Lauren

Lordina Unknown, possibly a feminised version of the word 'lord'

Loredana Unknown, possibly created by George Sand in her novel *Mattea*, where Loredana is the titular character's mother

Lorelai/Lorelei/Lorelie Old German: luring rock

Lorelei is a maiden from German mythology whose lover left her on a rock, so she turned into a spirit and lured sailors with her song to crash into the rock

Lorelle *See* Laurel

Loren *See* Lauren

Lorena/Lorenza Latin: from Laurentum, an ancient Roman city, or crowned with laurel

Loretta Italian (from loreto): laurel wood (name from flowers and trees)

Lori A diminutive form of Lorraine

Lorien Tolkien's Quenya: place of sleep. Also Tolkien's Nandorin: place of golden light. The name of Lothlórien, the forest where the Elves live. Also the name of Irmo, who lives in the Gardens of Lórien, which is in Valinor

Lorin *See* Lauren

Lorna Unknown, possibly named after Lorne, a district in historical Scotland

Lorraine Old English: from Lorraine, the Kingdom of Lothar, the kingdom of the famous army

Lorren *See* Lauren and Lorraine

Lotta/Lotte/Lotti/Lottie/Lotty A diminutive form of Charlotte

Lotus (name from flowers and trees, name from an English word)

Lou A diminutive form of Louise

Louanna A blend of Lou and Anna

Louella A blend of Lou and Ella

Louisa/Louise/Louisha/Louiza Old German: famous warrior

Lourdes A town in France and home of Our Lady of Lourdes, the Virgin Mary seen by Saint Bernadette Soubirous

Loveday A name that evolved from Leofdaeg, and a loveday is where enemies meet to settle disagreements

Lowena/Lowenna Cornish: joy, bliss

Lowri *See* Laura

Loza Spanish: porcelain. Also possibly a title of the Virgin Mary

Lua Portuguese: moon. Also the name of a minor Roman goddess

Luana A blend of Lou and Ana

Lubelihle Ndebele: beautiful flower

Lubna Arabic: perfume resin tree

Luchia/Luci/Lucia/Luciana/ Lucianna/Lucie/Lucienne/ Lucille/Lucinda/Lucja/Lucy Latin: light

Luella A blend of Lou and Ella. Known for being the fashion label founded by Luella Bartley

Luisa/Luiza *See* Louisa

Lujain Arabic: silver

Lukne Lithuanian: yellow water lily (name from flowers and trees)

Lula Manx: shining. A diminutive form of Louise

Lulu/Lulya Arabic: pearls. Also Native American: rabbit. Also a diminutive form of Louise

Luna Latin: moon. The Roman goddess of the moon

Lyba/Lybah *See* Laiba

Lydia Greek: from Lydia, a kingdom based in parts of modern day Turkey

Lyla/Lylah *See* Lila

Lyna *See* Lina

Lynda *See* Linda

Lyndsay/Lyndsey *See* Lindsay

Lynette *See* Eluned

Lynn/Lynne Welsh: lake

Lynsey *See* Lindsay

Lyra The constellation that is shaped

like a lyre. The name of the heroine, Lyra Silvertongue from the *His Dark Materials* trilogy by Philip Pullman

Lyric (name from an English word)

m

Maame A contraction of madame

Maanya Hindi (from many): good, orderly

Maaria/Maariah/Maariya/ Maariyah/Maarya *See* Maria

Maaya *See* Maya

Mabel/Mabelle/Mable Latin (from amabilis): worthy of love

Mabli A Welsh variant of Mabel

Macayla *See* Cayla

Macey/Maci/Macie *See* Macy

Mackenna *See* Kenna

Macy Unknown, possibly Old French: from Massy (geographical name, shifted from surname usage). Also possibly a feminine variant of Massius/Matthew, Hebrew: gift of Jehova

Madalaine/Madaleine/Madalena/ Madalin/Madalina/Madaline/ Madalyn/Maddalena *See* Magdalene

Maddi/Maddie A diminutive form of Maddison and Magdalene

Maddison Old English: Madde's son, Magdalene's son. *See also* Girls and Boys: Madison

Maddy A diminutive form of Maddison and Magdalene

Maddyson *See* Maddison

Madeeha/Madeha Arabic: praiseworthy, commendable

Madelaine/Madeleine/Madelene/ Madelin/Madeline/Madelyn/ Madelyne *See* Magdalene

Madi A diminutive form of Maddison and Magdalene

Madia/Madiha/Madihah *See* Madeeha

Madilyn *See* Magdalene

Madina/Madinah Persian: city *See also* Medina

Madisson/Madisyn *See* Maddison

Madiya/Madiyah *See* Madeeha

Madlen A Hungarian variant of Magdalene

Madyson *See* Maddison

Mae A diminutive form of Magdalene. *See also* Maia

Maebh *See* Meabh

Maeesha *See* Aisha

Maegan A diminutive form of Margaret

Maelys Breton: princess

Maeve An anglicised variant of Meabh

Magan Old English: prevail

Magda A diminutive form of Magdalene

Magdalena/Magdalene Hebrew: of Magdala, of the tower. The name of Mary Magdalene

Magenta (colour name, name from

an English word)

Maggie A diminutive form of Margaret

Maha/Mahak Arabic: wild cow, large eyes like a cow, beautiful eyes. Also Hindi: great

Mahala/Mahalia Hebrew: harp, pardon

Maham A city in India (geographical name)

Mahbuba Persian: beloved, favourite

Mahdiya/Mahdiyyah Arabic: rightly guided

Maheen Arabic: like the moon, fine, thin

Mahek Hindi: breath, fragrance

Mahera Arabic: expert, skilled

Mahfuza Arabic: the protected

Mahi Sanskrit: heaven and earth. *See also* Girls and Boys: Maahi

Mahika Sanskrit: frost, mist

Mahima Sanskrit: greatness

Mahira/Mahirah Sanskrit: sun

Mahisha Sanskrit (from mahisa): great, powerful

Mahiya Sanskrit: exultation, happiness, joy

Mahmuda Arabic: praise

Mahnaz Persian: moon's glory

Mahnoor Arabic: light of the moon

Mahreen Arabic: bright, beautiful, like the sun

Mahrosh Arabic: piece of the moon, pleasant, nice

Mahrukh Arabic: beautiful, like the moon

Mahum Arabic: moonlight

Mai *See* Mae

Maia Latin (from maius): greater. The Roman goddess of growth. Also the mother of Hermes in Greek mythology. *See also* Maja and Maya

Maicey/Maicie/Maicy *See* Macy

Maida/Maidah Arabic: beautiful

Maija *See* Maia, Maja and Maya

Maimoona/Maimoonah/ Maimuna Arabic: lucky

Mair A Welsh variant of Mary

Maira Arabic: moon, favourable. *See also* Mary

Maire An Irish variant of Mary

Mairead An Irish variant of Margaret

Mairi A Scottish variant of Mary

Maisa Arabic: walking proud. *See also* Macy and Maisha

Maisee/Maisey *See* Macy

Maisha Arabic: pretty

Maisie/Maisy *See* Macy

Maiya *See* Maia, Maja and Maya

Maizee/Maizey/Maizie/Maizy *See* Macy

Maja A diminutive form of Maria. *See also* Maia and Maya

Majka Polish (from maj): May

Makanaka Shona: being good, being beautiful

Makayla *See* Cayla

Makeda The Ethiopian variant for Queen of Sheba's name

Makenna *See* Kenna

Mala Hindi: garland, necklace

Malaeka/Malaika/Malaikah
Arabic: angels

Malak Arabic: angel

Malaya Sanskrit (from malai and
ur): town on the hill (geographical
name)

Malayeka *See* Malaika

Malayka *See* Malaika

Maleah/Maleeha/Maleehah *See*
Maliha

Maleeka/Maleekah *See* Malika

Malena Polish: raspberry (name
from flowers and trees). *See also*
Marlene

Malgorzata A Polish variant of
Margaret

Malia *See* Maria

Maliaka *See* Malaika

Maliha Arabic: praising, beautiful

Malika/Malikah Arabic: queen.
See also Girls and Boys: Malek

Malina/Malini Slovak/Slovene:
raspberry (name from flowers and
trees)

Malissa *See* Melissa

Maliyah *See* Maria

Malka/Malky A diminutive form
of Malika

Mallika *See* Malika

Mallory Unknown, possibly Old
French (from malheur): unlucky

Malwina Unknown, possibly
Scottish Gaelic (from maol and
mhìn): beautiful face. Also possibly
from Old German: friend of justice

Malyka *See* Malika

Mamie A diminutive form of Mary

Manaal *See* Manal

Manahil Arabic: spring of fresh
water

Manal Arabic: attainment,
achievement

Manar Arabic: guiding light

Mandy A diminutive form of
Amanda

Manel Hebrew: god is with us

Manha Arabic: gift of god

Manika Sanskrit: ruby, jewel
(gemstone name)

Manisha Sanskrit (from manisa):
idea, thought, wisdom

Mannat Punjabi: wish (Sikh name)

Manon A diminutive form of Marie

Manreet Punjabi: way of the mind,
traditional mind (Sikh name)

Manroop Punjabi: beauty of the
mind, beautiful mind (Sikh name)

Mansi Unknown

Manuela/Manuella *See* Emanuela

Mara/Marah Hebrew: bitter. Also
Arabic: happiness, joy. Also a
diminutive form of Marcella

Maram Arabic: aspiration, wish,
desire

Marcela/Marcelina/Marcella
Latin: of Mars, the Roman god
of war

**Marcey/Marci/Marcia/Marcie/
Marcy** A diminutive form of
Marcella

Mared A Welsh variant of Margaret

Margaret/Margarita/Margaux/ Margery/Margo/Margot/ Marguerite Greek: pearl (gemstone name)

Mari/Maria/Mariah/Mariam/ Mariama Unknown, possibly Latin: of Mars, the Roman god of war

Mariana/Marianna/Marianne A blend of Maria and Anna/Anne

Marie/Mariella/Marielle/ Mariem/Mariette/Mariha/ Marija/Marika See Maria

Marilyn A blend of Mary and Lynn

Marina/Marine Latin: of the sea. See also Maria

Marion See Maria

Marisa/Marisha/Marissa Latin: of the sea

Marium See Maria

Mariya/Mariyah The name of Mariya al-Qibtiyya, one of the prophet Muhammad's wives. See also Maria

Mariyam/Mariyum See Maria

Marjan/Marjana See Marianna

Marjorie See Margaret

Marla A diminutive form of Marlene

Marleigh A blend of Maria and Leigh. See also Girls and Boys: Marley

Marlena/Marlene A blend of Maria and Lene

Marney/Marnie Unknown, possibly from the village of Marigni (shifted from surname usage)

Marriyah See Maria

Marsha A diminutive form of Marcella

Marta/Martha Greek: lady, mistress

Martina/Martine/Martyna Latin: warlike

Marwa Arabic: a fragrant plant (name from flowers and trees). See also Marwah

Marwah The name of Al-Marwah, one of the hills in Mecca along with Al-Safa. See also Marwa and Moriah

Marwo Somalian: madame. See also Marwa

Mary/Marya/Maryah See Maria

Maryam/Maryama See Maria

Maryan/Maryann/Maryanne See Marian

Maryjane A blend of Mary and Jane

Maryum See Maria

Masal Turkish: fairy tale

Masha A diminutive form of Maria

Masie See Macy

Masooma/Masuma Arabic: innocent

Mataya Hebrew: gift of god

Mathilda/Mathilde See Matilda

Mathusha Unknown, possibly Sanskrit (from madhus): sweetness

Matilda/Matilde Old German: mighty in battle

Mattea A diminutive form of Martha. See also Girls and Boys: Mattie

Matylda *See* Matilda

Maud/Maude Shifted from the surname Maude. Also *See* Matilda

Maura/Maureen *See* Mary

Mavis (name from an English word) English: song thrush

Mawahib Arabic: talents

Maxine Latin: the greatest

May (name from an English word)

Maya/Mayah Sanskrit: illusion. Also Old Persian: generous. Also Hebrew (from ma'ayan): spring, brooke, stream. *See also* Maia and Maja

Mayar Unknown

Maycee/Maycie *See* Macy

Mayeda Unknown, possibly from Maeda, Japanese: in front of the field (shifted from surname usage). *See also* Maida

Mayesha *See* Maisha

Maymuna/Maymunah *See* Maimuna

Mayra *See* Mary

Maysa *See* Maisa

Maysie *See* Macy

Maysoon Arabic: beautiful face and body

Mayumi Japanese: various, including truth and beauty

Mayzie/Mazie *See* Macy

Mckayla *See* Cayla

Mckenna *See* Kenna

Mea A diminutive form of Maria

Meabh/Meadhbh Irish Gaelic: intoxicator. A queen in Irish mythology

Meadow (name from an English word)

Meagan/Meaghan A diminutive form of Margaret

Meah A diminutive form of Maria

Meda Native American: prophetess

Medi Welsh: September

Medina/Medine A city north of Mecca, and the city where the prophet Muhammad is buried. *See also* Madina

Meeka A diminutive form of Michaela

Meena Arabic: light

Meenakshi An avatar of Parvati, the gentle Hindu goddess

Meera Hindi: light. *See also* Mira

Meerab Hebrew: increase. One of Saul's daughters

Meesha A diminutive form of Michaela

Meg/Megan/Megane/Meggan A diminutive form of Margaret

Megha Hindi (from meghachchhadit): cloud, cloudy

Meghan/Meghann A diminutive form of Margaret

Meghna *See* Megha

Megi A diminutive form of Margaret

Meha *See* Maha

Mehak Arabic: fragrance

Mehar Arabic: kindness, benevolence

Mehek *See* Mehak

Meher *See* Mehar

Mehmoona Arabic: joyful, glad

Mehnaz Arabic: proud, moon-like

Mehr Arabic: full moon

Mehreen/Mehrin Arabic: loving

Mehvish/Mehwish Arabic: bright star, shining star

Mei Chinese: various, including beautiful. Also Japanese: various, including bright and sprouting. *See also* May

Meika *See* Maria

Meira *See* Mira

Meisha *See* Mysha

Melania/Melanie/Melany Greek: black, dark

Melek Arabic: angel. Also Hebrew: king

Melia A diminutive form of Amelia

Melika/Melike *See* Malika

Melina A diminutive of Carmela

Melinda A blend of Melissa and Linda

Melis A Turkish variant of Melissa

Melisa/Melisha/Melissa Greek: honey bee. A nymph in Greek mythology who discovered honey and used it to nurse Zeus

Melita Latin: Malta

Meliz *See* Melissa

Mellisa/Mellissa *See* Melissa

Melodie/Melody (name from an English word)

Melvina From Malleville (Latin and Old French, from mala and ville: bad town; shifted from surname usage)

Mena A daughter of the Hindu god Brahma

Menaal Arabic: flower of heaven

Menna *See* Mena and Mina

Mercedes/Mercedez Spanish (from mercedes): mercies

Merci/Mercy (name from an English word)

Meredith Welsh: great lord (shifted from surname usage)

Meriam *See* Maria

Meriel *See* Muriel

Meriem *See* Maria

Merin *See* Marine

Merissa *See* Marissa

Merle Old French: blackbird (shifted from surname usage)

Merryn A Cornish saint. *See also* Morwenna

Merve A Turkish name from a mountain in Mecca (geographical name). Also a diminutive form of Merveille

Merveille Old French: wonder, marvel

Meryem *See* Miriam

Meryl *See* Muriel

Mesha Sanskrit (from mesa): ram. Also a diminutive form of Michaela

Meya *See* Maia, Maja and Maya. Also a diminutive form of Maria

Mhairi A Scottish variant of Mary

Mia/Miah A diminutive form of Maria

Miami The city in Florida (geographical name)

Mica A diminutive form of Michaela

Micaela See Cayla and Michaela

Micha A diminutive form of Michaela

Michaela/Michaella Hebrew: who is like god. See also Girls and Boys: Michele

Michalina A Polish variant of Michaela

Micheala/Michela/Michelle See Michaela

Mickayla See Cayla

Mieka A diminutive form of Michaela

Migle Lithuanian: bluegrass (name from flowers and trees)

Mihaela See Michaela

Mihika Sanskrit: snow, fog, mist

Miia A diminutive form of Maria

Mija Spanish: sweet girl, my daughter

Mikaela See Cayla and Michaela

Mikah/Mikala/Mikalah A diminutive form of Michaela

Mikayla See Cayla and Michaela

Miki Japanese: various, including beautiful princess. Also a diminutive form of Michaela

Mikka A diminutive form of Michaela

Mikyla See Kyla and Michaela

Mila A diminutive form of Milena

Milana See Milena

Mildred Old English: mild strength

Mileigh Unknown (shifted from surname usage). See Girls and Boys: Miley

Milena Slavic (from mil): beloved, dear

Mili A diminutive form of Mildred and Millicent

Milica A Serbian variant of Milena

Milissa See Melissa and Milica

Milka Hebrew: queen. A sister of Sarah, and sister-in-law to Abraham

Milla A diminutive form of Milena

Millee/Milli A diminutive form of Mildred and Millicent

Millicent Old French: working strengh

Millie/Milly A diminutive form of Mildred and Millicent

Mimi A diminutive form of Maria

Mina Arabic: light, pearl

Minaal Arabic: reaching a destination

Minahil Arabic: air of paradise

Minal See Minaal

Mindy A diminutive form of Melinda

Minerva Latin: mindful, wise. The Roman goddess of wisdom

Minna See Mina and Minnah

Minnah Arabic: grace, kindness, blessing

Minnie A diminutive form of Wilhelmina

Mio Japanese: various, including

beautiful cherry blossom

Mira Latin: marvelous, wonderful Also a diminutive form of Amira and Miranda. *See also* Myra

Mirabel/Mirabelle Latin (from mirabilis): wonderous. Also the name of the mirabelle plum (name from flowers and trees)

Mirain *See* Maria

Miral Arabic: gazelle. *See also* Mireia

Miranda Latin (from mirandus): wondered, marvelled

Mireia Old French (from mirar): to admire

Mirella A Spanish variant of Mireia

Miri A diminutive form of Miriam

Miriam The sister of Moses. *See also* Maria

Mirin/Mirren/Mirrin/Mirryn Saint Mirin is an Irish monk who became a patron saint in Scotland. *See also* Merryn

Miruna Slavic: peace

Miryam *See* Maria

Misba/Misbah Arabic: innocent

Mischa A diminutive form of Michaela and Michelle

Mishaal/Mishal/Mishall/Mishel Arabic: light, beautiful

Mishk A diminutive form of Michaela and Michelle

Miski Mapudungun: honey

Missie/Missy A diminutive form of Melissa

Misty (name from an English word)

Mitzi A German diminutive form of Maria

Miya Japanese: various, including beautiful fight

Miyah Arabic: waters, coastal sea

Miyu Japanese: various, including beautiful reason and beautiful dusk

Modupe Yoruba: I thank god

Moesha Hebrew: to draw, draw out of the water

Mofiyinfoluwa *See* Fiyinfoluwa

Mohima *See* Mahima

Mohini Sanskrit (from moha): illusions, magical enchantment. The female avatar of the Hindu god Vishnu

Moira *See* Mary

Moli/Molli/Mollie/Molly A diminutive form of Margaret

Momena/Momina/Mominah/ Momna Arabic: faith, true belief

Mona Irish Gaelic (from muad): superior in rank and wealth. Also Arabic: wish, desire. Also Italian: an abbreviated form of Madonna, as used in the Mona Lisa. Also Old Norse (from máni): moon, a male personification of the moon in Norse mythology. Also a diminutive form of Monica. *See also* Monae

Monae Manx: the Isle of Man (geographical name)

Monalisa A blend of Mona and Lisa, named after the famous painting by Leonardo da Vinci

Monet From the surname of the artist Claude Monet (shifted from surname usage)

Monica/Monika/Monique Latin: to advise. Also Greek: unique

Monira Arabic: guiding light

Monisha *See* Manisha

Montana/Montanna Spanish (from montaña): mountain (shifted from surname usage). Also a state in the US (geographical name)

Moonisah Arabic: close friend

Morag Scottish Gaelic (from mòr): great, grand

Morayo Yoruba: I see joy

Morenike Yoruba: I have one to cherish

Morgana/Morgane/Morganne The name of Morgan le Fay from Arthurian legends. Also possibly from Morrígan, a goddess of war and strife from Irish mythology. *See also* Girls and Boys: Morgan

Moriah/Morium Hebrew: ordained by the lord. The mountain wher the sacrifice of Isaac took place. *See also* Marwah

Morsal Persian: sent, a sent letter

Morven Scottish Gaelic (from mòr and beàrn or binnean): sea gap, sea peaks. Also the name of a mountain and the Morvern peninsular in Scotland (geographical name)

Morwenna Cornish: sea fair, sea maiden. A Cornish saint

Motunrayo Yoruba: I found another joy

Moya An Irish variant of Mary

Moyinoluwa Yoruba: praising god

Moyosoreoluwa Yoruba: I am rejoicing at the gift of god

Muireann From Muirfhionn, Irish Gaelic (from muir and fionn): sea fair. The name of Muireann Muncháem, mother of Fionn mac Cumhail from Irish mythology

Mumina/Muminah Arabic: lovely, sweet

Mumtaz Arabic: distinguished

Muna Arabic: water. Also Amharic: faithful, steady. Also Hopi: gushing spring

Muneeba/Muneebah Arabic: consulting god

Muneera Arabic: bright, shining

Muniba/Munibah *See* Muneeba

Munira/Munirah *See* Muneera

Muntaha Arabic: the utmost

Muqadas/Muqaddas Arabic: holy

Muriel Irish and Scottish Gaelic (from muir and geal): sea bright

Murren/Murrin/Murron Unknown, possibly Irish and Scottish Gaelic (from muir): sea. Also a diminutive form of Marion and Muireann

Mursal Arabic: hurried. A type of haddith that has only been partially transmitted. *See also* Morsal

Musammat/Musammath Arabic: beaded thread. A type of poetry

with a repetitive rhythm
Muska Arabic: smile
Muskaan/Muskan Arabic: smiling
Mya/Myah *See* Maia and Maja
Myesha *See* Myiesha
Myfanwy Welsh (from annwyl): beloved
Myia/Myiah *See* Maia and Maja
Myiesha Arabic: blessed life
Myla/Mylah A diminutive form of Milena
Mylea/Mylee *See* Mileigh
Myleene Unknown, possibly a blend of Miley and Lene. The name of the singer Myleene Klass
Myleigh/Myley/Mylie *See* Mileigh
Myra/Myrah Greek: myrrh (name from flowers and trees)
Myriam *See* Maria
Myrtle (name from an English word, name from flowers and trees)
Mysha A diminutive form of Michelle

n

Naa Hebrew: pleasant
Naba Arabic: good, famous
Nabeeha *See* Nabiha
Nabeela/Nabeelah *See* Nabila
Nabiha/Nabihah Arabic: intelligent
Nabila/Nabilah Arabic: noble
Nada Arabic: dew, generous
Nadeen An Arabic variant of Nadine

Nadia/Nadine Greek: hope
Nadira/Nadirah Arabic: precious, rare
Nadiya/Nadiyah An Arabic variant of Nadia
Nadja/Nadya *See* Nadia
Naeema/Naeemah Arabic: blessing, happiness, peace, bliss
Naeve *See* Niamh
Nafeesa/Nafeesah/Nafisa/Nafisah Arabic: refined, precious
Nagina Arabic: precious gem
Nahida Persian (from na-heed): from Venus
Nahima *See* Naima
Nahla Arabic: bee
Naia Danish: little sister
Naila/Nailah Arabic: winner, achiever
Naima/Naimah Arabic (from na-eem): delight, pleasure
Naina Arabic: eyes
Naiomi *See* Naomi
Naira Arabic: shining
Naisha Unknown, possibly Sanskrit (from naiza): at night
Naiya Unknown, possibly Hindi (from naya): young, new
Najah Arabic: success
Najat Arabic: salvation, deliverance
Najibah Arabic: noble, distinguished
Najiyah Arabic: close friend
Najla Arabic: large eyes
Najma Arabic: star
Najwa Arabic: secret
Nakia Arabic: pure, faithful

Nakisha A blend of Natalia and Keesha

Nakita *See* Nikkita

Nalani Hawaiian: the heavens. *See also* Lani

Namira/Namra/Namrah Arabic: delicious water

Nanci/Nancie/Nancy A diminutive form of Ann

Nandi Sanskrit: pleasure, joy. Also the name of the bull that the Hindu god Shiva rides

Nandini Sanskrit: daughter

Nansi A diminutive form of Ann

Naoimh Irish Gaelic: holy, blessed

Naoise The nephew of king Conchobar mac Nessa from Irish mythology, now shifted into a feminine name

Naomi/Naomie Hebrew: pleasant, sweet. Ruth's mother-in-law

Nara The name of the city in Japan (geographical name)

Nardia *See* Nadia

Nargis Arabic: narcissus (name from flowers and trees)

Narin Turkish: delicate person

Narjis *See* Nargis

Naseema *See* Nasima

Nashwa Arabic: fragrance, elated

Nasima Arabic: zephyr

Nasra Arabic: helper

Nasreen/Nasrin Arabic: wild rose

Nastassja/Nasteha *See* Anastasia

Natacha *See* Natasha

Natalia/Natalie/Nataliya/Natalya Latin (from natalis): birthday, implying Christmas

Natania *See* Nathania

Natascha/Natasha/Natashia/Natasja/Natassia/Natassja/Natasza A Russian variant of Natalia

Nataya A Thai name

Natea A diminutive form of Natania

Nathalia/Nathalie *See* Natalia

Nathania Hebrew (from nathan and el): gift of god

Navdeep Punjabi: new light, new lamp (Sikh name)

Naveen/Naveena Punjabi: new, fresh (Sikh name)

Navjot Punjabi: new bright light (Sikh name)

Navneet Punjabi: always anew (Sikh name)

Navpreet Punjabi: new love (Sikh name)

Navreet Punjabi: new way (Sikh name)

Navya Sanskrit: new

Nawaal/Nawal Arabic: gift

Naya Hindi: new, young. *See also* Naia

Nayaab/Nayab Arabic: rare

Nayah *See* Naya

Nayana Sanskrit: eye, guiding, directing

Nayara Arabic: sun, shining

Nayeema *See* Naimah

Nayla *See* Naila

Naz Turkish: coy

Nazar From Nazareth (geographical name). Also Arabic: vow

Nazia Arabic: pure, honest

Nazifa Arabic: clean

Nazish Persian: beauty, pride

Nazli Arabic: delicate, beautiful

Nazma Arabic: star

Nazmeen/Nazmin Arabic: light

Nazneen Arabic: beautiful

Nazreen/Nazrin See Nasreen

Ndey Wollof: mother

Neah A diminutive form of Linnea

Neamh/Neave See Niamh

Nechama Hebrew: comfort

Neda Slovenian (from nedelja): Sunday

Neela See Nila

Neelam Persian: sapphire (gemstone name)

Neema See Nimah

Neena See Nina

Neesha See Nisha

Neeve See Niamh. See also Girls and Boys: Neev

Nefeli From Nephele, Greek: cloud. A cloud created in the form of the Greek goddess Hera

Neha Arabic: rain, love

Nehir Turkish: river

Neisha See Nisha

Neive See Niamh and Nieve

Nel/Nela/Nell/Nella/Nellie/Nelly A diminutive form of Eleanor and Helen

Neneh See Nina

Neriah Hebrew: god is my lamp

Nerissa/Nerys Greek (from nereis): Nereid, sea nymph

Nesta A Welsh variant of Agnes

Nethra Sanskrit (from netra): guide, leader

Neva/Nevaeh/Nevaya/Neve/Neveah/Nevie See Niamh

Neya See Naya

Ngozi Igbo: blessing

Nhi Vietnamese: little one

Nia/Niah/Niamh Irish Gaelic: bright, radiant. A goddess of the sea in Irish mythology

Niaomi See Naomi

Niara Swahili: high purpose

Niav See Niamh

Nichola/Nichole See Nicola

Nicki A diminutive form of Nicola

Nicol/Nicola/Nicole/Nicolette/Nicolle Greek: victory of the people. See also Girls and Boys: Nikola

Nida Arabic: call

Nidhi Sanskrit: treasure. The nine treasures of Kubera, the Hindu god of wealth, include jasmine and sapphire

Nieve Spanish (from nieves): snow. An aspect of the Virgin Mary, as María de las Nieves

Nihal Turkish: beloved, fresh, thin

Nika Greek (from nike): victory. The Greek goddess of victory, companion to Athena

Niketa/Nikhita See Nikkita

Niki A diminutive form of Nikkita

Nikisha A blend of Niki and Keesha

Nikitta *See* Nikkita

Nikki A diminutive form of Nikkita

Nikkita Greek (from aniketos): unconquerable. *See also* Girls and Boys: Nikita

Nikol/Nikole *See* Nicola

Nila Sanskrit: indigo (colour name)

Nilima Sanskrit (from niliman): blueness

Nimah Arabic: blessing

Nimco Cushitic: abundance, prosperity

Nimisha Sanskrit (from nimisa): twinkling

Nimo Unknown, possibly from Nemo, Latin: nobody

Nimra/Nimrah Arabic: pure

Nina Arabic: favour. Also Native American: strong. Also a diminutive form of Anna

Niomi *See* Naomi

Nirvana Sanskrit: extinguished, disappeared. The state in Hinduism and Buddhism where pain and suffering have been extinguished

Nisa Arabic: women

Nisanur Unknown, possibly Arabic and Turkish (from nisa and nur): woman of light

Nisha Sanskrit (from nisa): night, dream, vision

Nishat Arabic: happiness

Nishi Sanskrit (from nizi): strengthen

Nishka Sanskrit (from niska): gold

Nishma Unknown, possibly Sanskrit (from niskama): unselfish. Also possibly Sanskrit (from nihsiman): infinite, grand

Nissi Hebrew: sign *See also* Nishi

Nitya Sanskrit: eternal

Niva Hebrew (from niv): expression

Nixie Old German (from nix): water elf

Niya/Niyah *See* Nia

Niyati Sanskrit: destiny, fate

Nneka Igbo: mother is supreme

Nneoma Igbo: beautiful mother, good mother

Noella/Noelle French: Christmas

Noemi/Noemie *See* Naomi

Noha *See* Nuha

Nola A diminutive form of Finola

Non Welsh: nun

Noora Arabic: light

Nora/Norah A diminutive form of Eleanor

Noreen Arabic: bright

Norma Unknown, possibly Old German: from the North. Also possibly Latin: pattern

Nosheen/Noshin Arabic: sweet, nice

Noura *See* Noora

Nova Latin (from novus): new, the abbreviated form of nova stella, new star. Also Hopi: chasing butterflies

Noya Hebrew (from noy): beauty

Nuala A diminutive form of Fionnuala

Nuha Arabic: intelligence
Numa Persian: view, display
Nur Turkish: light
Nura *See* Noora
Nuria Catalan: from La Mare de Déu de Núria, an aspect of the Virgin Mary. Also Arabic: luminuous, radiant
Nusaiba/Nusaibah/Nusayba/ Nusaybah Arabic: noble
Nusrat/Nusrath/Nuzhat Arabic: help
Nya/Nyah *See* Nia
Nyima *See* Nimah
Nyla/Nylah Arabic: achiever
Nyomi *See* Naomi
Nyree From Ngaire, Mauri (from ngaere): soft, roll of the sea. Also possibly Mauri (from ngai): flax
Nyssa A character from Dr Who *See also* Nisa

Oceana/Oceane *See* Girls and Boys: Ocean (name from an English word)
Octavia Latin: eight, from the Octavius family, most notably of Gaius Octavius, emperor Augustus
Odette Old German: inherit
Ofelia *See* Ophelia
Ogechi Igbo: god's time
Ola Old Norse: ancestor's relic. Also a diminutive form of Aleksandra

Olanna Igbo: god's beauty, god's gold
Olga Old Norse: holy, dedicated to the gods
Olive/Olivia/Olivija/Oliwia (name from flowers and trees, name from an English word) Created by Shakespeare in *Twelfth Night*
Ololade Yoruba: the wealthy has arrived
Olsa The Olza river in Poland and the Czech Republic (geographical name)
Olta The name of Olta Boka, an Albanian singer
Oluchi Igbo: god's work
Oluwadara Yoruba: god is good to me. *See also* Girls and Boys: Oluwadarasimi
Oluwafunmilayo Yoruba: god has given me joy
Oluwafunmilola Yoruba: god has given me wealth
Oluwakanyinsola Yoruba: god has added sweetness to my wealth
Oluwakemi Yoruba: god pampers me
Oluwaseyifunmi Yoruba: god has given me this
Oluwateniola Yoruba: god has spread a mat of wealth
Oluwatofunmi Yoruba: god is enough for me
Oluwatosin Yoruba: god is worthy of worship

Oluwatoyin Yoruba: god is worthy of praise

Oluwatoyosi Yoruba: god is worth celebrating

Oluwatumininu Yoruba: god has comforted me

Olwen/Olwyn Welsh (from ol and gwyn): white footprints. The daughter of a giant in Welsh mythology who is courted by Culhwch; white flowers spring from every step she takes

Olympia Greek: from Olympos, the highest mountain in Greek, the home of the twelve Olympian gods in Greek mythology. Also the Greek sanctuary that is the birthplace of the Olympic games

Omaima *See* Umama

Omara/Omera Arabic: to live, to flourish

Omolara Yoruba: child of my family

Omolola Yoruba: child of wealth

Omotola Yoruba: this child equals wealth

Oona/Oonagh *See* Una

Opal (gemstone name, name from an English word)

Opeyemi Yoruba: I should be grateful

Ophelia Greek: help. Created by Jacopo Sannazzaro in his poem *Arcadia*, but better known as the girl who drowns from Shakespeare's *Hamlet*

Oriana/Orianna/Orianne Latin: gold

Orla/Orlagh/Orlaigh/Orlaith Irish Gaelic (from ór and flaith): gold soverign

Orlanda Old German: famous lands

Orli/Orly Hebrew: light is mine

Ornela/Ornella Italian: flowering ash tree (name from flowers and trees)

Ottilie/Otylia Old German: riches, wealth

Oyindamola Yoruba: honey mixed with wealth

Oyinkansola Yoruba: honey drops into wealth

Ozge Turkish: different

Ozlem Turkish: yearning

P

Pacha *See* Pasha

Pagan (name from an English word)

Page/Paige (name from an English word)

Paighton *See* Payton

Paiton *See* Payton

Pal *See* Paula

Palak Hindi (from palaka): eyelash

Paloma Latin (from palumbes): wood pigeon, dove

Palwasha Pashto: moon beam

Pamela Created by Philip Sidney for the character in *The Countess of Pembroke's Arcadia* to mean all sweetness

Panayiota Greek: Panagia, a title of the Virgin Mary

Pandora Greek: all giving. Also the first woman from Greek mythology who opened the box containing all the evils, and hope, into the world

Paola *See* Paula

Pari Persian (from paree): fairy

Parisa/Parise Persian (from paree): like a fairy

Parisha Possibly Sanskrit (from pariza): high lord. A name for the Hindu god Rama. *See also* Parisa

Pariss From Paris, the capital city of France. *See also* Girls and Boys: Paris

Parmis Persian: small cloud. A wife of Darius the Great

Parneet Punjabi: mystical like the guru

Parris *See* Pariss

Parsa Persian: devout

Parveen/Parvin Persian: star

Parys A town in South Africa, and a mountain in Wales (geographical name). *See also* Pariss

Pascale Latin (from pascha): Easter

Pascha/Pasha *See* Pascale

Pat A diminutive form of Patricia

Patience Latin: patience, endurance

Patrice/Patricia/Patricija/Patrycja Latin: patrician, noble

Patsy A diminutive form of Patricia

Paula/Paulina/Pauline Latin:

petite

Pavan Punjabi: sacred, pure (Sikh name). Also Sanskrit: protected

Pavandeep Punjabi: sacred lamp (Sikh name)

Pavneet Punjabi: always sacred (Sikh name)

Payal Hindi: anklet

Payge *See* Paige

Peace Latin: peace

Peaches Latin: Persian apple (name from flowers and trees)

Pearl Old French: pearl (gemstone name)

Pebbles Old English: pebble stones

Peggy A diminutive form of Margaret

Peighton Old English: from Peyton, possibly the village in Essex (shifted from surname usage). *See also* Girls and Boys: Payton and Peyton

Pelin Turkish: wormwood (name from flowers and trees)

Penelope Greek: threads. Also the name of the faithful wife of Odysseus from Greek mythology

Pennie/Penny A diminutive form of Penelope

Peony (name from flower and trees, name from an English word)

Pepper (name from flower and trees, name from an English word)

Perdita Latin: lost one. The heroine from Shakespeare's *The Winter's Tale*

Peri *See* Perri

Perla Italian: pearl (gemstone name)

Persephone The daughter of Demeter and wife of Hades in Greek mythology

Persia A name for Iran (geographical name)

Pessy Unknown

Peta Blackfood: golden eagle. *See also* Petra

Petal (name from flower and trees, name from an English word)

Petra/Petrina Latin (from petrus): rock

Phebe/Pheobe/Pheobie *See* Phoebe

Philippa/Phillipa/Phillippa Greek: friend of horses

Philomena Greek: friend of strength

Phoebe/Phoebie Greek: bright, shining, radiant (the name of a Titan in Greek mythology)

Phyllis Greek: green branches (a princess from Greek mythology, who changed into an almond tree after hanging herself)

Pia Latin (from pius): pious

Pinar Turkish: spring

Piper Old English: bagpipe or pipe players (shifted from surname usage)

Pippa A diminutive form of Philippa

Pixie (name from an English word)

Piya *See* Pia

Pola *See* Paula

Polina A Hungarian, Portuguese and Romanian variant of Paulina

Polly A diminutive form of Mary

Pollyanna A blend of Polly and Anna. A novel by Eleanor H. Porter, featuring an optimistic heroine of the same name

Pooja *See* Puja

Poonam Hindi (from punam): full moon

Poppi/Poppie/Poppy (name from flower and trees, name from an English word)

Porcha/Porchia/Porscha/Porsche/Porsha/Portia Latin: pig

Posy (name from flower and trees, name from an English word)

Prabhleen Punjabi: absorbed in god's love (Sikh name)

Prachi Hindi: east

Pranavi Sanskrit (from pranava): the sound of 'om'. A sacred sound in Hinduism and Buddhism

Praveena Hindi (from pravin): talented

Preena Unknown

Preeti Hindi (from priti): love, affection. *See also* Girls and Boys: Preet

Preeya/Pria *See* Priya

Primrose (name from flowers and trees, name from an English word)

Princess (name from an English word)

Prisca/Priscilla Latin: old, long lived

Prisha *See* Priya
Prithika/Pritika Hindi (from pritikar): endearing
Priya Sanskrit: beloved
Priyal *See* Payal and Priya
Priyanka *See* Priya
Promise (name from an English word)
Prudence (name from an English word)
Pui Thai: plump, fluffy, cute
Puja Sanskrit: honour, worship
Purdey Old French (from par dieu): by god (shifted from surname usage)
Pyper *See* Piper

q

Qudsia Arabic (from quds): holy, sacred
Queen/Queenie (name from an English word)

r

Raabia/Rabia Arabic: spring, breeze
Rabiah Arabic: garden, springtime
Rabiya Arabic: hill
Rachael/Racheal/Rachel/Rachelle Hebrew: ewe
Radeyah Arabic: content, satisfied
Radha/Radhika A friend of lover of the Hindu god Krishna
Radia/Radiyah *See* Radeyah
Rae A diminutive form of Rachel
Raeesa/Raeesah Arabic: princess, noble lady
Raeya *See* Raiya and Raya
Rafa A diminutive form of Raphaela
Rafaela/Rafaella/Raffaella/Rafia/ Rafiah *See* Raphaela
Raghad Arabic: comfortable, pleasant
Raha Arabic: peaceful
Rahaf Arabic: delicate, fine
Raheela An Arabic variant of Rachel
Raheema/Raheemah *See* Rahima
Rahela *See* Raheela
Rahima/Rahimah Arabic: kind, compassionate
Rahma/Rahmah Arabic: compassion, mercy
Raiha Arabic: fragrance
Raihana Arabic: fragrance of roses
Raima Arabic: happiness
Rain (name from an English word). *See also* Girls and Boys: Rayne
Raina *See* Regina
Rainbow (name from an English word)
Raine/Rainey A diminutive form of Regina
Raisa/Raisah/Raissa Arabic: captain, leader
Raiya Sanskrit: desiring riches. *See also* Raya
Rajni Punjabi: night (Sikh name)

Rajpreet Punjabi: love of the kingdom (Sikh name)

Rajvinder Punjabi: lord of the kingdom (Sikh name)

Rajvir Punjabi: warrior of the kingdom (Sikh name)

Raluca Unknown, used in Romania

Rama Aramaic: tall, high. Also a name of the Hindu goddess Lakshmi

Rameen Arabic: obedience

Rameesa/Rameesah/Rameesha/Ramisa/Ramisha Unknown, possibly Persian (from ramesh): cheerful, joyful. Also possibly from Rumaisa

Ramla/Ramlah A city in Israel (geographical name)

Ramneek Punjabi: beautiful (Sikh name)

Ramona Unknown, possibly Old German (from ragin and mund): protector, advice

Ramsha Arabic: beautiful, moon-like

Randa Arabic: fragrant tree

Raneem Arabic: reciting in a sing-song voice

Rani Sanskrit: queen

Rania/Raniya/Raniyah/Ranya Arabic: gazing

Raphaela/Raphaella/Raphaelle Hebrew: god is healer

Raquel A Spanish and Portuguese variant of Rachel

Rasha Arabic: young gazelle

Rashida Arabic: rightly guided

Rashmi Sanskrit (from razmi): ray of light

Raveena Punjabi: beauty of the sun (Sikh name)

Raven (name from an English word)

Ravina *See* Raveena

Ravneet Punjabi: always with the sun god (Sikh name)

Rawan Unknown, possibly from Rawah, Arabic: charm, beauty

Rawdah Arabic: garden, meadow

Raya Sanskrit: prince, royal. *See also* Raiya

Rayaan From al-Rayyaan, a gate to paradise

Rayah *See* Raya and Reyah

Rayana/Rayann/Rayanne *See* Rhiain and Rhiannon

Rayhana *See* Rehana

Rayna *See* Regina

Rayya Arabic: sated, no longer thirsting.

Raz Hebrew: secret

Razan Arabic: respect

Razia Arabic: delighted, content. *See also* Rida

Rea/Reah *See* Rhea

Reann/Reanna/Reanne *See* Rhiain and Rhiannon

Reba A diminutive form of Rebecca

Rebbecca/Rebeca/Rebecca/Rebeccah/Rebecka/Rebeckah/Rebeka/Rebekah/Rebekha/Rebekka/Rebekkah Hebrew: captivating, binding

Reeha Arabic: air

Reem Arabic: gazelle

Reema Arabic: white antelope

Reemas *See* Remas

Reena *See* Rina

Reenie *See* Irene and Renee

Reese From Rhys, Old Welsh (from rīs): ardour

Reet A diminutive form of Margaret

Reeya *See* Rhea

Regina Latin: queen

Reham Arabic: rain

Rehana/Rehanna Arabic: sweet basil (name from flowers and trees). *See also* Rhiannon. *See also* Girls and Boys: Reyhan

Reina *See* Regina

Rema *See* Rhema

Remas Arabic: heart of diamonds, diamonds and gold

Remi/Remie/Remmie/Remy A diminutive form of various names, including Ramona

Rena A diminutive form of Irena. *See also* Renee and Rina

Renad Unknown

Renae/Renai *See* Renee

Renata Latin (from renatus): reborn. *See also* Renee

Renay/Renee/Renie French (from renée): reborn. *See also* Renata. *See also* Girls and Boys: Rene

Renu A diminutive form of Renuka

Renuka A Hindu goddess who gave birth to one of the reincarnations of Vishnu

Resham/Reshma Hindi (from resham/reshami): silk, silky

Reva A diminutive form of Rebecca

Reya/Reyah Hebrew: close companion, scent, aroma, fragrance. *See also* Rhea

Reyhana *See* Rehana. *See also* Girls and Boys: Reyhan

Rezwana From Ridwan, Arabic: satisfaction, the name of an angel at the gates of paradise

Rhea Greek: flow. A Titaness who is the mother of Zeus in Greek mythology

Rheanna/Rheanne/Rheannon *See* Rhiain and Rhiannon

Rhema Greek: utterance, saying

Rheya/Rhia *See* Rhea

Rhiain Welsh (from rhiain): maiden. *See also* Girls and Boys: Rhian

Rhiana/Rhiane/Rhiann *See* Rhiain and Rhiannon

Rhianna/Rhiannah/Rhiannan/ Rhianne/Rhiannon/Rhianon The mother of Pryderi in Welsh mythology

Rhianwen Welsh (from rhiain and gwyn): fair maiden

Rhoda Ancient Greek: rose. Also from the island of Rhodes, named after roses (geographical name)

Rhona *See* Rona

Rhyanna/Rhyanne/Rhyannon *See* Rhiannon

Ria/Riah *See* Rhea

Riana/Riann/Rianna/Riannah/

Rianne/Riannon *See* Rhiain and Rhiannon

Richa Hindi: incantation. A type of mantra in Hindu scriptures

Richelle *See* Rochelle

Rida/Ridah Arabic: content, satisfied. *See also* Razia

Riddhi Hindi: prosperity, wealth

Ridha *See* Rida

Ridhi *See* Riddhi

Ridhima Sanskrit (from ridhama): love, spring

Rifat Arabic: high, exalted, joyous

Rifka *See* Rebecca

Riham *See* Reham

Rihana/Rihanna/Rihannah/ Rihannon *See* Rhiain and Rhiannon

Rijja Arabic: beauty of paradise

Rika Japanese: various, including pear flower

Rima *See* Reema

Rimini A city in Italy from where, the character Francesca da Rimini's husband in Dante's *Inferno* halls

Rimsha/Rimshah Arabic: bunch of flowers

Rina Hebrew (from rinnah): joy, praise

Rinesa Unknown, possibly a blend of Ria and Nessa

Riona/Rionach An Irish variant of Regina

Risha Arabic: rope to the well

Rishika Sanskrit (from rsi): inspired poet, Seer

Rita A diminutive form of Margaret

Ritaj Arabic: door. Also a way of referring to the Kaaba

Rithika/Ritika Sanskrit (from ritika): brass

Riva/Rivka/Rivky A diminutive form of Rebecca

Riya/Riyah *See* Rhea

Riyana *See* Rehana

Rizwana *See* Rezwana

Roanna *See* Rowanne

Robbyn Old German (from hrod): fame. *See also* Girls and Boys: Robin

Roberta Old German (from hrod and berhtaz): bright fame

Robynne *See* Robbyn

Rochel/Rochelle From La Rochelle, French (from roche): rock, stone (geographical name, shifted from surname usage)

Roda *See* Rhoda

Roha Arabic: soul, life

Rohima *See* Rahima

Rohini Sanskrit: Alderbaran A daughter of Chandra and the Hindu god Daksha

Roise/Roisin An Irish variant of Rosa

Rojda Kurdish: sunrise

Rojin Kurdish: sun, sunlight

Roksana A Croatian and Polish variant of Roxana

Roma Latin: Rome (geographical name). Also a name in English for Romani people

Romaana *See* Rumana

Romaisa *See* Rumaisa

Romana From Roman, of Rome. *See also* Romaana

Romani/Romanie/Romany *See* Roma and Romana

Romeesa/Romessa Arabic: beauty of paradise

Romey/Romie A diminutive form of Romana

Romilly/Romily Unknown, possibly from a place in France, such as Romilly-sur-Seine (geographical name, shifted from surname usage)

Romina *See* Romana

Romy *See* Romey

Rona Old Norse (from rogn): council, advice

Ronni A diminutive form of Veronica. *See also* Girls and Boys: Ronnie

Ronya A Russian diminutive form of Veronica

Rosa Latin: rose (name from flowers and trees)

Rosabel/Rosabella/Rosabelle Italian: beautiful rose

Rosaleen *See* Rosalind

Rosalia/Rosalie *See* Rosa

Rosalina/Rosalind/Rosaline/ Rosalyn Old German (hros and lind): weak horse. *See also* Rosa

Rosamund Old German (hros and mund): horse protection. *See also* Rosa

Rosanna/Rosanne A blend of Rose and Anna/Anne

Rose (name from flowers and trees, name from an English word)

Roseann/Roseanna/Roseanne *See* Rosanna

Rosella *See* Rosa

Rosemarie/Rosemary (name from flowers and trees, name from an English word)

Rosetta Italian: little rose (name from flowers and trees). *See also* Rosa

Rosey *See* Rose

Rosheen From Róisín, Irish Gaelic: little rose (name from flowers and trees)

Roshni Persian: lustre

Rosie *See* Rose

Rosina *See* Rosa

Roslyn *See* Rosalind

Rosy *See* Rose

Rowanne/Rowena From Ó Ruadháin, Irish Gaelic (from ruadh): red, red-haired. *See also* Girls and Boys: Rowan

Roxana/Roxann/Roxanna/ Roxanne From Roshanak, Persian: bright, beautiful, luminous beauty. A wife of Alexander the Great

Roxi/Roxie/Roxy A diminutive form of Roxanna

Roya Persian: dream, premonition

Roza *See* Rose

Rozalia *See* Rosa

Rozeena *See* Rozina

Rozerin Kurdish: golden

Rozina Persian: daily, of the day. *See also* Rosa

Rubee/Rubi/Rubie *See* Ruby

Rubina Hebrew: See, a son. *See also* Ruby

Ruby English: ruby (colour name and gemstone name)

Ruchi Sanskrit (from ruci): pleasure, wish, light, splendour, beauty

Rufaro Shona: happiness, joy

Rugile Lithuanian (from rugys): rye (name from flowers and trees). Lithuanian name day for Rugile: 15th August

Ruhena Arabic: sweet fragrance

Ruhi Hindi (from ruh): soul

Rukaiya/Rukaya *See* Ruqayyah

Rukhsaar/Rukhsar *See* Ruksar

Rukia/Rukiya Swahili: rising high

Ruksana *See* Roxana

Ruksar Arabic: cheeks, face

Rukshana *See* Roxana

Rumaanah *See* Rumana

Rumaisa/Rumaisah A traditional Arabic name, unknown, possibly meaning a bunch of flowers

Rumana Arabic: pomegranite (name from flowers and trees)

Rumaysa/Rumaysah *See* Rumaisa

Rumbidzai Shona: praise

Rumena Bulgarian: red, ruddy cheeks

Rumer The name of Rumer Godden who wrote, among others, *The Greengage Summer*

Rumeysa *See* Rumaisa

Ruo Chinese: various, including woman and small

Rupali Hindi: beautiful

Rupinder Sanskrit (from rupa): greatest beauty (Sikh name)

Ruqaiya/Ruqaiyah/Ruqaya/ Ruqayah/Ruqayya/Ruqayyah/ Ruqiya Arabic: gentle. The name of Ruqayyah bint Muhammad, the daughter of prophet Muhammad's wife, Khadija

Rushda Arabic: sensible

Rutendo Shona: faith

Ruth/Ruthie Unknown, possibly Hebrew: companion

Ruvarashe Shona: god's flower

Ruvimbo Shona: faith

Ruwaida/Ruwayda/Ruweyda Arabic: gently walking

Ruya Arabic: vision, sight

Ryanna/Ryhanna *See* Reyhana and Rihanna

Rym Arabic: gazelle

S

Saachi *See* Sachi

Saadia Arabic: tributary

Saaliha/Saalihah *See* Saliha

Saamiya *See* Samiya

Saanvi Sanskrit (A blend from sa and anvi): be guided, be followed

Saara/Saarah *See* Sarah

Saba Arabic: east wind. Also island

in the Caribbean (geographical name)

Sabaa/Sabaah/Sabah Arabic: morning. Also a state in Malaysia (geographical name)

Sabahat Arabic: beautiful, graceful

Sabba *See* Saba

Sabbah *See* Sabbah

Sabeeha/Sabeehah Arabic: beautiful, morning

Sabeeka *See* Sabika

Sabeen Arabic: both worlds

Sabena *See* Sabina

Sabha Arabic: pretty, graceful

Sabia *See* Sadhbh

Sabiha/Sabihah Arabic: dawn, arrival of morning

Sabika Arabic: bar made of gold or silver

Sabina/Sabine Arabic: sword. Also Latin: from Sabines in Italy (geographical name)

Sabira/Sabirah Arabic (from saber): patient

Sabirin *See* Sabrin

Sabiya *See* Sabiha

Sabreen/Sabreena/Sabrin/ Sabrina/Sabrine Welsh: the river Severn, once named Habren, after a princess from legends who drowned in the river. *See also* Sabira

Sachi Japanese: various, including happiness and colourful wisdom. Also a beautiful Hindu goddess of wrath with a thousand eyes

Sadaf Arabic: seashell

Sade Finish: ray of light. Also a diminutive form of Folasade

Sadhbh Proto-Celtic (from sŭādŭā): lovely lady. Also the mother of the great poet Oisín in Irish mythology

Sadia/Sadiah *See* Sadiya

Sadie A diminutive form of Sarah

Sadika/Sadiqah Arabic (from sadegh): truthful, honest

Sadiya/Sadiyah Arabic: happiness, luck

Saeeda Arabic: happy, lucky

Safa/Safaa/Safah Aabic: purity, clarity

Safeena *See* Safina

Saffa/Saffah *See* Safa

Saffi/Saffia/Saffie *See* Safia

Saffire *See* Saphire

Saffiya/Saffiyah *See* Safiya

Saffron (name from an English word, name from flowers and trees, colour name)

Safia/Safiah Arabic: pure, clear

Safina Arabic: boat, ark

Safiya/Safiyah/Safiye/Safiyya/ Safiyyah Arabic: pure, righteous. Also the name of Safiyya bint Huyayy, one of prophet Muhammad's wives

Safreen Arabic: pure love

Sagal Cushitic: morning star

Sage (name from an English word, name from flowers and trees)

Sahaana/Sahana Sanskrit (from sahana): tolerance, patience, endurance

Sahar Persian: dawn. *See also* Saher

Sahara Arabic: desert. The name of one of the world's largest deserts (geographical name)

Sahasra Sanskrit: thousand, infinite

Saher Persian (from sehr): bewitching, enchanting, charmer. *See also* Sahar

Sahiba Punjabi: companion, friend, the Guru (Sikh name). *See also* Girls and Boys: Sahib

Sahira/Sahra Sanskrit: mountain

Saiba/Saibah A narrator of hadith

Saida Arabic (from sa-eed): happy, lucky

Saima/Saimah Arabic (from sa-em): fasting, one who fasts. Also possibly from the Saimaa Lake in Finland (geographical name). *See also* Girls and Boys: Sami

Saina Persian: simurgh, a mythical bird that is part-dog and part-lion

Sainabou A Gambian variant of Zaynab

Saiqa Arabic: thunderbolt, storm

Saira/Sairah Arabic: wanderer, traveller

Sairish Arabic: flower

Saisha Unknown

Saiya Unknown

Saja Arabic: calm, queit

Sajeda/Sajida/Sajidah Arabic (from sajed): prostrating before god, bowing down to god

Sakeena/Sakina/Sakinah Arabic: tranquility, calm inspired by god

Sakura Japanese: cherry blossom (name from flowers and trees)

Saleena *See* Salena

Saleha Arabic: good, right

Salena *See* Selena

Salha/Saliha/Salihah *See* Saleha

Salima Arabic: safe

Salina *See* Selena

Sallie/Sally A diminutive form of Sarah

Salma/Salmah Arabic: peaceful

Salome Hebrew: peace. The stepdaughter of King Herod Antipas who asked for the beheading John the Baptist as a reward for her dancing

Saloni Hindi (from salona): pretty, beautiful

Salsabil Arabic: spring in paradise

Salwa Arabic: comfort, solace

Sama/Samaa/Samah Arabic: generosity

Samaira *See* Samra

Samanta Sanskrit: neighbour, captain. A title that was used by Indian nobility

Samantha Unknown, possibly Hebrew: god has listened. *See also* Samanta

Samara/Samarah Arabic: soft light

Samaya Sanskrit: pact, vow. The vow given when initiating into Esoteric Buddhism

Sameeah/Sameeha Arabic: generous

Sameen/Sameena/Sameenah *See*
Samina

Sameera/Sameerah/Samera *See*
Samira

Samia/Samiah Arabic: *See* Samiya

Samiha/Samihah *See* Sameeha

Samiksha Sanskrit (from samiksa):
understanding, perceiving, deep
insight

Samina Arabic (from samin):
precious, valuable

Samira/Samirah Arabic:
companion, entertaining
companion in nightly conversations

Samiya/Samiyah Arabic: high,
exalted, supreme

Sammie A diminutive form of
Samantha. *See also* Samiya.
See also Girls and Boys: Sammi

Samra/Samrah Arabic: tan-
coloured, light brown (colour
name)

Samreen Urdu: helpful, beneficial

Samreet Unknown, possibly Punjabi
(from sam/sarman and reet/preet)
(Sikh name): love of bravery,
bravery in love, way of bravery

Samsam *See* Zamzam

Samuella Hebrew: god has listened

Samya *See* Samiya

Sana/Sanaa/Sanah Arabic:
brilliance, splendour, radiance,
sublimity. *See also* Sanna

Sanam Hindi: friend, beloved

Sanaya Unknown, possibly Sanskrit:
ancient (shifted from surname

usage). Also possibly Hindi (from
sanajay): victory. Also made more
popular by the actress Sanaya Irani

Sanchia Latin (from sanctius): holy

Sandhya Telugu: twilight, dawn

Sandie A diminutive form of
Alexandra

Sandra A diminutive form of
Alexandra and Cassandra

Sangeeta Sanskrit (from samgita):
music

Sanha *See* Sana

Sania *See* Saniya

Sanika Sanskrit: flute

Sanita A Latvian diminutive form of
Susannah/Zuzanna

Saniya/Saniyah Arabic: splendid,
brilliant

Sanjana *See* Sanjna

Sanjida/Sanjidah Arabic: serious,
guarded

Sanjna A name for Saranyu, the
Hindu goddess of clouds

Sanna/Sannah A diminutive form
of Susannah

Santana From Santa Ana, Saint
Anna, whom many places are
named after (geographical name,
shifted from surname usage).
See also Anna

Santina Italian (from santino): saint

Sanvi *See* Saanvi

Sanya *See* Saniya

Saoirse Irish Gaelic: freedom

Saorla/Saorlaith Irish Gaelic (from
saer and flaith): freeborn sovereign,

noble woman

Saphia *See* Safiya

Saphira/Saphire *See* Sapphire

Saphron *See* Saffron

Sapna Sanskrit (from svapna), Latvian and Lithuanian: dream

Sapphira/Sapphire (gemstone name, name from an English word)

Sara Sanskrit: essence. *See also* Sarah

Sarah/Sarai Hebrew: princess

Saraya *See* Soraya

Sareena/Sarena *See* Serena

Saria/Sariah *See* Sariya

Sarika Hindi: thrush

Sarina *See* Serena

Sarish Arabic: morning

Sarita A Spanish variant of Sarah

Sariya/Sariyah Arabic: clouds at night

Saron A Swedish variant of Sarah

Sarra A Greek variant of Sarah

Sarrinah *See* Serena

Saskia Unknown, possibly Old German/Dutch (from Sas-/Sakser): Saxon

Sauda/Saudah *See* Sawda

Saule Latvian and Lithuanian: sun, the sun goddess who is married to the moon. Also French: willow (name from flowers and trees)

Savana/Savanah/Savanna/Savannah (name from an English word)

Savera Hindi: morning

Savina Latin (from Sabinus): the ancient Italian tribe, the Sabines

Sawda/Sawdah The name of Sawda bint Zam'ah, one of the wives of prophet Muhammad

Saya Japanese: various, often including the character for sand

Sayeda/Sayeeda Arabic: mistress, lady

Sayma *See* Saima

Saynab *See* Zaynab

Sayyeda *See* Sayeda

Scarlet (colour name, name from an English word). *See also* Scarlett

Scarlett/Scarlette/Scarlotte From Escarlate, Old French: scarlet cloth, dyer of scarlet cloths (shifted from surname usage). *See also* Scarlet

Scout (name from English word, term of endearment)

Seana An Irish variant of Jeana

Seanan *See* Shanon

Seanna An Irish variant of Jeana

Seda Turkish: voice, echo

Sedef Turkish: mother of pearl (gemstone name)

Seema Hindi (from sima): boundary, horizon. *See also* Sima

Seerat Arabic: history, biography, story of your life

Sefora *See* Zipporah

Sehar/Seher/Sehr Urdu: dawn. *See also* Sahar and Saher

Sehrish Persian: sunrise

Sejal Sanskrit (from sajala/sujala): water, sweet water

Selen/Selena/Selene/Selin/Selina/

Seline The Greek goddess of the moon. *See also* Celina

Selma Old German: protected by gods

Sema Turkish: sky. *See also* Seema

Semra A Turkish variant of Samra

Sena/Senna (name from flowers and trees) Swahili: beautiful. The name of senna plants come from Arabic, from sana. *See also* Sana

Seona/Seonaid A Scottish variant of Jeana

Sephora *See* Zipporah

Sera A diminutive form of Seraphina. *See also* Sarah

Serafina *See* Seraphina

Serah *See* Sarah

Seraphina Hebrew: seraphim, fiery ones

Seraya Unknown, possibly from the masculine name Seraiah, Hebrew: god's prince, god's warrior

Sereena *See* Serena

Serena/Serene/Serenity/Serenna Latin: tranquil, calm

Serife Turkish (from şerif): sacred

Serin *See* Seren

Serina/Serine *See* Serena

Serish *See* Sehrish

Setareh Persian: star

Setayesh Persian: to praise

Sevval Turkish: tenth month of the Arabic lunar calendar

Shabana/Shabina Arabic and Persian (from shab/shabān): dark, night. Also possibly Persian (from shubbān): young person, youth

Shabnam Hindi (from shabanam): dew

Shada Arabic: aroma

Shade (name from an English word)

Shadi Arabic: singer

Shadia The stage name of the Egyptian actress Fatima Ahmad Kamal. *See also* Shadi

Shafia Arabic: mercy, compassion

Shahad *See* Shahida

Shahana Persian (from shāhāna): royal, magnificent

Shahd Arabic: honey

Shahed *See* Shahida

Shaheena *See* Shahina

Shahida Arabic: witness. Also Persian (from shāhīda): pious, righteous

Shahina Persian (from shāhīn): royal falcon. *See also* Girls and Boys: Shaheen

Shahnaz Persian (from shah and nāz): king's pride, royal glory, royal grace. Also possibly Persian (from shahnāz): a musical note

Shaila Sanskrit (from zaila): hill, mountain

Shaima A daughter of Halima Al-Sadiyah, who was prophet Muhammad's wet nurse

Shaina *See* Shana

Shaira Arabic: poet

Shaista From Khaista, Pashto: beautiful. Also possibly a variant of Shagufta, Persian (from shigufta):

calm, patient

Shajeda *See* Sajeda

Shakeela *See* Shakila

Shakera *See* Shakira

Shakia Unknown

Shakila Arabic: beautiful, handsome

Shakira/Shakirah Arabic (from shaker): thankful, grateful, content

Shalini Hindi (from shalin): modest

Shama Arabic: lamp, light, candle

Shamaila *See* Shamila

Shamara Unknown, possibly Sanskrit (from samara): battle, war, accompanied by god. *See also* Samara and Shamira

Shamila Arabic (from shamil): complete, united, joint

Shamima Arabic: fragrant, sweet smell, perfume

Shamira Hebrew: flint, thorn

Shamiso Shona: miracle, great surprise

Shams/Shamsa Arabic: sun. Also from Shamash, the Mesopotamian sun god

Shana Yiddish (from shayn/sheyn): beautiful, lovely. Also an Irish or Welsh variant of Jeana

Shanade/Shanae/Shanai/Shanay An anglicised variant of Sinead

Shanaya *See* Sanaya and Shania

Shanaye *See* Shanay and Shanaya

Shanaz *See* Shahnaz

Shanea *See* Shania

Shaneen A blend of Shanay and a feminine ending

Shanel/Shanell/Shanelle *See* Chanel

Shaney *See* Shanay

Shani Hebrew: scarlet, crimson. Also Hindi: Saturday. A celestial being from Hindu astrology corresponding to Saturn

Shania/Shaniah Unknown. The stage name that Shania Twain took, possibly from Ojibwa: on my way

Shanice A blend of Shanay and a feminine ending

Shanie *See* Shanay and Shani

Shaniece/Shanika/Shanine/ Shaniqua/Shanique/Shanise A blend of Shanay and a feminine ending

Shaniya/Shaniyah *See* Shania

Shanna A diminutive form of Shoshana. *See also* Shana

Shannagh Irish Gaelic (from sinnach): fox. From Lough Shannagh, the lake of the fox, located in Northern Ireland (geographical name)

Shannah *See* Shanna

Shannan *See* Shanon

Shannay *See* Shanay

Shannel/Shannelle *See* Chanel

Shannen *See* Shanon

Shannia *See* Shania

Shannice A blend of Shanay and a feminine ending

Shannyn/Shanon Gaelic: wise one, little owl. *See also* Girls and Boys:

Shannon

Shantae/Shantay *See* Chantay

Shantaya Sanskrit (from zantaya): calming

Shante *See* Chante

Shantel/Shantell/Shantelle *See* Chantal

Shanti Sanskrit (from zanti): peace, calm, rest

Shanya *See* Shania

Shanza/Shanzay From Shahzani, Persian (from shāh and zan): the king's bride

Shara *See* Sarah and Sharon

Sharandeep Punjabi: lamp of the Guru's shelter (Sikh name)

Sharanya Sanskrit (from zaranya): yielding protection, yielding help

Shardae/Sharday An anglicised variant of Sade, the diminutive form of Folasade

Shardonnay *See* Chardonnay

Shareen A blend of Sharon and a feminine ending

Sharelle A blend of Sharon and a feminine ending. *See also* Cheryl

Shari *See* Cherie

Sharice *See* Cerise

Sharifa Arabic: noble, protector Sharif was used as a tribal title

Sharika A form of the Hindu goddess Durga

Sharla A diminutive form of Charlene and Charlotte

Sharlene *See* Charlene

Sharlotte *See* Charlotte

Sharmaine *See* Charmaine

Sharmila Hindi: shy, coy

Sharmin/Sharmina Persian (from sharmi): shy, bashful, pretending to be shy, bashful

Sharn A diminutive form of Sharna. Please note that in some parts of Scotland, sharn/sharny means dung/covered in dung

Sharna Sanskrit (from zarana): help, protection, shelter, refuge. *See also* Sharon

Sharnay/Sharne/Sharney/Sharni/ Sharnie A diminutive form of Sharna. Please note that in some parts of Scotland, sharn/sharny means dung/covered in dung

Sharon Hebrew: forest. The name of the plain in Israel (geographical name)

Shasmeen *See* Jasmin

Shauna/Shaunagh An anglicised variant of Sinead

Shauneen A blend of Shauna and a feminine ending

Shauni/Shaunie A diminutive form of Shauna

Shaunna/Shaunnah/Shawna *See* Shauna

Shawnee A diminutive form of Shauna

Shayla/Shaylah *See* Sheila

Shaylee/Shayleigh/Shayley A diminutive form of Sheila

Shayma/Shaymaa *See* Shaima

Shayna *See* Shana

Shazia Arabic: precious, rare, unique

Shazmeen/Shazmin *See* Jasmin

Shaznay The stage name of Tricia Lewis, a former member of All Saints

Sheema *See* Shaima

Sheena A Scottish variant of Jane

Sheereen *See* Shireen

Sheila *See* Cecilia and Celia

Sheindy A diminutive form of Sheindel, which is a variant of Shana

Shekinah Hebrew: dwelling, in the presence of god, the female aspect of god

Shelbi/Shelbie/Shelby Possibly Old English (salig and leah): willow clearing

Shelina *See* Selene

Shellbie/Shellby *See* Shelby

Shelley/Shellie/Shelly Old English (from scylf and leah): ledge clearing (shifted from surname usage). Also a diminutive form of Michelle

Shenae/Shenai/Shenay From shehnai, a flute-like instrument mostly used in India, Iran and Pakistan

Shenaya *See* Shania

Shenelle *See* Chanel

Shenice A blend of Shanay and a feminine ending

Sheree *See* Sherry

Shereen A blend of Sharon and a feminine ending

Sherelle *See* Sharelle

Sheri *See* Sherry

Sherice *See* Cerise

Sherie *See* Sherry

Sherise *See* Cerise

Sherri/Sherrie/Sherry The wine named after Jerez, the place in Spain where it is made (geographical name). *See also* Cherie

Sheryl *See* Cheryl

Sheza Sanskrit (from zesa): result, end, survivor

Shi Chinese: various, including poetry

Shian/Shiann/Shianne *See* Sian

Shifa Arabic: remedy, cure

Shifra Hebrew: fair, beautiful. A midwife who helped Hebrew children during Exodus

Shikha Sanskrit (from zikha): peak, crest, pinnacle

Shilah *See* Sheila

Shilpa Sanskrit (from zilpa): art, craft

Shira Hebrew: poetry

Shireen/Shirin Persian (from shīrīn): sweet, gentle, gracious

Shirley Old English (from scir and leah): country of meadows (shifted from surname usage)

Shivani A name for Parvati, as she is the wife of the Hindu god Shiva

Shiza *See* Sheza

Shola Yoruba: blessed

Shona/Shonagh A Scottish variant

of Joan

Shontelle *See* Chantal

Shorna An anglicised variant of Sinead

Shoshana A variant of Susanna

Shree Sanskrit (from zri): radiance, beauty

Shreena Sanskrit (from zrina): night

Shreeya/Shreya/Shriya Sanskrit (from zriya): happiness, prosperity

Shruthi/Shruti Sanskrit (from zruti): word, sound, listening, wisdom. The sacred text in Hinduism

Shu Chinese: various, including pretty, beautiful girl

Shukri Arabic: thanks, grateful

Shuma Unknown, possibly Sanskrit (from suma): heaven, sky

Shyan/Shyann/Shyanna/Shyanne *See* Sian

Shyla/Shylah *See* Sheila

Sia *See* Ziya

Sian/Siana/Siani/Sianna/Sianne A Welsh variant of Jane

Siannon *See* Shanon

Sibel A Turkish variant of Sybil

Sicily The name of the Italian island (geographical name)

Siddhi Sanskrit: perfection, accomplishment, success

Sidhra Sanskrit: perfect, successful. *See also* Sidra

Sidonie From Sidon, a city in Phoenicia, which is in modern day Lebanon (geographical name)

Sidra/Sidrah The name of the sidra tree, found in Qatar, which grows despite the harsh desert conditions. *See also* Sidhra

Siena/Sienna English: orange-red (colour name). Also the name of the Italian city (geographical name)

Sierra Spanish: mountain range

Sigourney Unknown (shifted from surname usage). The name of Sigourney Howard, a character who is Jordan's aunt, mentioned in F. Scott Fitzgerald's *The Great Gatsby*, who inspired Sigourney Weaver to take on this stage name

Sihaam/Siham Arabic: arrows

Sila Turkish: home, returning home, returning to loved ones. Also Sanskrit (from zila): virtue, integrity

Silan Croatian: strong, powerful

Silke A German diminutive form of Cecilia and Celia

Silvana Latin (from silva): forest, wood. The Roman god, Silvanus, protects forests, woods and fields

Silver (name from an English word)

Silvia/Silvie *See* Sylvia

Sima Unknown, possibly Hebrew (from *See*mhah): joy. *See also* *See*ma

Simar Punjabi: absorbed in god, absorbed in the remembrance of god (Sikh name)

Simarpreet Punjabi: lovingly

remembering god (Sikh name)

Simge Turkish: symbol

Simi A diminutive form of Similoluwa and Simisola

Similoluwa Yoruba: rest in the Lord

Simisola Yoruba: rest in wealth

Simona Hebrew: one who hears. *See also* Girls and Boys: Simone

Simra/Simrah Arabic: paradise, heaven

Simrandeep Punjabi: lamp of remembrance (Sikh name)

Simranjeet Punjabi: winning remembrance (Sikh name)

Simranjit Punjabi: victory of remembrance (Sikh name)

Simranpreet Punjabi: loving remembrance (Sikh name)

Simrat/Simreet Punjabi: meditate (Sikh name)

Simren *See* Simran

Simrit *See* Simrat

Simron/Simrun *See* Simran

Sinai The Sinai Peninsula in Egypt, the possible location of the biblical Sinai Mountain, where Moses received the Ten Commandments (geographical name)

Sindy A diminutive form of Cynthia

Sinead/Sinéad An Irish variant of Jeanette. *See also* Jane

Sinem Turkish: my heart

Siobhan Irish Gaelic: Jane

Siofra Irish Gaelic: changeling, sprite

Siona Hebrew (from Zion): Jerusalem (geographical name). *See also* Girls and Boys: Zion

Sioned A Welsh variant of Joan

Sireen The wife of Hassan ibn Thabit, one of prophet Muhammad's companions

Siri From Sigrid (Old Norse: fair victory)

Siria Greek: scorching bright (a feminine form of Sirius, the brightest star in the constellation)

Sirine *See* Serena

Sita Sanskrit: furrow

Sitara Hindi: star

Siti Malay: miss, girl

Siwan Welsh: Joan

Siya Unknown

Siyana Unknown

Siyona Sanskrit (from syona): tender, pleasant, gentle

Skaiste Lithuanian (from skaisti): bright, beautiful, pure

Skarlett *See* Scarlett

Skie From the word 'sky'. *See also* Girls and Boys: Sky

Skyla/Skylah/Skylar/Skyrah Dutch: scholar. *See also* Girls and Boys: Skyler

Smilte Lithuanian: sandwort (name from flowers and trees)

Sneha Hindi: love

Sobia The name of the nurse who brought up prophet Muhammad

Soffia/Sofi *See* Sophia

Sofia Arabic: beautiful. *See also* Sophia

Sofie/Sofija *See* Sophia

Sofiya *See* Sofia and Sophia

Soha Arabic: star

Sohana *See* Suhana

Solange Latin: religious. The name of a French shepherdess who became a saint. Also the name of Solange Knowles

Soliana A blend of Sol and Liana

Soma Sanskrit: a ritual drink made from a plant that grants immortality. Also a Hindu god connected to the moon, as the moon is the cup for soma

Somaya *See* Sumayyah

Somer *See* Summer

Somia *See* Sumayyah

Sommer *See* Summer

Sona Hindi: gold

Sonakshi A name of the Hindu goddess Parvati

Sonal/Sonali Hindi: golden

Sonia *See* Sona. *See also* Sophia

Sonique French: sonic. Also a stage name created by the DJ Sonia Clarke

Soniya/Sonja/Sonya *See* Sonia

Sookie *See* Suki

Sophia/Sophie/Sophina/Sophiya/ Sophy Greek: wisdom

Sora Japanese: sky

Soraia/Soraiya/Soraya/Sorayah Persian: princess

Sorcha Manx, Irish and Scottish Gaelic: bright

Soroh *See* Sarah

Sorrel (name from flowers and trees, name from an English word)

Soumaya *See* Sumayyah

Srishti Sanskrit: nature, creation

Sriya *See* Shriya

Sruthi Sanskrit: road, path, flow

Stacey/Stacie/Stacy Greek: stable. Also a diminutive form of Anastasia

Star/Starla/Starr Old English: star

Stefani/Stefania/Stefanie/Steffi *See* Stephanie

Stela/Stella Latin: star

Stephanie/Stephany/Stephenie Greek: crown Stevi/Stevie. A diminutive form of Stephanie

Su Chinese: various, including simple. Also Turkish: water

Suad Arabic: happiness, good fortune

Subhana Arabic: pure, chaste

Sude A diminutive form of Sudenaz

Sudenaz Unknow, possible from Sarvenaz (Persian: a type of tall and slender tree)

Sue A diminutive form of Susan

Sufia Arabic: intellectual. *See also* Sophia

Suha Arabic: a star in Ursa Minor

Suhaila Arabic: gentle

Suhana/Suhani Hindi (from suhānā): pleasant

Suhayla *See* Suhaila

Sukaina Arabic: calmness. The name of Sukayna bint Husayn, one of the prophet Muhammad's great granddaughters

Sukhleen Punjabi: engrossed in peace (Sikh name)

Sukhmani Sikh name: brings peace to mind, a Sikh prayer (Sikh name)

Sukhpreet Punjabi: one of loves peace (Sikh name)

Suki/Sukie A diminutive form of Susan

Sultana Arabic: king

Sumaira *See* Samra

Sumaiya/Sumaiyah *See* Sumayyah

Suman Sanskrit: good mind

Sumaya/Sumayah/Sumayya/ Sumayyah The name of Sumayyah bint Khayyat, the first martyr in Islam

Sumer *See* Summer

Sumera *See* Sumaira

Sumeya/Sumia/Sumiya *See* Sumayyah

Summa/Summah/Summar *See* Summer

Summaya/Summayah/ Summayyah *See* Sumayyah

Summer (name from an english word)

Suna Turkish: duck, drake

Sunaina Hindi (from sundara and nainā): beautiful eyes

Sundara/Sundari Hindi and Sanskrit: beautiful

Sundas/Sundus Arabic: silk brocade

Sunita Sanskrit: wisdom, prudence

Sunnah Arabic: usual practice, the way of life based on the teachings of prophet Muhammad

Supriya Sanskrit: darling, lovely woman

Suraiya/Suraiyah *See* Suriya

Suranne Sanskrit (from surana): happiness, delight

Suraya/Surayya/Sureya *See* Suriya

Suri Persian (from sooree): red rose Also Sanskrit: thinker, sage, goddess. *See also* Sarah

Surina *See* Suri

Suriya Sanskrit: the sun. A Hindu sun god. *See also* Girls and Boys: Surya

Susan/Susana/Susanna/Susannah/ Susie/Suzan/Suzanna/ Suzannah/Suzanne/Suzi/Suzie/ Suzy Hebrew: lily (name from flowers and trees)

Swara Sanskrit (from svara): tones (the seven notes from the Hindu music scale)

Sybil/Sybille Greek: prophetess

Sydnee/Sydni/Sydnie Old English: wide island (shifted from surname usage). *See also* Girls and Boys: Sydney

Syed/Syeda Arabic: descendants of Muhammad, from the title Sayyid

Syesha *See* Sasha

Sylvia/Sylvie/Sylwia Latin: spirit of the woods

Symone *See* Simona

Symran *See* Simran

Syra *See* Cyra

Syriah *See* Siria

t

Tabassum/Tabasum Arabic: smiling

Tabatha/Tabetha/Tabitha Aramaic: gazelle. *See also* Dorcas

Tabu A diminutive form of Tabassum

Taegan *See* Teagan

Taela *See* Taylar

Tahani Arabic: congratulations

Tahera *See* Tahira

Tahia Arabic: dance

Tahira/Tahirah Arabic: pure, chaste

Tahiya/Tahiyah Arabic: greetings

Tahlia *See* Talia

Tahmeena *See* Tahmina

Tahmida Arabic: praising god

Tahmina Persian: wife of Rostam from the epic poem Shahnameh

Tahnee *See* Tawny

Tahreem Arabic: respected

Taia *See* Taja

Taiba/Taibah Arabic: refrain from evil, repentant

Taija/Taijah *See* Taja

Taila English: tiler (shifted from surname usage). *See also* Girls and Boys: Tyler

Taina *See* Tanya

Taisha *See* Aisha

Taiya/Taiyah *See* Taja

Taiyewo Yoruba: the first to taste the world (given to the elder twin).
See also Girls and Boys: Kehinde

Taja Persian (from taj): crown

Takara Japanese: treasure (rarely used in this form as a name)

Tala Native American: wolf

Taleah *See* Talia

Taleen A blend of the 'Ta' sound and Eileen

Tali Arabic: rising star

Talia/Taliah Hebrew: dew of god

Talisa/Talisha/Talitha Spanish: noble

Taliya/Taliyah/Tallia/Talliah *See* Talia

Tallie A diminutive form of Talia and Tallulah

Tallula/Tallulah Native American: leaping water

Tally A diminutive form of Talia and Tallulah

Talor *See* Taylar

Talula/Talulah/Talulla *See* Tallulah

Talya *See* Talia. Also a village in India (geographical name)

Tamana/Tamanna Arabic: to wish, to hope

Tamar/Tamara Hebrew: date palm (name from flowers and trees)

Tameka *See* Tamika

Tamera *See* Tamara

Tami/Tamia A diminutive form of Tamsin

Tamica/Tamika Japanese: from Tamiko, various, including beautiful child

Tamima/Tamimah Arabic (from

130

tameem): strong

Tamina A river in Switzerland (geographical name)

Tamira *See* Tamara

Tammi/Tammie/Tammy A diminutive form of Tamsin

Tamsin/Tamsyn/Tamzen/ Tamzin/Tamzyn *See* Thomasina

Tana A diminutive form of Tatiana and Titania. Also a lake in Ethiopia and a place in Norway (geographical name)

Tanaya *See* Tanya

Taneesha/Taneisha A blend of Tanya and Aisha

Tanem Unknown, possibly from birtanem, Turkish for my one and only

Tanesha A blend of Tanya and Aisha

Tania A diminutive form of Tatiana and Titania. *See also* Tanjia

Tanika *See* Tamika and Tania

Tanisha/Tanishka A blend of Tanya and Aisha

Tanita A blend of Tanya and Anita

Tanith From Tanit, a Phoenician moon and war goddess

Taniya A diminutive form of Tatiana and Titania. *See also* Tanjia

Tanjia Arabic: salvation

Tanjina *See* Tanjia

Tansy (botanical name, name from an English word). Also Hopi: name of a flower

Tanvi Persian: slender and delicate

woman

Tanwen Unknown, possibly Welsh (from tana and gwyn): slender and fair

Tanya A diminutive form of Tatiana and Titania. *See also* Tanjia

Tanyaradzwa Shona: found comfort, where tears are wiped away

Tanyel *See* Daniela

Tanzeela/Tanzila Arabic (from enzil): descent

Tanzina Unknown, possibly from Tanzania (geographical name)

Taome A modernised and shifted variant of Naome

Taqwa Arabic: pious, devout

Tara/Tarah Sanskrit: star, darling

Taran Punjabi: saviour, heaven (Sikh name). Also Welsh: thunder

Tarandeep Punjabi: lamp of heaven

Tariro Shona: hope

Tarryn/Taryn Unknown, possibly from Tyrone, a county in Northern Ireland (geographical name)

Tasfia Unknown, possibly from Tzvi (Hebrew: deer)

Tasha A diminutive form of Natasha

Tashana A blend of Tasha and Shana

Tasia A diminutive form of Anastasia

Taslima Arabic: greetings

Tasmia Arabic: name of god

Tasmeen/Tasmeena/Tasmin/ Tasmina *See* Tamsin. *See also* Jasmin

Tasmiyah *See* Tasmia

Tasneem/Tasneema Arabic: spring in paradise

Tasnia Arabic: praise, admire

Tasnim/Tasnima *See* Tasneem

Tatiana/Tatiyana Latin: from Tatius, the name of king Titus Tatius

Tatum Old English: from Tata (shifted from surname usage)

Tatyana *See* Tatiana

Tavia A diminutive form of Octavia

Tawny Old French: tan-coloured (colour name)

Taya/Tayah/Tayana A diminutive form of Tatiana

Tayba/Taybah/Tayiba/Tayibah *See* Tayyiba

Tayjah *See* Taja

Taylah/Taylar Old English: to cut (shifted from surname usage). *See also* Girls and Boys: Taylor

Taymar *See* Tamar

Taysha *See* Aisha

Tayyaba/Tayyabah/Tayyeba/Tayyiba/Tayyibah Arabic: kind, good-natured

Tazkia Arabic: to purify

Tazmeen/Tazmin Arabic: adding, combining

Tea A diminutive form of Teresa

Teagan/Teagen/Teaghan Irish Gaelic (from tadg): poet

Teah *See* Tia

Tean An uninhabited island near Cornwall (geographical name)

Teanna A diminutive form of Tatiana and Christiana

Teegan *See* Teagan

Teeya *See* Tia

Tegan/Tegen *See* Teagan

Tehila/Tehilla/Tehillah Hebrew: praise, adoration

Tehreem Arabic: respect

Tehya Unknown, possibly Zuni: precious. *See also* Tia

Tehzeeb Arabic: etiquette

Teia *See* Tia

Teigan/Teighan *See* Teagan

Teisha *See* Tisha

Teja A diminutive form of Doroteja, a form of Dorothea. *See also* Tejal

Tejal Hindi (from tej): bright

Teleri Tolkien's Quenya: the hindmost, the name of the third and last of elf clan to arrive in Aman, the Undying Lands

Temidayo Yoruba: joy is mine

Temilola Yoruba: wealth is mine

Tempany The name of the Australian actress Tempany Deckert, possibly from the word 'tempest'

Temperance (name from an English word)

Tenisha *See* Tanisha

Teodora *See* Theodora

Teona/Teoni *See* Theona

Teresa/Tereza Greek: harvest

Teri/Terri/Terrie A diminutive form of Teresa

Tesni Welsh (from tes): warmth,

heat haze

Tess/Tessa A diminutive form of Teresa

Texas Caddo: friends. The name of the US state (geographical name)

Teya/Teyah A diminutive form of Teyana

Teyana A diminutive form of Tatiana and Christiana

Teyla The name of Teyla Emmagan from Stargate Atlantis

Thahmina *See* Tamina

Thaila Unknown, possibly from Thailand. *See also* Thalia

Thais Greek: bandage. The name of a courtesan who accompanied Alexander the Great

Thalia Greek: to blossom. The muse of comedy, and also one of the three Graces from Greek mythology

Thamanna *See* Tamana

Thamina *See* Samina and Tamina

Thandeka Xhosa: pleasant, desirable

Thandie A diminutive form of Thandiwe

Thandiwe Xhosa: loving one

Thania *See* Tanya

Thaslima *See* Taslima

Thea A diminutive form of Dorothy

Theadora *See* Theodora

Theia Greek: goddess (a Titan in Greek mythology)

Thekra Arabic: memory

Thelma Greek: will

Theodora Greek: god's gift

Theona Greek: god's name. The sister of Hecuba from Greek mythology

Theresa/Therese *See* Teresa

Thi Vietnamese: from the family of

Thia A diminutive form of Dorothy

Thomasina Aramaic: twin

Thu Vietnamese: autumn

Tia/Tiah Spanish: aunt (made more popular by the brand Tia Maria). Also diminutive form of Cynthia

Tiahna A diminutive form of Tatiana and Christiana

Tiamii Created by Katie Price and Peter Andre for their daughter by combining Thea and Amy

Tian Chinese: various, including sky. *See also* Tiana

Tiana/Tianah/Tiani/Tianie/ Tiann/Tianna/Tiannah/Tianne A diminutive form of Tatiana and Christiana

Tiara Latin: headdress of Persian kings

Tiarna Irish Gaelic (from tigerna): lord, superior

Tiaunna A blend of Tia and Anna

Tiegan *See* Teegan

Tienna A modernised and shifted variant of Sienna

Tierna Spanish: tender

Tierney Irish Gaelic (from tigerna): lords of (shifted from surname usage)

Tierra Spanish: earth

Tiffani/Tiffanie/Tiffany Greek:

born on the day of the Theophania feast

Tiger Old English: tiger. Also a diminutive form of Tigerlily

Tigerlily/Tigerlilly A name derived from the tiger lily flower (name from flowers and trees)

Tiggy A diminutive form of Antigone, the daughter of Oedipus

Tihanna/Tijana Serbian: peaceful, quiet

Tila *See* Tilia

Tilda A diminutive form of Matilda

Tileah/Tilia Old English: lime tree (name from flowers and trees)

Tilley/Tilli/Tillie/Tilly A diminutive form of Matilda

Timara *See* Tamara

Timea A character name created by the Hungarian author Mór Jókairom from Euthymia (Greek: good natured)

Tina Old English: river

Tinisha Shona: god is with us *See also* Girls and Boys: Tinashe

Tionne The name of Tionne Solusar from *Star Wars*

Tirion Welsh: kind, tender, gentle. Also Tolkien's Sindarin: of the watch (the name of the city Tirion upon Túna)

Tirzah Hebrew: my delight (a daughters of Zelophehad from the Torah)

Tisha A diminutive form of Latisha

Titania Greek: giant. Also the queen of fairis from Shakespeare's *A Midsummer Night's Dream*

Titilayo Yoruba: eternal happiness

Tiya *See* Tia

Tiyana/Tiyanna *See* Tiana

Tna *See* Tina

Tola A diminutive form of Antonia

Toni/Tonia A diminutive form of Antonia

Tonicha *See* Antonia

Tonie A diminutive form of Antonia

Tonisha *See* Antonia

Tonya A diminutive form of Antonia

Tooba Arabic: good news

Topaz Greek: topaz (gemstone name)

Torey A diminutive form of Victoria

Tori Japanese: various, including bird (rarely used in this form as a name) and peaches and plums. Also a diminutive form of Victoria

Toria/Torie/Torri/Torrie A diminutive form of Victoria

Tova/Tove Old Norse: beautiful Thor

Toyah A diminutive form of Victoria

Tracey/Tracy French: from Tracy-Bocage (shifted from surname usage)

Trenyce From Lashundra Trenyce Cobbins, the stage name of a finalist from *American Idol*

Trina A diminutive form of Katrina

Triniti/Trinity Latin: trinity, triad

Trisha A diminutive form of Patricia

Trishna Sanskrit (from trsna): a Buddhist concept of thirst and desire

Trixie A diminutive form of Beatrice

Tru/Trudi/Trudie/Trudy A diminutive form of Gertrude

Truly Other English: true

Tuana Turkish: first drops of rain in paradise

Tuba Latin: trumpet

Tuesday Old English: day of Tiw, the Norse of justice and combat

Tugce Turkish: gems from the queen's throne

Tula A diminutive form of Tallulah

Tulip Turkish: shaped like a turban (name from flowers and trees)

Tulisa/Tulisha From Tula Paulinea Contostavlos, the self-coined name of the British singer

Tulsi Sanskrit (from tulasi): holy basil (name from flowers and trees)

Twila/Twyla English: twilight

Tyana/Tyanna/Tyanne See Tiana

Tye A diminutive form of Tyra. Also a city in Texas (geographical name)

Tyesha/Tyisha See Aisha and Tisha

Tyna Named from the River Tyne (shifted from surname usage). See also Tina. See also Girls and Boys: Tyne

Tyra/Tyrah Old English: Thor's battle

u

Ugne Lithuanian: fire

Ula/Ulla A diminutive form of Ulrica

Ulrica/Ulrika Old German: power

Uma Sanskrit: various, including flax, friend, light, night and sky. A name of the gentle Hindu goddess Parvati

Umaima/Umaimah See Umama

Umaira/Umaiza Arabic: long life

Umama/Umamah Arabic: young mother (the name of Umamah bint Zainab, granddaughter of prophet Muhammad)

Umarah See Umaira

Umayma/Umaymah See Umama

Umayrah See Umaira

Umayyah A narrator of hadith

Umera See Umaira

Ummayah/Ummayyah See Umayyah

Umme Arabic: mother

Una Irish Gaelic (from úan): lamb Also Latin: one

Unaisah/Unaysah Arabic: friendly

Unique Latin: only, single

Unity Latin: oneness

Urooj Arabic: exaltation

Uroosa Arabic: bride, heroine

Ursula/Urszula Latin: little bear

Urte Old German: good with a sword. Also a diminutive form of

Dorothea

Urvi Sanskrit: heaven and earth, wide

Uswa/Uswah Arabic: habit, usual practice. Also Urdu: good manners

Uzma Arabic: greatest

Vaidehi Princess of Videhas. Also one of the names of Sita, the avatar of the Hindu goddess Laksmi

Vaishali Hindi: ancient city of King Vishal (the ancient capital of Licchavi in ancient India)

Vaishnavi Sanskrit (from vaisnavi): female worshipper of Vishnu. Also the sister of the Hindu god Vishnu

Vakare Lithuanian: in the evening

Valencia/Valentina/Valentine/ Valeria/Valerie/Valerija/Valery Latin: healthy, strong

Vaneeza/Vanesa/Vanessa Hebrew: star (created as A blend of Esther and Vanhomrigh by Jonathan Swift)

Vani A diminutive form of Evangelina. Also a town in Georgia (geograpical name)

Vania A diminutive form of Evangelina

Vanisha *See* Vanessa

Vanshi/Vanshika Hindi: to the future

Varsha Hindi: rainy season, a ritu in the Hindu calendar

Veda *See* Vidya

Vedika Sanskrit: alter

Velvet (name from an English word)

Venessa *See* Vanessa

Venetia/Venice Latin: city of canals (geographical name)

Venus Latin: the Roman goddess of love

Vera Russian: faith. Also Latin: truth

Verity Latin: truth

Verona A diminutive form of Veronica. Also a city in Italy (geographical name)

Veronica/Veronika Latin: true image

Vesper Latin: everything

Vesta Latin: the Roman goddess of the home

Vicki/Vickie/Vicky A diminutive form of Victoria

Victoire/Victoria/Victory Latin: victory

Vida *See* Vita

Vidhi Sanskrit: method, manner, destiny

Vidya Sanskrit: knowledge. Also a name of the Hindu goddess of knowledge, Sarasvati

Vienna Latin: the capital of Austria (geographical name)

Vikki A diminutive form of Victoria

Viktoria/Viktorija *See* Victoria

Vilte Lithuanian: a dimiuitive form of Viltaute, people of hope

Vinisha *See* Vanessa

Viola *See* Violet Also the instrument from the violin family

Violet/Violeta/Violetta/Violette French: violet (name from flowers and trees, also colour name)

Virginia Latin: virgin, maiden. Also a US state (geographical name)

Vita Latin: life. Also a city in Sicily (geographical name)

Vittoria *See* Victoria

Vivian/Viviana/Vivianne/Vivien/ Vivienne Latin: living

Vrinda *See* Brenda

Wafa Arabic: loyalty

Waheeda/Wahida Arabic: unique

Wajeeha/Wajiha/Wajihah Arabic: distinguished

Wallis Old English: from Wales

Wanessa *See* Vanessa

Wania/Waniya Arabic: gift of god

Warda Pashto: rose

Wareesha/Warisa Arabic: heiress

Waseema/Wasima Arabic: beautiful, graceful

Wednesday Old English: day of Woden, or Odin

Wendy Old English: friend. Also a diminutive form of Gwendolyn

Weronika *See* Veronica

Whitney Old English: white water

Wiktoria *See* Victoria

Wilhelmina/Willa Old German: protection, helmet

Willow Old English: rolling. Also the name of willow trees (name from flowers and trees)

Winifred Welsh (from gwyn and frewi): fair frewi, where frewi is of uncertain origins. Also the name of Saint Winifred, a Welsh noble woman who was beheaded and restored to life, forming a holy well where her head had fallen)

Winnie A diminutive form of Winifred and Winona

Winona Native American: first born daughter

Winter Old English: fourth season

Wynter *See* Winter

Xanthe/Xantha/Xanthia Greek: blonde

Xara *See* Zara. *See also* Sara

Xena/Xenia Greek: stranger, guest

Xsara *See* Zara

Ya Chinese: various, including elegant. *See also* Yaa

Yaa/Yaaba/Yaayaa Akan: born on a

Thursday

Yael *See* Jael

Yagmur Turkish: rain

Yalda Arabic: longest night, winter solice

Yan Chinese: various, including swallow, feast and bright. *See also* Jan

Yana *See* Yoana

Yara Arabic: butterfly. *See also* Iara

Yaren A district in Nauru (geographical names)

Yasemin *See* Jasmin

Yashica/Yashika *See* Jessica

Yashvi Hindi: fame

Yasmeen/Yasmin/Yasmina/ Yasmine *See* Jasmin

Yasna Avestan: worship (the name of the sacred Avesta text)

Yazmin/Yazmine *See* Jasmin

Ye Chinese: various, including night and leaf

Yelda Turkish: longest night of the year

Yelena *See* Helen

Yesim Turkish: jade (gemstone name)

Yetunde Yoruba: return of the mother, rebirth of a deceased woman

Yezda Kurdish: unknown

Yitty *See* Kitty

Yoana Hebrew: god is kind

Yocheved *See* Jochebed

Yolanda Greek: violet (name from flowers and trees)

Yousra *See* Yusra

Ysabel/Ysabella/Ysabelle/Ysobel *See* Elizabeth

Yue Chinese: various, including exceed and moon. Also Japanese: various, including sunset

Yumi Japanese: various, including abundant beauty. Also Chinese: various

Yumna Arabic: blessed, lucky

Yun Chinese: various, including luck and cloud

Yuna Japanese: various, including gentle heart, moon maiden and summer dream. Also Chinese: various. Also a river in the Dominican Republic (geographical name). *See also* Jean

Yusra/Yusrah Arabic: state of ease

Yvaine The heroine in *Stardust* by Neil Gaiman, who is a fallen evening star

Yvette/Yvetta *See* Yvonne

Yvie A diminutive form of Yvonne *See also* Eve

Yvonne Old German: yew (name from flowers and trees)

Z

Zaakirah *See* Zakira

Zaara *See* Zara

Zadie *See* Zaida

Zafirah Arabic: successful

Zahara Arabic: flower, bright

Zahida Arabic: pious

Zahira/Zahirah Arabic: brilliant, shining

Zahra/Zahraa/Zahrah *See* Zahara

Zaiba/Zaibaa *See* Zayba

Zaida Arabic: abundance, growth

Zaima Arabic: leader

Zaina Arabic: beauty. *See also* Xena

Zainab *See* Zaynab

Zainah *See* Zaina

Zaineb/Zainub *See* Zaynab

Zaira/Zairah *See* Zara

Zakia/Zakiah *See* Zakiya

Zakira/Zakirah Arabic: speaker

Zakiya/Zakiyah/Zakiyyah Arabic: bright, clever

Zamzam The well in Mecca, on the route of the Hajj, where god revealed a source of water to Hagar

Zana *See* Zaina and Sanna

Zanna *See* Sanna

Zaneta Hebrew: god is gracious

Zanib *See* Zaynab

Zantha *See* Xanthe

Zara/Zarah Hebrew: radiance

Zareen/Zareena *See* Zarin

Zaria/Zariah *See* Sara and Zara. Also a city in Nigeria (geographical name)

Zarin/Zarina Persian: golden

Zariya Arabic: beauty, light

Zarrah *See* Sara

Zarrin *See* Zarin

Zayba Persian: beautiful

Zayna *See* Zaina

Zaynab Arabic: desert flower. Also the names of Zaynab bint Khuzayma and Zaynab bint Jahsh, both wives of the prophet Muhammad, and the name of Zaynab bint Muhammad, daughter of Muhammad

Zaynah *See* Zaina

Zeba/Zeena A diminutive form of Zenobia

Zeenat *See* Zinat

Zefira Hebrew: morning

Zehra *See* Zahara

Zeina *See* Xena

Zeinab *See* Zaynab

Zelal Arabic: shadow

Zelda A diminutive form of Griselda

Zelia/Zelie A diminutive form of Cecilia

Zena Amharic: news. Also a diminutive form of Zenobia

Zenab *See* Zaynab

Zenaide Unknown

Zenia *See* Xena. Also a diminutive form of Zenobia

Zenobia Greek: life of Zeus

Zerda Persian: fennec fox

Zeta/Zetta Hebrew: olive (name from flowers and trees)

Zeynab/Zeynep *See* Zaynab

Zhanae/Zhane *See* Jane

Zhara *See* Zara

Zia *See* Ziya

Zian *See* Jane. Also Chinese (as Zi'an): various

Zifira *See* Zefira

Zikra/Zikrah *See* Thekra
Zilan Kurdish: named after the
  Zilan Valley in Turkey. Also (as
  Zi'lan): various
Zina *See* Xena
Zinat Arabic: beauty, decoration
Zineb Arabic: beautiful, flower
Zinia/Zinnia Latin: plant named
  after the botanist Johann Gottfried
  Zinn (name from flowers and
  trees)
Zippora/Zipporah Hebrew: bird
  Also the name of the wife of
  Moses
Zita Greek: seeker. Also the name
  of an Italian patron saint of maids
  and servants
Ziva Hebrew: radiant, bright. Also
  the same of the Slavic goddess of
  love
Ziya Arabic: light
Zobia Arabic: gift of god
Zoe/Zoee/Zoey/Zoeya Greek: life
Zofia *See* Sophia
Zoha Arabic: light
Zohal Pashto: moon of another
  planet
Zohra Arabic: blossom
Zoie *See* Zoe
Zola/Zolia Italian: earth
Zosia *See* Sophia
Zowie *See* Zoe
Zoya/Zoyah Arabic: life. *See also*
  Zoe
Zsofia *See* Sophia
Zuba *See* Azuba

Zubaida/Zubaidah Arabic: little
  butter ball. Also the name of
  Zubaidah bint Ja`far ibn Mansur,
  an Abbasid princesses
Zuha/Zuhaa/Zuhal Arabic:
  adornment, dawn
Zuhaira Arabic: small flower
Zuhra/Zuhrah *See* Zahara
**Zulaikha/Zulaikhah/Zulaykha/
  Zuleika/Zuleikha/Zulekha**
  Arabic: fair, lovely
Zunaira/Zunairah Arabic: flower of
  paradise
Zuri *See* Suri
Zuzana *See* Susannah
Zuzanna *See* Susannah
Zyana Hebrew: heaven blessed

Boys' names

a

Aaban The eighth month of the Iranian calendar. Also the angel of iron in Persian mythology

Aadam *See* Adam

Aaden *See* Aden

Aadi *See* Adi

Aadil *See* Adil

Aadit *See* Adit

Aaditya *See* Aditya

Aahil Arabic: honourable judge

Aakash *See* Akash

Aamir *See* Amir

Aaqib *See* Aqib

Aaqil Arabic: intelligent

Aaran *See* Aaron

Aarav *See* Arav

Aarib *See* Areeb

Aarish *See* Arish

Aariyan *See* Aryan

Aariz Arabic: leader, ruler

Aarnav *See* Arnav

Aaron Hebrew: high, exalted. The name of Aaron the Priest, the older brother of Moses

Aarondeep Punjabi: the lamp of Aaron (Sikh name)

Aarron *See* Aaron

Aarush *See* Arush

Aaryan *See* Aryan

Aashir Arabic: living

Aasim Arabic: protector

Aatif *See* Atif

Aayan *See* Ayan

Aayush *See* Ayush

Abaan Unknown, an old Arabic name

Abas/Abass/Abbas Arabic: furious lion

Abd Arabic: servant

Abdal/Abdalla/Abdallah/Abdel/ Abdellah Arabic: slave of Allah

Abdelrahman *See* Abdur-Rahman

Abdi *See* Abd

Abdifatah Arabic: slave of the Conquerer

Abdihakim *See* Abdul-Hakeem

Abdikarim *See* Abdul-Kareem

Abdimalik *See* Abdul-Malik

Abdinasir Arabic: slave of the Helper. *See also* Nasir

Abdiqani Arabic: slave of the Rich

Abdirahim *See* Abdur-Raheem

Abdirahman *See* Abdur-Rahman

Abdishakur Arabic: slave of the All-Thankful

Abdou/Abdoulie/Abdul *See* Abdallah

Abdulaahi/Abdulah/Abdulahad/ Abdulahi *See* Abdallah

Abdul-Azeez/Abdul-Aziz Arabic: slave of the The Mighty or The Honourable. *See also* Aziz

Abdulaziz *See* Abdul-Aziz

Abdulbasit Arabic: slave of the Expander

Abdul-Hadi Arabic: slave of the Guide. *See also* Hadi

Abdulhadi *See* Abdul-Hadi

Abdul-Hakeem Arabic: slave of the Wise One. *See also* Hakeem

Abdulkadir *See* Abdulqadir

Abdul-Kareem Arabic: slave of the Most Generous. *See also* Kareem

Abdulkarim *See* Abdul-Kareem

Abdulla/Abdullaah/Abdullah/ Abdullahi/Abdullahi *See* Abdallah

Abdulmajid Arabic: slave of the All-Glorious

Abdul-Malik Arabic: slave of the King. *See also* Malik

Abdulmalik *See* Abdul-Malik

Abdulqadir Arabic: slave of the Powerful. *See also* Kadir

Abdulraheem/Abdulrahim *See* Abdur-Raheem

Abdul-Raheem *See* Abdur-Raheem

Abdulrahman/Abdulrehman *See* Abdur-Rahman

Abdul-Rahman *See* Abdur-Rahman

Abdulsalam Arabic: slave of the Saviour and the All-Peaceful As-Salam is one of Allah's 99 names, meaning Saviour and All-Peaceful, and reciting it repeatedly is believed to help cure sickness

Abdulsamad Arabic: slave of the Eternal. *See also* Samad

Abdulwahab Arabic: slave of the Gifter and Bestower. *See also* Wahab

Abdur *See* Abdallah

Abdurahman/Abdurrahmaan/ Abdurrahman *See* Abdur-Rahman

Abdur-Raheem Arabic: slave of the Most Merciful. *See also* Rahim

Abdur-Rahmaan/Abdur-Rahman Arabic: slave of the Most Beneficent and Most Gracious. *See also* Rahman

Abdus *See* Abdallah

Abe A diminutive form of Abraham

Abed *See* Abid

Abel Hebrew: herdsman or breath. The son of Adam and Eve who was killed by his older brother Cain

Abhay Sanskrit (from abhi and abhaya): fearless

Abhijot Sanskrit (from abhijit): victorious

Abhinav Sanskrit (from abhinava): new, fresh, young

Abhiraj Sanskrit: reigning everywhere

Abhiram Sanskrit: delighted

Abhishek Hindi: consecration, annoitment

Abid/Abidur Arabic: worshipper,

adorer

Abir Arabic: strong, aroma

Abishan Hebrew: gift of god

Abraar Arabic: gift, obedience

Abraham/Abrahim Hebrew: father of many. Abraham's name was originally Abram (Hebrew: high father), but it was changed by god

Abu Arabic: father

Abu-Bakr/Abubakar/Abubaker/ Abubakr Arabic: father of the young camel

Abul *See* Abu

Abyan Arabic: clearer

Ace (name from an English word). Also a diminutive form of Alexander

Acer From ace, meaning someone who aces

Achilles Greek: grief of the people. The Greek hero during the Trojan War whose only weakness was a point on his ankle, which had not been protected by the waters of the Styx

Adal *See* Adel

Adam/Adamas Hebrew: man. The first man created by god

Adar Hebrew: the sixth month in the Hebrew calendar

Adarsh Hindi: ideal

Adas *See* Adam

Adebayo Yoruba: the crown is mixed with joy

Adedamola Yoruba: the crown is mixed with wealth

Adedayo Yoruba: the crown of joy

Adeeb Arabic: refined, well-mannered, learned, scholar

Adeel Arabic: same age, matching

Adel Persian: righteous, noble

Adem *See* Adam

Ademide Yoruba: my crown has arrived

Ademola Yoruba: the crown is given to me

Aden *See* Adam

Adetokunbo Yoruba: the crown arrived from over the sea

Adham Arabic: black, black horse

Adi Hebrew: jewel. *See also* Adiy

Adib Arabic: well-mannered, courteous

Adil Arabic: fair, just, righteous

Adin Hebrew: slender or ornament

Adison Old English: son of Adam (shifted from surname usage). *See also* Girls and Boys: Addison

Adit Sanskrit (from adita): boundless, entire, happy

Adithya/Aditya Sanskrit: belonging to Aditi, a Hindu sky goddess and celestial mother. *See* Adit

Adiy The name of Khubayb ibn Adiy, a companion of prophet Muhammad. *See also* Khubaib

Adiyan Arabic: religions, ways of life

Adnaan/Adnan The name of the ancestor of prophet Muhammad, and the father of the Adnanite Arabs

Adomas *See* Adam

Adon A diminutive form of Adonis

Adonis Greek: lord. The youth whom the Greek goddess Aphrodite fell in love with. He was subsequently killed by a wild boar, and anemones grew from his blood

Adrian/Adriano/Adrians Latin: from Hadria, a city in Italy

Adriel Hebrew: flock of god

Adrien *See* Adrian

Adrijus/Adris *See* Adrian

Advait Sanskrit (from advaita): unique, sole

Advaith Sanskrit (from advaidha): free from malice, not divided

Advay/Advik Sanskrit (from advaya): unique, ultimate truth

Adyan *See* Adiyan

Aedan *See* Aidan

Aelfred *See* Alfred

Aengus *See* Angus

Aeron Welsh: berry. *See also* Girls and Boys: Erin

Afan/Affaan/Affan Arabic: modest

Afif Arabic: chaste, modest, virtuous

Afonso *See* Alfonso

Afraz Persian: move higher

Aftab Arabic: the sun

Afzal Arabic: better, superior

Agastya Sanskrit: mountain thrower. One of the seven sages, and a grandson of Brahma

Agha Arabic: honourable man

Ahaan Sanskrit (from ahana): dawn

Ahad Arabic: unique. A name of Allah

Ahamed *See* Ahmad

Aharon *See* Aaron

Ahmad/Ahmed/Ahmet Arabic: the most praised. A name of the prophet Muhammad

Ahnaf Arabic: club-footed. The name of Ahnaf ibn Qais, whose tribe accepted Islam after being sent a missionary from prophet Muhammad

Ahren/Ahron *See* Aaron

Ahsan Arabic: beautiful, handsome, perfection, excellence

Ahyan Arabic: era, age, time

Aidan/Aiden/Aidyn An anglicised variant of Aodhan

Ailbe Irish: white

Airon/Aironas *See* Aeron

AJ/AJai A blend of two letters from the alphabet

Ajani Yoruba: he who wins the fight

Ajay *See* AJ

Ajeet/Ajit Sanskrit: unconquered. A name for the Hindu gods Shiva and Vishnu

Ajmal Arabic: very beautiful

Ajwad Arabic: more generous

Akaash/Akash Sanskrit (from akasha): sky

Akbar Arabic: greater, honourable

Akeeb *See* Aqib

Akeel *See* Akil

Akeem Arabic: wise

Akhil *See* Akil

Akib *See* Aqib

Akif Arabic: devoted, dedicated

Akil Arabic: thoughtful

Akim *See* Akeem

Akin Turkish: flood, stream

Akiva The name of Akiva ben Joseph, an influential rabbi. *See also* Jacob

Akmal Arabic: more complete

Akram Arabic: more noble, more generous

Aksel *See* Axel

Akshaj A name of the Hindu god Vishnu

Akshar/Akshat/Akshay/Akshayan Sanskrit (from aksara): letter, syllable. Also Hindi (from akṣaya): everlasting. A name of Brahma, the Hindu creator god

Al-Ameen/Al-Amin/Alamin *See* Amin

Alan/Aland Unknown, possibly Old English: little rock

Alasdair/Alastair Scottish Gaelic: Alexander

Alban Latin: white. Also Scottish Gaelic: Scotland (geographical name)

Albert/Alberto Germanic: noble, bright, white

Albi/Albie A diminutive form of Albert

Albin From the Albus family (Latin: white)

Albion Greek: the name for Great Britain

Alby A diminutive form of Albert

Alden *See* Alvin

Aldo Latin: tall. Also Old German: old, noble

Alec A diminutive form of Alexander

Aled Welsh: offspring

Aleem *See* Alim

Alejandro *See* Alexander

Alek/Aleks A diminutive form of Alexander

Aleksandar/Aleksander/ Aleksandr/Aleksandrs *See* Alexander

Alen *See* Alan

Alessandro *See* Alexander

Alessio *See* Alexei

Alex A diminutive form of Alexander

Alexanda/Alexander/Alexandr/ Alexandre/Alexandro/ Alexandros/Alexandru Greek: defender of men

Alexei/Alexey Greek: to help. *See also* Girls and Boys: Alexi

Alexzander *See* Alexander

Alf/Alfi/Alfie A diminutive form of Alfred

Alfonso Old German: noble and ready

Alfred/Alfredo Old English: elf council

Alfy A diminutive form of Alfred

Alhaji Arabic: a Hajji, a title given to those who have been on the Hajj

Ali Arabic: high, sublime. The name of Ali ibn Abu Talib, cousin of prophet Muhammad

Alieu Fulani: strong. This is usually used within the Fulani royal family

Alim Arabic: scholar

Alisdair/Alistair/Alister *See* Alasdair

Alix A diminutive form of Alexander

Aliyaan/Aliyan Hebrew: rising, exalted

Aliyu *See* Ali

Allan/Allen *See* Alan

Allister *See* Alasdair

Alonso/Alonzo *See* Alfonso

Alp Turkish: brave

Alper Turkish: brave men

Alperen Turkish: small

Alpha Greek: the first letter of the alphabet

Altin Turkish: gold

Alun *See* Alan

Alvaro Old German: guard of all

Alvin/Alwyn From the family of Ealdwine (Old English: old friend)

Alyaan/Alyan Arabic: sky, heaven

Amaad Arabic: pillar of support

Amaan Arabic (from aman): peace, tranquility, safety

Amaar *See* Amar

Amad/Amadou/Amadu *See* Ahmad

Amanuel *See* Emanuel

Amanveer/Amanvir Punjabi: one who fights for peace (Sikh name)

Amar Arabic: work, order. Also Punjabi: the immortal one (Sikh name)

Amare/Amarii Latin: everlasting

Amarpal Punjabi: protector of the immortal one (Sikh name)

Amaru Quechua: serpent. The name of Túpac Amaru, the Inca monarch who was killed by the Spanish invaders (the name Túpac means brilliant). Also the name of Túpac Amaru II, who led an uprising against the Spanish rulers. The rapper Túpac Amaru Shakur was named after these men

Amarveer Punjabi: warrior of the immortal one (Sikh name)

Ambrose From Ambrosia (Greek: food and drink of the gods)

Ameen Arabic: faithful. *See also* Amin

Ameer Arabic: chief, prince. *See also* Amir

Amen Hebrew: so be it. *See also* Ameen and Amin

Amer *See* Ameer and Amir

Amiel/Amil Hindi: untouchable

Amin/Amine/Aminul/Aminur Arabic: safe, secure, protected. *See also* Ameen

Amir Arabic: full of life, prosperous *See also* Ameer

Amish Sanskrit (from amisha): gift, beautiful

Amit Sanskrit (from amita): immeasurable, infinite. A name of the Hindu elephant god Ganesha

Amjad Persian: noble, honourable

Ammaar *See* Amar

Ammad *See* Amaad and Ahmad

Amman *See* Amaan

Ammar *See* Amar

Amogh Hindi: unwavering, unerring

Amon From Amun, the Egyptian king of god. A king of Judah

Amos Hebrew: to carry

Amr Arabic (from omr): long lived Also possibly Arabic (from amr): command, order, commander, chief

Amrik Punjabi: god of the sky (Sikh name)

Amritpal Punjabi: protected by the nectar of immortality (Sikh name)

Anakin The name of Anakin Skywalker from *Star Wars*

Anand Sanskrit: rejoice, delight

Anas/Anass *See* Anes

Anay A name of the Hindu god Vishnu

Anders A Danish, Norwegian and Swedish variant of Andrew

Anderson Old English: son of Anders (shifted from surname usage)

Andre A French variant of Andrew

Andreas *See* Andrew

Andrei A Romanian and Russian variant of Andrew

Andrej A Czech and Slovenian variant of Andrew

Andres An Estonian variant of Andrew

Andrew Greek (from andreios): man, manly. *See also* Girls and Boys: Andrea

Andrey A Romanian and Russian variant of Andrew

Andrzej A Polish variant of Andrew

Andy A diminutive form of Andrew

Aneeq Arabic: beautiful

Anees/Aneesh *See* Anis

Aneil *See* Anil

Aneirin A Welsh bard who served as a court poet in Scotland

Anes Arabic (from anees): close friend, companion, friendly, kind

Aneurin *See* Aneirin

Angad Sanskrit (from aggada): arm bracelet. The name of the second Guru (Sikh name)

Angelo Italian: angel

Angelos Latin: angels

Angus Irish Gaelic (oín and gus): one strength

Anil Sanskrit (from anila): wind, air

Aniq Arabic: elegant, smart

Anirudh Sanskrit: uncontrolled. A grandson of Krishna who was loved by the princess Usha

Anis/Anish Arabic: good natured

Ankit Sanskrit (from agkita): marked, with auspicious marks

Ankush Hindi (from anakush): goad, drive forth

Anoop Sanskrit (from anupa): marshy, watery, cherish, preserve. Also Hindi (from anupam): unparelleled, incomparable

Ans *See* Ansh

Ansel Old German (from ansand helm): god's helmet, god's protection (shifted from surname usage)

Ansh Sanskrit (from amz): part of, divide, distribute

Anson Old English: son of Agnes (Ancient Greek, from agnós: pure, chaste)

Anthony/Antoine/Anton/ Antoni/Antonio/Antonios/ Antony/Antwon/Antwone Latin: from the Antonius family, most notably that of Marcus Antonius

Anuj Sanskrit (from anuja): little brother

Anush Hindi: morning star

Anwar Arabic: bright, light

Anzar Arabic: looks, glances

Aodhan Irish Gaelic (from áed): fire

Aqeeb *See* Aqib

Aqeel Arabic: the best. *See also* Akil

Aqib Arabic: successor

Aqil *See* Aqeel

Ara The name of the Armenian hero, Ara the Beautiful

Arad Persian: he who brings

Arafat A mountain in Mecca (geographical name, shifted from surname usage)

Aram An area in Syria (geographical name)

Aran A group of islands on the west side of Ireland (geographical name)

Arandeep *See* Arundeep

Aras Sanskrit: cedar. Also a river that flows through Armenia, Azerbaijan, Iran and Turkey (geographical name)

Arash The name of Arash the Archer, a hero in Iranian folklore

Arav Sanskrit (from arava): quiet

Arbaaz Unknown, possibly Sanskrit (from arvaza): quick, fast. Also possibly Sanskrit (from arapas): safe, unharmed

Arbab Arabic: lord, master

Arbaz *See* Arbaaz

Arber Old English (from herebeorg): shelter, harbour (shifted from surname usage)

Archer (name from an English word, shifted from surname usage)

Archey A diminutive form of Archibald

Archibald Old German (from ercan and bald): truly bold

Archie/Archy A diminutive form of Archibald

Arda Turkish: to follow, to come after, chisel, marking stake

Ardi An Estonian variant of Arthur

Ardil *See* Adil

Ardit Albanian (from ar and ditë): golden day

Areeb Arabic: wise

Aren Armenian: from god. *See also* Aaron

Ares Unknown, possibly Ancient Greek (from arē): ruin. The Greek god of war

Arhaan Sanskrit (from arhana): worship, honour

Arham A Jain variant of Om

Ari Albanian (from ar): bear, gold. Also Armenian: brave. Also Bororo: moon. Also Old Norse: eagle. Also Swahili: eager, keen. Also Turkish: bee. Also a Finnish variant of Adrian. *See also* Aris and Aryeh

Arif Arabic (from aref): intelligent, full of knowledge

Arijus Lithanian: aria, air

Arin *See* Aaron

Arion A divine and immortal horse in Greek mythology

Aris Greek (from áristos): the best A diminutive form of Aristotle, the name of the Greek philosopher

Arish Arabic: palm huts. The largest city in Sinai (geographical name)

Ariyan *See* Aryan

Ariz *See* Aris

Arjan/Arjen Albanian (from ar and jetë): golden life. Also a Dutch variant of Adrian. *See also* Arjun

Arjun Sanskrit (from arjuna): silver. From Arjuna, the Hindu hunter and hero, whose name reflects his purity and shining fame

Arkadiusz A Polish variant of Arcadius, Greek: of Arcadia, from the land of bears

Arlan/Arlen *See* Harlan

Arley/Arlie Old English (from hoer and leah): rock clearing (shifted from surname usage). *See also* Girls and Boys: Harley

Arlind Albanian (from ar and lind): born from gold

Arlo Old English: unknown, possibly temple hill. *See also* Girls and Boys: Harlow

Armaan/Arman Persian: desire, longing. Also Kazakh: dream. Also possibly Armenian (from ar): gold, or Armenian (from ari): brave. *See also* Girls and Boys: Harman

Armand A French variant of Herman, Old English (from here and man): army man

Armandas A Lithuanian variant of Armand

Armando An Italian, Portuguese and Spanish variant of Armand

Armin A prince of Persia. Also a German variant of Arminius, from the same root as Armand

Arminas A Lithuanian variant of Arminius, from the same root as Armand

Arnas Basque: breath

Arnav Sanskrit (from arnava): from the sea. Also Turkish: hare

Arnie/Arno A diminutive form of Arnold

Arnold Old German (from arn and wald): eagle ruler, eagle power

Aro An Igbo god of judgement

Aron *See* Aaron and Arun

Aronas A Lithuanian variant of Aaron

Aroon *See* Arun

Arran/Arren/Arron *See* Aaron

Arry *See* Ari
Arsalaan/Arsalan *See* Aslan
Arsh Persian: throne, heaven and earth
Arshad/Arshan Persian (from arshad): elder, most brave
Arshman Urdu: angel of Arsh, angel of heaven and earth. *See also* Arsh
Arslaan/Arslan *See* Aslan
Art A diminutive form of Arthur
Artan Turkish: remaining. Also Old Persian (from ard): truth
Artem From Artemisios, Greek: to the Greek goddess Artemis
Arthur Celtic: bear king
Artie A diminutive form of Arthur
Artin Persian: righteous. A king of the Median Empire
Artur/Arturo/Arturs *See* Arthur
Arun Hindi: sun
Arundeep Punjabi: lamp of the sun (Sikh name)
Arush Sanskrit (from arushi): red mare, dawn
Arvin Persian: experiment, test
Arvind Sanskrit (from aravinda): lotus, copper
Arwel Unknown, possibly Welsh: prominent
Aryaan *See* Aryan
Aryaman Sanskrit: close friend. A Hindu sun god, the son of Aditi
Aryan Sanskrit (from arya): worthy, noble, wise, polite. *See also* Girls and Boys: Arya
Aryeh Hebrew: lion

Asa Hebrew: healer. A king of Judah
Asad Arabic: lion
Asadullah Arabic: lion of god
Asam/Aseem *See* Asim
Ash (name from flowers and trees, name from an English word). A diminutive form of Ashley. *See also* Girls and Boys: Ashley
Ashan Sanskrit (from asan): rock, stone
Ashar Arabic: ten. Also possibly from Ashur, Hebrew: box wood Ashur is one of Noah's grandsons *See also* Girls and Boys: Asher
Ashaz Unknown, possibly Arabic (from asas): nightwatch
Ashden/Ashdon Old English (from ash and dun): ash hill (shifted from surname usage)
Ashfaq Urdu: noble prince
Ashir *See* Ashar
Ashish Sanskrit (from azis): blessing, prayer, wish
Ashraf Arabic: His Excellency, greatest
Ashveer Punjabi: bravery of hope (Sikh name)
Ashvin/Ashwin Sanskrit (from azvini): the stars that form the head of Aries. Also from Ashvin, the seventh month of the Hindu calendar
Asif Arabic (from asef): strong, stormy
Asim Arabic (from asem): defender, protector

Aslam Old English (from hoeslum): hazel (shifted from surname usage)

Aslan Turkish: lion, man as brave as a lion. Also the name of the great lion in C. S. Lewis's *Narnia*

Assad *See* Asad

Astin/Aston From Asketill, Old Norse (from ós and ketill): god's sacrificial cauldron (shifted from surname usage)

Aswin *See* Ashwin

Ata Arabic: gift, giving. Also Turkish: father

Atal Hindi: strong, unwavering

Ateeq Arabic: old, ancient

Atharv/Atharva From Atharvan, the name of a Hindu Vedic sage

Atif Arabic: compassion, sympathy

Atticus Greek: from Attica, a region of Greece

Attila Unknown, possibly Turkish: the from Volga river. The name of Attila the Hun, the famous king of Huns who managed to invade Italy

Augustas/Augustin/Augustine/ Augustus Latin: great

Aum *See* Om

Aun A Scandinavian variant of Edwin

Aurelien A French variant of Aurelio

Aurelio Latin (from aurum): gold

Auryn is a magical amulet in Michael Ende's *The Neverending Story*, known as 'The Gem and The Glory'

Austen/Austin/Austyn Old English: of Augustine (shifted from surname usage)

Avais Unknown, possibly from Avis, Latin: bird. *See also* Uwais

Avi A diminutive form of Avraham

Avik Hindi (from avikal): untroubled

Avinash Punjabi: evernal, immortal (Sikh name)

Avraham/Avram/Avrohom *See* Abraham

Avtar Punjabi: incarnation of god (Sikh name)

Awab Urdu: Repentant, turn to god

Awad Arabic: reward

Awais *See* Uwais

Axel From Aslakr, Old Norse (from ós and lác): god's sacrifice

Axl The stage name of Axl Rose, the lead singer of Guns N' Roses. *See* Axel

Ayaan *See* Ayan

Ayaaz *See* Ayaz

Ayan Sanskrit (from ayana): solice. Also Arabic: clear, visible. Also a Tamil name for the Hindu god Brahma

Ayaz Sanskrit (from ayas): gold, steel, iron. Also Turkish: cold night air

Aydan Turkish (from ay and dan): from the moon

Ayden/Aydin *See* Aiden and Aydan

Ayham Persian (from ayam): ancient days, ancient one

Ayobami Yoruba: joy is mine

Ayodeji Yoruba: my joy has doubled

Ayodele Yoruba: joy has come home

Ayoob An Arabic variant of Job

Ayotunde Yoruba: joy has returned

Ayoub An Arabic variant of Job

Ayrton Old English (from ea and tun): town by the water (shifted from surname usage)

Ayub An Arabic variant of Job

Ayush Sanskrit (from ayus): long life

Ayuub An Arabic variant of Job

Ayyan *See* Ayan

Ayyub An Arabic variant of Job

Azaan *See* Azan

Azad Persian (from azadeh): free, free-born, free-minded

Azam *See* Azim

Azan Arabic: a call to prayer

Azeem *See* Azim

Azeez *See* Aziz

Azhar Arabic: shining, luminous. Also exists in a slightly different form, closer to Azhaar, as a name for girls (Arabic: flowers, blossoms)

Azim Arabic: defender. Al-Azim is one of Allah's 99 names, meaning The Great One, and reciting it is believed to help gain respect from others. Azim has connotations of great respect

Aziz/Azizur Arabic (from az): cherished, beloved. Al-Aziz is one of Allah's 99 names, meaning The Mighty or The Honourable, and reciting it regularly is believed to help ensure independence from others. Aziz has connotations of strength and power

Azlaan/Azlan An Arabic variant of Aslan

Azriel Hebrew: help of god. The name of the Archangel of Death

b

Babatunde Yoruba: father has come again

Baden A region in Germany (geographical name)

Bader Welsh: son of Adam (shifted from surname usage). *See also* Badr

Badr Arabic: full moon

Balal Sanskrit (from bala): power

Balazs Hungarian: lisping. *See also* Girls and Boys: Blaise

Baldeep Punjabi: lamp of power (Sikh name)

Balraj Punjabi: powerful king (Sikh name)

Balthazar Hebrew: may Ba'al protect the king. The name of one of the Three Wise Men. *See also* Caspar and Melchior

Baptiste French: baptist. In honour of John the Baptist

Barack Arabic: blessing

Bardia The name of Bardiya, a Persian prince who was the son of Cyrus the Great

Baris Turkish: peace

Barnabas/Barnaby Aramaic: son of the prophet, or son of consolation. The name given to the man who became Saint Barnabas after he gave away all his possessions

Barney A diminutive form of Barnabas

Baron (name from an English word)

Barra/Barrie/Barry A diminutive form of Fionnbharr and Barrfhionn (Irish Gaelic, from barr, barrán and finn: fair head of hair)

Bartek A diminutive form of Bartlomiej

Bartholomew/Bartlomiej Greek: son of Talmai, son of the furrow. The name of one of the twelve apostles of Jesus

Bartosz A diminutive form of Bartlomiej

Bashar/Bashir Arabic: bringer of good news

Basil (name from flowers and trees, name from an English word). Also Arabic: brave

Basit Arabic: extender, a meter in poetry

Bassam Arabic: smiling

Bastian A diminutive form of Sebastian

Batu Turkish: prevailing. Also Mongolian: firmness

Batuhan Turkish: prevailing ruler

Bawan Unknown, possibly Kurdish (from bawer): faith

Baxter Old English: a female baker (shifted from surname usage)

Bear (name from an English word)

Beck Old German: brooke, stream (shifted from surname usage)

Beckett Old German: little brooke (shifted from surname usage)

Beckham Old English: from near Becca's homestead (shifted from surname usage). Also the surname of David Beckham (footballer name)

Bede Old English: prayer. The name of a sainted English monk

Bedwyr Welsh, unknown. The knight who returns Excalibur to the Lady of the Lake in Arthurian legend

Belal See Balal and Bilal

Ben A diminutive form of Benjamin and Benedict

Benaiah Hebrew: Jehova builds up

Benas A diminutive form of Benedikt

Bence A diminutive form of Vincent

Benedict/Benedikt Latin: blessed

Beniamin See Benjamin

Benicio See Benedict

Benito Spanish: blessed

Benjaman/Benjamen/Benjamin/ Benjamyn Hebrew: son of the right hand. The youngest son of Jacob and brother of Joseph, originally named son of my pain, as his mother died shortly after his birth

Benji A diminutive form of Benjamin

Benjiman *See* Benjamin

Benjy A diminutive form of Benjamin

Benn A diminutive form of Benedict and Benjamin (shifted from surname usage)

Bennett *See* Benedict (shifted from surname usage)

Benny A diminutive form of Benedict and Benjamin

Benoit *See* Benedict

Benson Old English: son of Ben (shifted from surname usage)

Bentley Old English: bent grass clearing (shifted from surname usage). Also various place names (geographical name)

Benton Old English: bent grass enclosure (shifted from surname usage). Also various place names (geographical name)

Benyamin *See* Benjamin

Berat Turkish: purifying. Also the name of a county in Albania (geographical name)

Berdan Turkish: provider of equality

Berk/Berkan Turkish: strong, sturdy

Berkay Turkish: strong man, like the moon

Bernard/Bernardo Old French: bold as a bear

Bernie A diminutive form of Bernard

Bertan Turkish: beautiful, strong, like the dawn

Bertie A diminutive form of Albert

Bertram Old German: bright raven

Berzan Kurdish: wise man

Betzalel Hebrew: in the shadow of god. The architect for the Tabernacle

Bevan Welsh: son of Evan (shifted from surname usage)

Bhavesh Sanskrit (from bhava and iz): master of the world

Bhavik Sanskrit (from bhavika): righteous, happy

Bhavin Sanskrit: future

Bhavya Sanskrit: grand, future, what is to come

Bilaal/Bilal Arabic: freshness

Bilawal Persian: without equal, pure

Bill A diminutive form of William

Billal *See* Bilal

Binyamin/Binyomin *See* Benjamin

Bjorn Old Norse: bear

Blade (name from an English word)

Bladen Various place names (geographical name)

Blain/Blaine Irish and Scottish Gaelic (from blá): yellow (shifted from surname usage)

Blakely Various place names (geographical name). *See also* Girls and Boys: Blake

Blane/Blayne *See* Blain

Blayze/Blazej French: lisping. *See also* Girls and Boys: Blaise

Bleddyn Welsh (from blaidd): wolf

Blend (name from an English word)

Bleu French: blue

Boaz Hebrew: swift

Bob A diminutive form of Robert. *See also* Girls and Boys: Bobbie

Bode/Boden Old English: shelter (shifted from surname usage)

Bodhi/Bodie A diminutive form of Boden

Bogdan Slavic: given by god

Bora/Boran Turkish: gale, violent storm, hurricane. Also Cornish (from bora): dawn, daybreak

Boris Turkish: wolf

Boruch Hebrew: blessed

Borys *See* Boris

Boston Various place names, including the city in Massachusetts (geographical name)

Botond Hungarian: mace-wielding warrior

Boubacar Arabic: small camel

Bowen Welsh: son of Owen (shifted from surname usage)

Boyd Scottish Gaelic (from buidhe): yellow

Brad/Bradd A diminutive form of Bradly

Braden Irish Gaelic (from bratán): salmon

Bradlee/Bradleigh/Bradley/ Bradly Old English: broad clearing

Brady From the Brádaigh family (Scottish Gaelic, from bradach: pilfering; shifted from surname usage)

Brae A diminutive form of Braedan

Braedan/Braeden/Braedon/ Braiden/Braidon *See* Braden

Brajan *See* Brian

Bram A diminutive form of Abraham

Brandan/Branden/Brandon Old English: gorse hill (shifted from surname usage). Also various place names (geographical name)

Brandonlee A blend of Brandon and Lee, possibly after the actor Brandon Lee

Brandyn/Brannan/Brannon *See* Brandon

Braxton Old English: Bracca's town (shifted from surname usage)

Bray (shifted from surname usage). Also a several place names (geographical name)

Brayan *See* Brian

Braydan/Brayden/Braydon *See* Bradon

Breandan/Brendan/Brenden/ Brendon *See* Brandan

Brennan Irish Gaelic: descendant of Braonán (shifted from surname usage)

Brent Celtic: from a steep hill (shifted from surname usage)

Brenton Old English: Bryni's homestead (shifted from surname usage)

Bret/Brett Old English: Breton

Brian Unknown, possibly Celtic: hill, high, exalted

Brice Latin: speckled (shifted from surname usage)

Bright (name from an English word)

Briley Old English: briar clearing (shifted from surname usage)

Brinley *See* Brynley

Brock Old English: badger (shifted from surname usage)

Broden Unknown (shifted from surname usage)

Brodey Unknown (shifted from surname usage). *See also* Girls and Boys: Brodi/Brodie/Brody

Bronson Old English: son of Brown (shifted from surname usage)

Bruce Old French: from Brix, from the willowlands

Bruno Old German: brown

Bryan *See* Brian

Bryce *See* Brice

Brychan The name of a legendary Welsh king. Also the name of a Cornish saint who has 24 children

Bryn/Brynley/Brynn Welsh (from bryn): hill

Bryson Old English: son of Brice (shifted from surname usage)

Buddy (name from an English word, term of endearment)

Burak Arabic: lightning. The mythological creature that transported the prophet Muhammad to heaven

Burhan Arabic: proof

Burhanuddin Arabic: proof of the religion

Buster (name from an English word, term of endearment)

Byran/Byron Old English: at the cattle sheds (shifted from surname usage). The surname of the poet George Gordon Byron, known as Lord Byron

C

Cadan Unknown, possibly from the Cathán family (Irish Gaelic, from cathaigid: battle, fight; shifted from surname usage)

Cade Old English: round (shifted from surname usage)

Caden/Cadyn/Caeden *See* Cadan

Cael/Caelan Irish Gaelic: slender

Caeleb *See* Caleb

Caelen *See* Cael

Caelum Latin: chisel. The name of a constellation

Caesar Latin: hair. Most famously, the name of Julius Caesar, where it evolved into an imperial title

Cahal *See* Cathal

Cahir *See* Cathair

Cai A diminutive form of Gaius

Caian The name of a Welsh saint who was a descendant from the king of Brecknock

Caidan/Caiden/Caidon *See* Cadan

Cailan/Cailean/Cailen Scottish Gaelic: young dog

Cain/Caine Hebrew: metalsmith or acquired. The son of Adam and Eve who killed his younger brother Abel and was marked by god and forced to become a wanderer

Caio *See* Gaius

Caira *See* Cairo and Ciaran

Cairn Scottish Gaelic: heap of stones (shifted from surname usage)

Cairo Arabic: the victorious. The name of the city in Egypt

Cairon *See* Cairo and Ciaran

Caius *See* Gaius

Cal A diminutive form of Calvin

Calam *See* Cailan

Calan Welsh Gaelic: calend, division of the year. *See also* Cailan

Cale A diminutive form of Caleb

Caleb Hebrew: dog. A Hebrew spy sent to Canaan along with Joshua

Calem/Calen *See* Cailan

Calib *See* Caleb

Callam/Callan/Callen/Callum/ Callun/Calum *See* Cailan

Calvin Old French: bald

Camaron Scottish Gaelic (from cam and sròn): crooked nose (shifted from surname usage). *See also* Girls and Boys: Cameron

Camden Old English: enclosed valley (shifted from surname usage). Also an area in London (geographical name)

Cameran *See* Camaron

Camaron *See* Camaron

Camilo Latin: from the Camillus family (Latin: in religious services)

Campbell Scottish Gaelic (from cam and béul): crooked mouth (shifted from surname usage)

Camran/Camren/Camron/ Cam'ron *See* Camaron

Can Turkish: life, soul

Canaan Unknown, possibly Hebrew: lowlands. The Land of Canaan is of importance in the bible

Cane A Welsh variant of Cathan. *See also* Cain

Caner Turkish: loved from the heart

Caodhan *See* Cadan

Caoimhin Irish Gaelic (from caomh): beautiful, gentle

Caolan/Caolin *See* Caelan

Caomhan Irish Gaelic (from cabhán): hollow

Carl *See* Charles

Carlin Scottish Gaelic: commoner, one of low birth (shifted from surname usage)

Carlin stones are connected to witches and Cailleach, the divine hag associated with winter

Carlisle Old English: fort of Lugus, a Celtic god. A city in Cumbria (geographical name)

Carlito/Carlo/Carlos *See* Charles

Carlson Old English: son of Carl (shifted from surname usage)

Carlton *See* Charlton

Carrick Scottish Gaelic: rock (shifted from surname usage)

Carson Unknown, possibly from Carlson (shifted from surname usage)

Carter Old English: user of carts (shifted from surname usage)

Carwyn Welsh: fair love

Cary From the Ciardha family (Irish Gaelic, from ciar: black)

Cash Old French: box maker (shifted from surname usage)

Casimir Slavic: destroyer of the great

Cason *See* Carlson

Caspar/Casper Persian: treasurer. The name of one of the Three Wise Men. *See also* Balthazar and Melchior

Caspian From the Caspian Sea, named after the Caspi people who lived near the sea (geographical name). Also the name created by C. S. Lewis for Prince Caspian of *Narnia*

Cass A diminutive form of Caspian and Casslan

Cassian/Cassius Latin: empty

Castiel Hebrew: my cover is god

Cathair Irish Gaelic: man of the battle

Cathal Irish Gaelic: ruler of the battle

Cathan Irish Gaelic: battle

Cathaoir *See* Cathair

Cauley *See* Macauley

Cavalli Italian: horseman, knight (shifted from surname usage)

Cavan From Caomhánach, Old Gaelic: hollow (shifted from surname usage). *See also* Caomhan

Cavell Old French: bald person (shifted from surname usage)

Caven *See* Cavan

Caydan/Cayden/Caydn/Caydon *See* Cadan

Caylan *See* Cailan

Cayleb *See* Caleb

Caylem/Caylen/Caylum *See* Cailan

Cecil Latin: way of the blind

Cedric Created by Sir Walter Scott for the novel *Ivanhoe*, in which Cedric the Saxon is the father of Wilfred of Ivanhoe

Ceiran/Ceiron *See* Ciaran

Cellan *See* Caelan

Celt (name from an English word)

Cem Turkish: ruler, bringing together

Cemal Turkish: beautiful face

Cerith A type of mollusk with slender, horn-shaped shells with spiral patterns

Cesar/Cezary *See* Caesar

Chace Old English: huntsman (shifted from surname usage). *See also* Girls and Boys: Chase

Chad/Chadd Welsh: battle

Chae/Chai Thai: victory, success

Chaim Hebrew: life

Chan Chinese: various, including steep and proud

Chandan Sanskrit (from chandana):

charming

Chandler Old English: candle maker, candle seller (shifted from surname usage)

Chandon Arabic (from chand): moon

Channing Unknown (shifted from surname usage)

Charalambos Greek: shine from happiness

Charbel Aramaic: story of god

Charlee A blend of Charles and Lee

Charles Old German: man, warrior

Charlton Old English: town of freemen (shifted from surname usage)

Chas A diminutive form of Charles

Chayce/Chayse See Chace

Chaz A diminutive form of Charles

Chen Chinese: various, including dawn and dust

Cheng Chinese: various, including sincere, accomplished and city

Chester Latin: land for military defence (shifted from surname usage). Also named after the city in Cheshire

Chetan Sanskrit (from cetana): consciousness

Chey See Chae

Chibueze Igbo: god is king

Chibuikem Igbo: god is my strength

Chidubem Igbo: god is my guide

Chigozie Igbo: god blesses

Chijioke Igbo: god holds creation

Chinedu Igbo: god guides

Chinedum Igbo: god guides me

Chinonso Igbo: god is near

Chirag Hindi: light

Chris A diminutive form of Christian and Christopher

Christiaan/Christian/Christiano Latin: follower of Christ

Christo A diminutive form of Christopher. See also Christos

Christophe/Christopher Greek: bearer of Christ

Christos Greek: anointed. In Greek, when referring to Jesus, the name is spelt with an accent: Christós

Chukwudi Igbo: god is there

Chukwuebuka Igbo: god is great

Chukwuemeka Igbo: god has done something great

Chukwuka Igbo: god is greater

Chun Chinese: various, including pure and spring

Cianan Irish Gaelic: ancient. See also Girls and Boys: Cian

Ciaran/Ciaron/Cieran/Cieron Scottish Gaelic (from ciaradh): darkening, twilight. Also Irish Gaelic (from cíar): dark, murky, black

Cillian Irish Gaelic: church

Cinar Turkish: broad-leafed tree

CJ/CJay A blend of two letters from the alphabet

Clarence Latin: clear. Associated with the royal family from Clarence House, the official residence of the Prince of Wales

Clark/Clarke Old English: clerk, scribe (shifted from surname usage)

Claude/Claudio Latin: crippled

Clay (name from an English word) **Old** English: clay worker (shifted from surname usage)

Clayton Old English: town of clay (shifted from surname usage)

Clement Latin: gentle, merciful

Clifford Old English: ford by the cliff (shifted from surname usage)

Clint A diminutive form of Clinton

Clinton From Glinton, a village in England (shifted from surname usage)

Clive Old English: cliff (shifted from surname usage)

Clyde From the river Clyde in Scotland (shifted from surname usage). Also known as a first name from the duo Bonnie and Clyde

Cobain/Coban/Coben Unknown, possibly from Cobham in Kent (shifted from surname usage). Also known for being the surname of Kurt Cobain

Cobey/Cobi/Cobie/Coby A diminutive form of Cobain

Coel See Cole

Coen/Cohan/Cohen Hebrew: priest (shifted from surname usage)

Colbie/Colby See Coleby

Cole Old English: charcole (shifted from surname usage)

Coleby Old Norse: dark town (shifted from surname usage)

Colin A diminutive form of Nicholas. See Cailean

Coll See Cole

Collin/Collins See Colin

Colm Latin: dove

Colt (name from an English word)

Colton Old English: town of charcoal (shifted from surname usage)

Colum See Colm

Conagh/Conah See Connor

Conaill/Conal/Conall Irish Gaelic: strong wolf

Conan Irish Gaelic: little wolf

Conar See Connor

Conchor/Conchur Unknown, possibly from the word 'conquer'

Coner See Connor

Conlan Irish Gaelic: like hound and lion (shifted from surname usage)

Conleth Irish Gaelic: chaste fire

Conn Irish Gaelic: chief

Conna/Connagh/Connah/ Connaire See Connor

Connal/Connall See Conall

Connan See Conan

Connar See Connor

Connel/Connell See Conell

Conner See Connor

Connlaodh See Conleth

Connor/Conor Irish Gaelic: dog lover

Conrad Old German: brave council

Constantin A French variant of

Constantine

Constantine Latin: constant

Constantinos A Greek variant of Constantine

Conway Welsh: holy water (shifted from surname usage). Also from River Conwy in Wales

Cooper Old English: barrel maker (shifted from surname usage)

Coran Unknown, possibly Latin (from cornu): horn. *See also* Corin

Corban/Corben/Corbin/Corby/Corbyn Old French: raven

Cordell Old English: cord maker (shifted from surname usage)

Coree/Corey/Cori/Corie Unknown (shifted from surname usage). Also Quechua: gold

Corin Latin: spear

Corley Unknown (shifted from surname usage)

Cormac Irish Gaelic: son of defilement

Cornelius Latin (from cornu): horn, symbolising strength and courage

Corran *See* Coran

Correy/Corrie/Cory *See* Corey

Cosimo/Cosmo Greek: order

Craig Scottish Gaelic: rocks

Crispin Latin: curly hair

Cristian/Cristiano *See* Christian

Cruz Spanish: cross

Cuba Named after the country (geographical name)

Culann/Cullan/Cullen Old French: from Cologne (shifted

Curt A diminutive form of Curtis

Curtis Old French: courteous

Cyle *See* Kyle

Cynan Welsh (from cynanu): enunciate. The bardic name Sir Albert Evans-Jones

Cyprian From Cyprus, associated with the Greek goddess of love, Aphrodite, where she was born. Also the name of Saint Cyprian, bishop of Carthage

Cyril Greek: lord

Cyron Unknown (shifted from surname usage). *See also* Cyrus

Cyrus Greek: young

d

Daanish Arabic: wisdom, learning

Daanyaal/Daanyal *See* Daniel

Dafydd A Welsh variant of David

Dagan/Dagon Hebrew: grain. A Semitic god of agriculture and, later, fish. Also one of the Elder Things in Lovecraft's Cthulhu Mythos, where it is worshipped alongside Cthulhu and Hydra

Dahir The name of Raja Dahir, the last Hindu king of Sindh who died fighting an Arab invasion led by Muhammad bin Qasim

Daine *See* Dane

Dainton Unknown (shifted from

surname usage)

Daire Irish Gaelic: oak grove, oak wood. The name of many kings and heroes in Irish mythology, including Dáire Doimthech. *See also* Girls and Boys: Derry

Daithi An Irish variant of David

Daiton *See* Dayton

Daiyaan/Daiyan Arabic: mighty ruler

Daksh Hindi: expert, master, able

Daley Irish Gaelic: Ó Dálaigh, descendant of Dálach (shifted from surname usage). Traditionally, the family is associated with poetry, and many members of the family were well-known bards in Ireland and Scotland

Dalton Old English (from dæl and tun): valley settlement (shifted from surname usage)

Dalvin Unknown, possibly a modernised and shifted variant of Alvin or Calvin

Damani/Damari/Damarni Unknown, possibly from Damaris (Greek, from damalis: calf)

Damian Greek (from damao): to tame

Damien A French variant of Damian

Damion *See* Damian

Damon Greek (from damazō): to tame, to subdue. Also associated with loyal friendship in the story of Damon and Pythias from Greek mythology. Pythias was accused of plotting against the tryant Dionysius I and sentenced to death. He asked to be allowed to say goodbye to his family. Damon took Pythias's place in prision on the understanding that should Pythias not return to face the executioner then Damon would be killed in his place. On Pythias's return the tyrant was moved to forgiveness by the strength of the friendship

Dan Hebrew: to judge. Also Chinese: various, including red and daybreak. Also Japanese: various, including sphere and man. A son of Jacob who founded an Israelite tribe, the Tribe of Dan. Also a diminutive form of Daniel

Danar Unknown, possibly created in *Star Trek* for Gul Danar and Roga Danar. Also Irish Gaelic: Danish, Dane

Danas *See* Daniel

d'Andre French: of André, from André, son of André (shifted from surname usage). *See also* Andre

Dane Old English (from Dene): Danish, from Denmark. *See also* Dean

d'Angelo Italian: of Angelo, from Angelo, son of Angelo, angel's (shifted from surname usage). *See also* Angelo

Daniaal/Danial An Arabic variant

of Daniel

Daniel Hebrew (from daniyél): god is my judge. A prophet whose tales form the Book of Daniel, in which Daniel was thrown into a lion's den for praying the orders of King Darius, but was unharmed by the lions

Daniele An Italian variant of Daniel

Danielis/Danielius/Daniels/ Daniil/Danil/Danila/Danilo *See* Daniel

Danish *See* Daanish

Daniyaal/Daniyal An Arabic variant of Daniel

Danny A diminutive of Daniel

Dantae/Dante Italian: lasting. The name of Dante Alighieri, who wrote *The Divine Comedy*

Danyaal/Danyal/Danyar/Danyl *See* Daniel

Daoud An Arabic variant of David

Daragh *See* Daire. *See also* Girls and Boys: Darragh

Dardan Albanian (from dardhë): pear

Dardania was a region now located in modern day Kosovo, Republic of Macedonia and Albania

Daren *See* Darren

Darian/Darien A modernised and shifted variant of Darius and Dorian

Darin *See* Darren

Dario *See* Darius

Darion *See* Darren

Darius/Dariush/Dariusz Persian: wealthy. Also Arabic: to learn

Darnel/Darnell/Darnelle Unknown, possible Old English: hidden (shifted from surname usage)

Darran *See* Darren

Darrel/Darrell Old French: from Airelle, the place of huckleberries (shifted from surname usage). *See also* Darren

Darren Unknown, possibly related to Daragh or Darrell (shifted from surname usage). *See also* Daragh and Darrell

Darryl *See* Darrell

Darsh A diminutive form of Darshan. Also possibly Sanskrit (from darza): new moon

Darshan Sanskrit (from darzana): sight, vision, philosophy. A vision and a blessing that passes between a diety and a worshipper in Hinduism

Darwin Unknown, possibly Old English (deor and wine): dear friend. Also possibly Old English (from derva): oak (shifted from surname usage). The surname of Charles Darwin, the author of *On the Origin of Species*

Daryan A city in Iran (geographical name). *See also* Darian

Daryl/Daryll *See* Darrell

Dashiell Unknown. The name of Dashiell Hammett, an author whose work includes *The Maltese Falcon*, who was named after his mother's surname, De Chiel

Dastan Persian (from dâstân): story, legend

Daud An Arabic variant of David

Dave/Davey/Davi A diminutive form of David

David Hebrew: beloved. The King of Israel and King of Jews

Davide An Italian variant of David

Davie A diminutive form of David

Davin *See* Devin

Davinder Punjabi: king of gods (Sikh name)

Davis Old English: son of David (shifted from surname usage)

Davy A diminutive form of David

Dawda A Gambian variant of David

Dawid/Dawood/Dawoud *See* David

Dawson Old English: son of Daw, which was a diminutive form of David (shifted from surname usage)

Dawud An Arabic variant of David

Dax A spa town in the south of France (geographical name). Also the surname given to Trills in *Star Trek* who join with Dax, an ancient and wise being, in symbiosis

Dayle Old English: valley (shifted from surname usage). *See also* Girls and Boys: Dale

Dayne *See* Dane

Dayton Old English (from dic and tun): ditch town, town with a moat (shifted from surname usage)

Dayyan Persian: judge, rewarder

De Chinese: various, including earth and morality

Deacan/Deacon Ancient Greek (from diākonos): minister, servant. The title of a Christian cleric who ranks just below a priest

Deaglan The name of Saint Deaglan, also known as Declán of Ardmore, one of the saints who spread Christianity through Ireland before the arrival of Saint Patrick

Deakon *See* Deacon

Dean Old English (from dene): valley (shifted from surname usage)

DeAndre *See* d'Andre

Deano A pet form of Dean. *See also* Dino

Decklan/Declan/Decland/Declyn An anglicised form of Deaglan

Deegan From O'Duibhginn (Irish Gaelic, from dub/dubh/duib and cenn: dark head; shifted from surname usage)

Deejay A blend of two letters from the alphabet. Also from the term for 'disc jockey'

Deen *See* Dean

Deep Sanskrit (from diip): lamp, flame, glow

Deepak Sanskrit (from diipaka): lamp, light

Deian A diminutive form of Dafydd

Deimantas Lithuanian: diamond

(gemstone name)

Deiniol A Welsh variant of Daniel

Deio A diminutive form of Dafydd

Deion A diminutive form of Dionysius, from Dionysus, the god of wine from Greek mythology. *See also* Girls and Boys: Dion

Deivid A Brazilian variant of David

Deividas A Lithuanian variant of David

Dejan Unknown, possibly from De Jan: of Jan, from Jan, son of Jan (shifted from surname usage). A name popular among those of Serbian heritage. *See also* Girls and Boys: Jan

DeJean From De Jean: of Jean, from Jean, son of Jean (shifted from surname usage). *See also* Girls and Boys: Jean

Dejon Unknown, possibly from De Jon: of Jon, from Jon, son of Jon (shifted from surname usage). *See also* Jon

Deklan *See* Decklan

Del A diminutive form of Derek

Delano From De Lano: of Lano, from Lano, son of Lano (Lano is possibly French, from l'aulnaie: alder; shifted from surname usage). In the US, the Delano family is of great prominence, and includes Franklin Delano Roosevelt

Delroy Unknown, possibly from Del Roy: of Roy, from Roy, son of Roy (shifted from surname usage).

See also Roy

DeMarco From De Marco: of Marco, from Marco, son of Marco (shifted from surname usage). *See also* Marco

Demari/Demario From De Mario: of Mario, from Mario, son of Mario (shifted from surname usage). *See also* Mario

Demetri/Demetrius Ancient Greek: of the earth mother, of Demeter, the goddess of harvest from Greek mythology

Demir Turkish: iron

Demitri *See* Demetri

Denas *See* Denis

Dene *See* Dean

Denholm Old English (from denu and ham): valley dwelling. A village near the Scottish borders (geographical name)

Denim French (from de Nîmes): from the French city Nîmes (geographical name). A term better known for the cotton twill textile that originated from the city

DeNiro From De Niro: of Niro, from Niro, son of Niro (Niro is Italian, from nero: black; shifted from surname usage). The surname of the actor Robert De Niro

Denis/Deniz French: Dionysius. Named after Saint Denis rather than the Greek god of wine, Dionysus

Denley Old English (from denu and

leah): valley clearing (shifted from surname usage)

Dennis *See* Denis

Denny A diminutive form of Denis

Denon Unknown (shifted from surname usage). The title of the French artist, author and diplomat Dominique Vivant, known as Baron de Denon

Denton Old English (from denu and tun): valley town (shifted from surname usage). The name of several villages and towns in English (geographical name)

Denzel/Denzil Unknown (shifted from surname usage). Also possibly from Denzell in Cornwall (geographical name). The name of the actor Denzel Washington allegedly comes from Dr Denzel, the man who delivered his father

Dereece From De Reece: of Reece, from Reece, son of Reece. *See also* Girls and Boys: Reece

Derek From Theodoric, Old German (from theud and ric): ruler of people

Deren Turkish (from dare): administrator, collector. *See also* Darren

Deri a modernised and shifted variant of Derry, which is a diminutive form of Diarmaid. *See also* Girls and Boys: Derry

Derick *See* Derek

Derin *See* Darren

Dermot An anglicised form of Diarmaid

Deron/Derren *See* Darren

Derrick *See* Derek

Deshaun/Deshawn From De Shaun/De Shawn: of Shaun/Shawn, from Shaun/Shawn, son of Shaun/Shawn. *See also* Shawn

Desmond From Ó Deasmhumhnaigh, Irish Gaelic: from South Munster (shifted from surname usage)

Dev Sanskrit (from deva): deity, god

Devansh Sanskrit (from devamza): portion of a god, partial reincarnation of a god

Devante Unknown, possibly from De Vante: of Vante, from Vante, son of Vante, where Vante is also of unknown origins. *See also* Devontae

Devesh Sanskrit (from deveza): chief of the gods, king of the gods. A name for the Hindu god Shiva

Devin From Ó Damháin (Irish Gaelic, from dam: fawn). Also possibly Turkish (from dev): giant

Devlin From O'Dobhailein, Irish Gaelic (from dobail): unlucky (shifted from surname usage)

Devontae/Devonte Unknown, possibly from De Vontae/Vonte: of Vante, from Vontae/Vonte, son of Vontae/Vonte, where Vontae/Vonte is also of unknown origins. *See also* Devante

Devraj Sanskrit (from devaraj): king of the gods

Devran Turkish: time, wheel of fortune, fate

Dewan Persian (from dīvān): house of documents. A historical title held by councillors or high-ranking officials in various countries

Dewi A diminutive form of Dafydd

Dexter Latin: right, right-hand side, skillful, fortunate, proper. Also Old English (from dighester): dyer, female cloth dyer (shifted from surname usage)

Deyaan Unknown, possibly Hindi (from daya): ruth, mercy, compassion

Dhairya Sanskrit: calmness, constancy, courage

Dhani Hindi (from dhan): wealth, riches

Dhanish Sanskrit (from dhanez): rich man, king of wealth. Also possibly Hindi (from dhanesh): stork

Dhanyaal/Dhanyal Sanskrit (from dhanya): fortunate, healthy, rich, blessed

Dharam Punjabi: righteous, religious, dutiful (Sikh name)

Dhaval Sanskrit (from dhavala): white, dazzling, handsome

Dheer Hindi (from dhir): calm, patient

Dhian Punjabi: absorbed in concentration (Sikh name)

Dhilan/Dhillon Dhiren Hindi (from dhire): quietly, softly

Dhru/Dhruv Sanskrit (from dhruva): pole star. As a child, the prince Dhruva was able to meet the Hindu god Vishnu through his devotion, and after a long and successful reign, he became the pole star

Dhyan Sanskrit (from dhyai/dhayati): contemplation, meditation

Dhyey Hindi: aim, goal

Diago See Diego

Diarmaid/Diarmuid Irish Gaelic (from dī and format, leading to the earlier form of diformenti): without envy, without jealousy. The name of Diarmuid Ua Duibhne, a warrior from Irish mythology who wields two swords and two spears, has a love spot on his forehead, and runs away with Grainne under her geis despite her being engaged to Fionn, Diarmaid's much older lord

Diego A Spanish variant of Jacob. See also Santiago

Diesel Unknown (shifted from surname usage). The fuel, diesel, is named after Rudolf Diesel, as he invented the diesel engine. Also the surname chosen by the actor Vin Diesel, whose real name is Mark Vincent

Dieter Old German (from thiot

and heri): army of people. Also a diminutive form of Dietrich, a German variant of Derek

Digby Old English (from dīc and býr): ditch settlment (shifted from surname usage). Also the name of several villages and towns in England and elsewhere (geographical name)

Dilanas Unknown

Dillan/Dillon *See* Dylann

Dilraj Punjabi: king of the heart (Sikh name)

Dimitri/Dimitrios/Dimitris Greek: related to the Greek goddess of harvest, Demeter

Dino A diminutive form of Edoardo and many names ending in 'dino'. *See also* Deano

Diogo *See* Diego

Dipesh Hindi: the sun

Dixon Old English: son of Dick, where Dick is a diminutive form of Richard. *See also* Richard

Dlyan *See* Dayyan

Diyar Kurdish: clarity. Also Kurdish (from diyarî): gift

DJ *See* Deejay

Djamel *See* Jamil

Django Romani: I wake. The gypsy nickname taken on by the Belgian jazz musican Jean Reinhardt, better known as Django Reinhardt d'Mari. *See* DeMari

Dolton A village in Devon (geographical name). *See also* Dalton

Domanic *See* Dominic

Domantas Lithuanian (from a blend of davimas and sumanus): giving and smart. Lithuanian name day for Domantas: 4th August

Domas A diminutive form of Dominykas, a Lithuanian variant of Dominic. Lithuanian name day for Domas: 8th August. *See also* Dominic

Domenic/Domenico *See* Dominic

Domhnall *See* Donald

Dominic/Dominick/Dominik/ Dominiks/Dominique/ Dominykas/Domonic Latin: belonging to god

Don A diminutive form of Donald

Donal/Donald Celtic: ruler of the world

Donatas Lithuanian: gift from god

Donato Italian: gift from god

Donell *See* Donald

Dong Chinese: various, including wlnter and east

Donnacha/Donncha *See* Duncan

Donnell *See* Donald

Donnie/Donny A diminutive form of Donald

Donovan Irish Gaelic (from donn and dubh): dark brown (shifted from surname usage)

Dontae/Dontay/Donte *See* Dante

Dorian Greek: from Doris. Possibly created as a name by Oscar Wilde for the novel *The Picture of Dorian*

Gray

Doruk Turkish: mountain top

Doug A diminutive form of Douglas

Dougal Scottish Gaelic (from dubh and gall): dark stranger

Dougie A diminutive form of Douglas

Douglas Scottish Gaelic: dark river

Dov A diminutive form of Dovid

Dovid/Dovydas *See* David

Doyle From Ó Dubhghaill (Irish Gaelic, from dub/dubh/duib and gallda: dark foreigner; shifted from surname usage)

Drake Old English (from draca): snake, dragon (shifted from surname usage). Also Old English (from andraca): duck king, male duck

Draven Unknown (shifted from surname usage). The surname of Eric Draven from the film adaptation of *The Crow*, possibly as a play on the word 'raven'

Dray Old English: a horse-drawn cart. Also possibly from Drogo (Old Dutch: phantom). *See also* Drey

Dre A diminutive form of Andre This variant is adopted by rapper Andre Romelle Young, better known as Dr Dre

Dren Albanian (from dre): deer

Drey Old English: squirrel's nest. *See also* Dray

Drilon/Drin The name of the longest river in Albania, both known as the River Drilon and The Drinn (geographical name)

Dru A diminutive form of Andrew

Duaine/Duane From the family of Dubhán (Irish Gaelic, form dubh: black, dark)

Dudley Old English: Dudda's clearing (shifted from surname usage)

Duke (name from an English word)

Duncan Scottish Gaelic: brown warrior

Dusan Slavic: soul, spirit

Dwain/Dwaine/Dwayne *See* Duane

Dwight Unknown (shifted from surname usage)

Dyako The first king of the Media, in mordern day Iran, also known as Deioces

Dyfan *See* Damon

Dylann/Dyllan/Dylon Welsh (from dy and llanw): tide, flow. *See also* Girls and Boys: Dylan

Dziugas Lithuanian (from dziuga): happy, jolly. A giant from Samogitian legends

e

Eamon/Eamonn *See* Edward

Earl (name from an English word)

Easa Unknown, possibly Irish Gaelic (from eas/easa): waterfall, rapid,

from a waterwall, from a rapid.
Place names historically near
waterfalls in Ireland, such as
Foxford, which is known as Béal
Easa, often contain this element

Eashan See Eshan

Eason Old English: son of Aythe
(shifted from surname usage)

Eathan See Ethan

Eban/Eben A diminutive form of
Ebenezer

Ebenezer Hebrew: stone of the help.
From Eben-Ezer, a place
mentioned in the Books of
Samuel, near Shiloh

Ebrahim See Abraham

Ebrima A Gambian variant of
Abraham

Ebubechukwu Igbo: god's glory

Ed A diminutive form of Edward

Edan Possibly Aramaic: watered,
fruitful. See also Girls and Boys:
Eden

Eddie A diminutive form of Edward

Eddison Old English: son of Adam
(shifted from surname usage)

Eddy A diminutive form of Edward

Edgar Old English: rich spear,
blessed spear

Edison See Eddison

Ediz Turkish: high

Edmond/Edmund/Edoardo See
Edward

Edon See Edan

Edouard See Edward

Edric Old English: rich ruler,

blessed ruler

Edson See Eddison

Eduard/Eduardo See Edward

Edvinas See Edwin

Edward Old English: rich guard,
blessed guard

Edwin/Edwyn Old English: rich
friend, blessed friend

Eesa/Eesaa/Eesah/Eessa An
Arabic variant of Jesus, Hebrew:
god saves

Efan A Welsh variant of John.
See also Girls and Boys: Evan

Efe Turkish: tough guy, older brother
In southwest Anatolia, Efe is used
as a title for those who lead certain
groups of swashbuckling village
soliders

Efraim See Ephraim

Egan From Mac Aodhagáin, Irish
Gaelic (from áed): fire, bright
(shifted from surname usage)

Ege Turkish: guardian. The Aegean
Sea is named this in Turkish
(geographical name)

Ehan A diminutive form of
Ehalaivan, a variant of Ekalavya,
a skilled archer in Hindu
mythology

Ehren German: honour

Ehsaan/Ehsan Persian: goodness,
favour

Eifion Old Welsh (from afon/
eifion): river (shifted from surname
usage)

Eimantas Lithuanian (from eiti and

sumanus): go smart, be clever, be intelligent

Eisa/Eisah/Eissa *See* Eesa

Eitan/Eithan *See* Ethan

Ekam Punjabi: oneness, the one, united (Sikh name)

Ekampreet Punjabi: love for oneness of god (Sikh name)

El An ancient name for god. Also possibly from the letter 'L'

Elan French (from élan): spirit, zeal. Also Native American: friendly

Elden/Eldon Unknown (shifted from surname usage). The name of several villages in England (geographical name)

Elgan Welsh: bright circle

Elian Unknown, possibly Latin (from helios): sun. Also a Welsh saint of Llanelian

Elias Hebrew: Jehova is god. *See also* Girls and Boys: Elijah

Eliezer Hebrew: god is my help. A son of Moses and also the name of Eliezer of Damascus

Elimelech Hebrew: god is king. A man who appears in the Book of Ruth

Elio Latin (from helios): sun

Eliot/Eliott An Old French variant of Elias. Also unknown (shifted from surname usage)

Elisei Hebrew: my god is salvation. *See also* Girls and Boys: Elisha

Eliyohu *See* Elias

Eljay A blend of two letters of the alphabet

Ellias *See* Elias

Elnathan Hebrew: god has given

Elon Hebrew: oak

Elozor A Polish variant of Eliezer

Elson From Aethelswithtun, Old English: Aethelswith's town, noble strength's town (shifted from surname usage). Also possibly from Elleston, a variant of Elias's town. *See also* Elias

Elton From Elphinton, which is from Aethelflaedtun, Old English: Aethelflaed's town, noble beauty's town (shifted from surname usage). Also possibly Old English (from ael): eel town

Elvin *See* Alvin

Elvis Unknown, possibly from Elwes (shifted from surname usage). Also possibly from Alvíss, a dwarf in Norse mythology. Also possibly an anglicised variant of Ailbe. Best known as the name of Elvis Presley. *See also* Ailbe

Elwood Old English (from ellern): a wood of elder trees (shifted from surname usage)

Ely Hebrew (from eli): lofty and high. Also a city in England, near Cambridge (geographical name)

Elyas *See* Elias

Emaad/Emad Arabic: support, pillar

Emanuel Hebrew: god is with us

Emeka A diminutive form of Chukwuemeka

Emil/Emile Latin: rival

Emilian A Romanian variant of Emile

Emiliano An Italian and Spanish variant of Emile

Emilijus A Lithuania variant of Emile

Emilio An Italian and Spanish variant of Emile

Emilis A Lithuania variant of Emile

Emils A Latvian variant of Emile

Emin Turkish: trustworthy, strong, certain

Emir Arabic: to command. *See also* Amir

Emirhan Turkish, possibly from Emir and Khan. *See also* Emir and Khan

Emlyn A Welsh variant of Emile

Emmanuel *See* Emanuel

Emmerson Old English: Amery's son. *See also* Girls and Boys: Emerson

Emmet/Emmett From the feminine name Emma, Germanic: universal (shifted from surname usage)

Emran An Arabic variant of Amram, the father of Moses

Emre Unknown. A Turkish name

Emrys A Welsh variant of Ambrose

Emyr *See* Emir

Enda Irish Gaelic (from én): bird

Endrit Albanian (from dritë): light

Enes/Enis Unknown, possibly Turkish (from enişte): brother-in-law. *See also* Ennis

Enoch One of the earlier generations of man after Adam who was taken to walk with god

Enrico/Enrique *See* Henry

Enzo An Italian variant of Heinz, a diminutive form of Heinrich, which is a German variant of Henry

Eoghan Unknown, possibly Irish Gaelic (from eó and gein): born form a tree. Also possibly an Irish variant of Eugene

Eoin An Irish variant of John

Ephraim Hebrew (from efráyim): fruitful. A son of Joseph who formed the Tribe of Ephraim

Eray Unknown, possibly Turkish (from er and ay): brave man of the moon

Erdem Turkish: virtue

Erdi Turkish: finished, fulfiled a purpose. Also possibly Turkish (from er): brave man

Eren Turkish: become one with god, saint, mystic

Erfan *See* Irfan

Eric/Erick Old Norse (from ei and ríkr): eternal ruler, ever powerful

Erik A Croatian, Czech, Hungarian, Russian and Scandinavian variant of Eric

Erikas A Lithuanian variant of Eric

Erion/Erjon Albanian (from erë and Jon): wind from the Ionian Sea

Erkan Turkish: great men, high officials

Ernest (name from an English word). Old German (from ernust): serious, solomn

Ernesto An Italian, Portuguese and Spanish variant of Ernest

Ernie A diminutive form of Ernest

Erol Turkish (from er): brave man. *See also* Errol

Eron Old German: to honour, to help

Errol Unknown, possibly from the village in Scotland (geographical name, shifted from surname usage). *See also* Erol

Ervin A Croatian and Hungarian variant of Irwin, which is from Old English (from eofor and wini): friend of boars

Erwin A German variant of Irwin, which is from Old English (from eofor and wini): friend of boars

Eryk *See* Eric

Esa/Esaa/Esah *See* Eesa

Eshaan/Eshan Arabic: in god's grace

Espen A Norwegian variant of Ásbjørn, Old Norse (from áss and bjorn): bear of god

Essa *See* Eesa

Essien Fante: sixth born son. Also Efik/Ibibio: belongs to everyone

Esteban A Spanish variant of Stephen

Ethan/Ethen Hebrew (from etán): strong, long-lived

Etienne A French variant of Stephen

Euan *See* Eoghan

Eugene Ancient Greek (from eugenios): well born

Eunan An anglicised variant of Adomnán, Irish Gaelic: little Adam. Also the name of an Irish saint. *See also* Adam

Evander Ancient Greek (from Euandros): good man. Also a Welsh variant of Ivor

Evans Welsh: son of Evan

Evren Turkish: universe, creation, cosmos

Evyn *See* Efan

Exauce French (from exaucer): to fulfil a wish

Eyad *See* Iyad

Eythan *See* Ethan

Ezekiel Hebrew: god strengthens. A prophet in the Old Testament who wrote the Book of Ezekiel

f

Faaris *See* Faris

Fabian Latin: bean (name from flowers and trees). *See also* Fabio

Fabien A French variant of Fabian

Fabio Latin: bean (name from flowers and trees). *See also* Fabian

Fabricio Latin (from faber): workman, smith

Fabrizio A Basque and Italian

variant of Fabricio

Fadi Arabic: redeemer

Fadil Arabic: virtuous, generous

Fahad/Fahd Arabic: leopard

Faheem/Fahim Arabic: intelligent, scholarly

Faisal Arabic: decisive

Faiyaz Arabic: overflowing, bountiful

Faiz Arabic: victorious

Faizaan Arabic: grace

Faizal *See* Faisal

Faizan *See* Faizaan

Falak Arabic: astronomy

Fallon From O' Fallamhain, Irish Gaelic: leader (shifted from surname usage). Also possibly Old English (from fullere): cloth dresser (shifted from surname usage)

Faraaz *See* Faraz

Farai Shona: rejoice

Faraj Arabic: remedy, improvement

Faran *See* Farhan

Faraz Persian: height, ascent

Fardeen Persian (from fardīn): first month in the Persian calendar

Fareed *See* Farid

Fares *See* Faris

Farhaan *See* Farhan

Farhad Persian: good tempered, thoughtful. A legendary architect who fell in love with the princess Shirin, and killed himself when he believed that she had died

Farhan Persian (from farāhat): clever, elegant, stately

Farid Arabic: unique, precious gem, imcomparible

Faris Arabic: knight, horseman, Persian

Farley Old English (from fearn and leah): fern clearing (shifted from surname usage)

Faron *See* Farron

Farooq Arabic: one who can tell truth from lies. The title of Umar, known as Farooq the Great, one of prophet Muhammad's companions

Farran *See* Farron

Farrell From Fearghal, Irish Gaelic (fer and galus): courageous man (shifted from surname usage)

Farren *See* Farron

Farris From O' Fearghusa, Irish Gaelic (from fear and gus): man of vigour (shifted from surname usage)

Farron Latin (from ferro): iron, blacksmith (shifted from surname usage)

Faruq *See* Farooq

Farzan Persian: wise, learned

Fatih Arabic: conquerer, taker

Faustas Latin (from faustus): favourable, fortunate, lucky

Favour (name from an English word)

Fawad Arabic: heart, mind, soul

Fawaz/Fawwaz Arabic: successful

Fayez *See* Faiz

Faysal Arabic: judge, arbiter

Fayzaan/Fayzan *See* Faizaan

Fazal Arabic (from fazl): grace, virtue

Fazan Unknown, possibly Old French (from fazon): fashioner (shifted from surname usage). *See also* Faizaan

Fearghal Irish Gaelic (fer and galus): courageous man. The name of two kings of Connacht. *See also* Farrell

Federico An Italian and Spanish variant of Frederick

Feliks *See* Felix

Felipe A Portuguese and Spanish variant of Philip

Felix Latin: happy, lucky

Fenn Old English (from foenn): bog, fen (shifted from surname usage)

Fenton Old English (from foenn and tun): bog town, fen town (shifted from surname usage)

Ferdinand Old German (from fardhand nandh): daring journey. Also possibly Old German (from fridh and nandh): peaceful and brave

Fergal *See* Fearghal

Fergus Irish Gaelic (from fer and gus): man of vigour

Fernando A Spanish variant of Ferdinand

Feroz Persian: victorious, triumphant, prosperous

Fezaan/Fezan *See* Faizaan

Fiachra Irish Gaelic (from fiach): raven

Fidel Latin (from fidelis): faith, loyalty, trust

Filip/Filipe/Filippo *See* Philip

Finan From O' Fionnain, Irish Gaelic (from fionn): fair (surname usage)

Finbar/Finbarr From Fionnbharr (from fionn and barr/barrach): fair topped, fair headed, fair haired

Findlay/Findley From Fionnlagh, Irish Gaelic (from fionn and láth): fair warrior (shifted from surname usage)

Finian *See* Finan

Finlay/Finlee/Finleigh/Finley *See* Findlay

Finn An anglicised variant of Fionn

Finnan *See* Finan

Finnbar *See* Finbar

Finnegan From O' Fionnagain, Irish Gaelic (from fionn): fair (shifted from surname usage)

Finnian *See* Finan

Finnlay/Finnley *See* Findlay

Fintan From Fionntan, Irish Gaelic (from fionn): fair. The name of Fintan mac Bochra the Wise, a seer from Irish mythology

Finton *See* Fenton

Fionn Irish Gaelic: fair

Fionnan *See* Finan

Fionntan/Fiontan *See* Fintan

Firas Arabic: observant, understanding

Firat Turkish: the Euphrates river (geographical name)

Fiyinfoluwa Yoruba: give god the

glory

Fizaan/Fizan *See* Faizaan

Flavio/Flavius Latin (from flavus): yellow, blond

Fletcher Old French (from fleche): arrow, fletcher (shifted from surname usage)

Flinn From O Floinn, Irish Gaelic (from flann): red (shifted from surname usage)

Flint (name from an English word). Also possibly Old English (from flinty): hard hearted, like the rock (shifted from surname usage)

Florian Latin (from florus): bright, shining. Also possibly Latin (from flora): flowers

Florin A Romanian variant of Florian

Floyd *See* Lloyd

Flyn/Flynn *See* Flinn

Forbes Unknown, possibly Irish Gaelic (from foirb): land, estate (shifted from surname usage). Known for the Scottish journalist B. C. Forbes who founded the magazine that bears his name

Ford Old English: ford, shallow river (shifted from surname usage)

Forhad *See* Fuad

Forrest Old English (from forest): woods around a manor (shifted from surname usage)

Fortune (name from an English word)

Foster Old French (from fustrier): wood worker (shifted from surname usage)

Fox (name from an English word, shifted from surname usage)

Fraiser/Fraizer Unknown, possibly Old French (from fraise): sheer or strawberries

Fran A diminutive form of Frank and Francesco

Francesco An Italian variant of Francis

Francis Latin (from Franciscus): from France. *See also* Franek

Francisco A Spanish variant of Francis

Franciszek A Polish variant of Francis

Franco An Italian and Spanish variant of Frank

Francois A French variant of Francis

Franek Latin (from Franciscus): from France (shifted from surname usage). *See also* Francis

Frank Old English (from franka): a Frank, a Germanic people who use spears and javelins, also called franka

Frankey A diminutive form of Frank. *See also* Girls and Boys: Frankie

Franklin/Franklyn Old English (from frankelein): free man, freeholder (shifted from surname usage)

Franky A diminutive form of Frank. *See also* Girls and Boys: Frankie

Franz A German variant of Francis

Fraser/Frasier/Frazer/Frazier *See* Fraiser

Fred/Freddy A diminutive form of Frederick. *See also* Girls and Boys: Freddie

Frederic/Frederick/Frederico/ Frederik Germanic: peaceful ruler

Fredi A diminutive form of Frederick

Fredric/Fredrick/Fredrik *See* Frederick

Frey Old Norse (from freyr): lord. The Norse god of virility and kingship

Fuad Arabic: heart

Furkan/Furqaan/Furqan Arabic: the criterion. Al-Furqan is the 25th chapter of the Qur'an, and deals with the deciding factors between good and evil

Fynlay/Fynley *See* Finlay

Fynn An anglicised variant of Fionn

Fynnley *See* Finlay

g

Gabe A diminutive form of Gabrielius

Gabrielius/Gabriels Hebrew: warrior of god, strength of god. *See also* Girls and Boys: Gabriel

Gael Of Gaelic heritage

Gagandeep Punjabi: light of the sky (Sikh name)

Gage/Gaige Unknown, possibly Old English: gauger, measurer (shifted from surname usage). Also possibly from greengage plums (name from flowers and trees)

Gaius Roman name, unknown, possibly Latin (from gaudere): rejoice. Also possibly Greek (from gaia): earth

Garan Cornish: crane

Gareth Unknown, possibly Welsh (from garth): rock jutting over the sea. Sir Gareth is a nephew of Arthur's and a knight of the Round Table

Garin Unknown, possibly Welsh (from garan): crane

Garion Unknown, possibly Scottish Gaelic (from gearran): a type of horse

Garrett An Old English variant of Gerard

Garry A diminutive form of Gareth and Gerard

Garth *See* Gareth

Gary A diminutive form of Gareth and Gerard

Garyn *See* Garin

Gaspard A French variant of Caspar

Gaurav Hindi: pride, honour

Gavin From Gawain, possibly Welsh (from gwalch): hawk. Also possibly Welsh (from gwyn): fair. Sir Gawain is a nephew of Arthur's and a knight of the Round Table

Gavinder *See* Gurinder

Gavriel *See* Gabrielius

Ged A diminutive form of Gerard

Gene/Geno A diminutive form of Eugene

Geoffrey Unknown, possibly Old German (from gawia and frid): peace of the land. Also possibly a variant of Godfrey

Geordan Hebrew (from yarden): flowing down. *See also* Girls and Boys: Jordan

Geordie A diminutive form of George

George/Georgi/Georgie/ Georgio/Georgios Greek: farm worked

Geraint Possibly from Gerontius, Latin: old man. The lover of Enid from Arthurian legends

Gerald Germanic: ruler of the spear

Gerard/Gerrard Old German (from ger and hard): strong spear, brave spear

Gerry A diminutive form of Gerard

Gershon Hebrew: temporary resident

Gerwyn Unknown, possibly Welsh (from caru and gwyn): fair love *See also* Gavin

Gethin/Gethyn Unknown, possibly Old Welsh (from cryf and udd): strong lord (shifted from surname usage)

Ghulam Arabic: boy, youth, servant, page

Giacomo An Italian variant of Jacob

Gian A diminutive form of Giovanni

Giancarlo An Italian variant of John-Charles

Gianluca An Italian variant of John-Luke

Gianni A diminutive form of Giovanni

Gibril *See* Gabrielius

Gideon Hebrew: warrior, destroyer. A judge in the Hebrew bible

Gil A diminutive form of Gilbert

Gilbert Old German (from gisil and beraht): noble, bright and famous youth

Giles Unknown, possibly Latin (from aegis): shield, protection from goatskin

Gino A diminutive form of Eugene

Gio A diminutive form of Giorgio and Giovanni

Giorgio An Italian variant of George

Giovanni An Italian variant of John

Giulio An Italian variant of Julius

Giuseppe An Italian variant of Joseph

Gleb Old Norse: heir of god. The name of a Russian saint. Along with his brother Boris the two are also known as Roman and David

Glen/Glenn *See* Glyn

Glory (name from an English word)

Glyn/Glynn Welsh (from glyn): valley, glen (shifted from surname usage)

Gobind The name of the tenth Guru (Sikh name)

Godfrey Old German (from god and fred): good peace

Godwin Old German (from god and wine): good friend, good protector (shifted from surname usage)

Goncalo The name of a Portuguese saint. Also from Gonçalo alves, tigerwood (name from flowers and trees)

Goodluck The name of Goodluck Jonathan, the President of Nigeria

Goran Slavic (from gora): mountain, high, highlander

Gordon Old Gaelic (from gor and dun): large fort (shifted from surname usage)

Govind Sanskrit (from govinda): cowherd. A name for the Hindu god Krishna

Gracjan Polish (from gracja): grace Polish name day for Gracjan: 18th December

Grady Irish Gaelic (from grádach): beloved, distinguished (shifted from surname usage)

Graeme/Graham From Grantham, possibly Old English (from grand and ham): gravel homestead (geographical name, shifted from surname usage)

Granit Unknown, possibly from the word 'granite'

Grant/Grantas Latin (from grandis): large (shifted from surname usage)

Gray (colour name, name from an English word, shifted from surname usage)

Grayson Old English (from greyve and son): son of a steward (shifted from surname usage)

Great (name from an English word)

Greg/Gregg A diminutive form of Gregor and Gregory

Gregor/Gregory Greek (from gregorien): wakeful, watchful (shifted from surname usage)

Greig A Scottish variant of Gregor

Greyson *See* Grayson

Griff A diminutive form of Griffin and Griffith

Griffin/Griffith An anglicised variant of Gruffudd

Gruff A diminutive form of Gruffudd

Gruffudd/Gruffydd Unknown, possibly Old Welsh (from gruff and udd): dragon lord (shifted from surname usage)

Grzegorz A Polish variant of Gregory

Guilherme/Guillaume A French variant of William

Gulam *See* Ghulam

Guled Cushitic: victory

Guney Turkish: south, from the south (shifted from surname usage)

Gurdeep Punjabi: lamp of the Guru

(Sikh name)

Gurdev Punjabi: almighty Guru (Sikh name)

Gurdit Punjabi: given by the Guru (Sikh name)

Gurinder Punjabi: lord, Guru (Sikh name). *See also* Girls and Boys: Gurvinder

Gurjeet Punjabi: victory of the Guru (Sikh name)

Gurjeevan Punjabi: life as ordained by the Guru (Sikh name)

Gurjit/Gurjot *See* Gurjeet

Gurkaran Punjabi: ray of light from the Guru (Sikh name)

Gurkirat Punjabi: singing praises of the Guru (Sikh name)

Gurman Punjabi: meditating words of the Guru (Sikh name)

Gurmukh Punjabi: following the words of the Guru (Sikh name)

Gurnoor Punjabi: divine light of the Guru (Sikh name)

Gurpal Punjabi: protected by the Guru (Sikh name)

Gurpreet Punjabi: love of the Guru (Sikh name)

Gurshaan/Gurshan Punjabi: finding peace through the Guru (Sikh name)

Gurtaj Punjabi: grandeur of the Guru (Sikh name)

Gurveer Punjabi: warrior of the Guru (Sikh name)

Gurvir *See* Gurveer

Gus A diminutive form of Augustus or Gustav

Gustas A Lithuanian variant of Gustav

Gustav Unknown, possibly Old Norse (from got and staff): support of the Geat tribe of Swedes. Also possibly Slavic (from gost and slava): guest of glory. The name of several Swedish kings

Gustavo An Italian, Spanish and Portugues variant of Gustav

Gustavs A Latvian variant of Gustav

Guto A diminutive form of Gruffydd

Guy Old German (from wido): wood

Gwilym A Welsh variant of William

Gwion The name of the Welsh poet Gwion Bach, who later took the name Taliesin

Gwydion Old Welsh: forest, trees The name of Gwydion fab Dôn, a magician from Welsh mythology

Gwyn Welsh: fair

h

Haadi *See* Hadi

Haamid *See* Hamid

Haaris *See* Harith

Haaroon An Arabic variant of Aaron

Haashim *See* Hashim

Haashir *See* Hashir

Haaziq Arabic: sharp, skillful, clever

Habeeb/Habib/Habibur Arabic (from habib): beloved, darling, sweetheart

Haden *See* Hayden

Hadi Arabic: leader, guide. Al-Hadi is one of Allah's 99 names, meaning Guide, and reciting it is believed to help gain spiritual knowledge

Hadleigh Old English (from haeth and leah): heather clearing (geographical name, shifted from surname usage)

Hadyn *See* Hayden

Hafeez/Hafiz Arabic: guardian, protector

Haidar Arabic: lion

Haiden *See* Hayden

Haider *See* Haidar

Haitham Arabic (from haisam): young eagle, young vulture

Hakan Arabic: leader. Also Native American: fire

Hakeem/Hakim Arabic: doctor, philosopher, sage. Al-Hakeem is one of Allah's 99 names, meaning Wise One, and reciting it is believed to help overcome difficulties

Hal A diminutive form of Harold and Henry

Haleem *See* Halim

Halil A Turkish variant of Khalil

Halim Arabic: patient, tolerant

Hallam/Hallum Old English (from halh): nook, valley (geographical name, shifted from surname usage)

Hamas Arabic: enthusiasm

Hamdaan/Hamdan Arabic: one who praises, one who elugises

Hamed/Hameed/Hamid Arabic: all praiseworthy. Al-Hamid is one of Allah's 99 names, meaning All Praisworthy, and reciting it is believed to help gain love and praise

Hamilton Old English (from hamel and dun): bare, treeless hill (geographical name, shifted from surname usage)

Hamim Arabic: good friend

Hamish Arabic: intelligent, clever, sharp

Hammaad/Hammad Arabic: praising

Hamsa/Hamse Sanskrit: goose, swan. The hamsa bird represents the balance of life

Hamza/Hamzah Arabic: lion The name of Hamza ibn 'Abd al-Muttalib, prophet Muhammad's uncle

Han Turkish: khan. Also Chinese: various, including courageous

Hanad Cushtic: full of vigour, youthful

Hanif Arabic: true believer, one true faith

Hano A diminutive form of Johan

Hans A diminutive form of Johannes

Hanson Old English: son of John (shifted from surname usage)

Hanzala/Hanzalah The name of one of prophet Muhammad's scribes, possibly named after a species of tree

Hao Chinese: various, including proud

Hardev Punjabi: man of god (Sikh name)

Hardy Old English (from hardi): bold, hardy (shifted from surname usage)

Harees *See* Harith

Hari Sanskrit: tawny, green (colour name). A name for the Hindi god Vishnu

Haris *See* Harith

Harish/Harishan Sanskrit (from harisa): joy. Also possibly Sanskrit (from hari and iza): lord Vishnu. *See also* Hari

Harison *See* Harrison

Harith Arabic: provider, cultivator

Harjas Punjabi: singing god's praises (Sikh name)

Harjeet Punjabi: victory of god (Sikh name)

Harjeevan Punjabi: living life to god (Sikh name)

Harjinder Punjabi: life that is granted by god (Sikh name)

Harkirat Punjabi: praise of god (Sikh name)

Harlan/Harland Old English (from har and land): grey land (shifted from surname usage). Also possibly Old English (from hara and land): land full of hares (shifted from surname usage)

Harlem Unknown, from Haarlem, a city in the Netherlands, where Harlem in New York is named after (geographical name)

Harlen *See* Harlan

Harminder Punjabi: house of god (Sikh name)

Harold Old English (from here and weald): ruler of the army

Haron/Haroon/Haroun An Arabic variant of Aaron

Harri/Harrie A diminutive form of Henry

Harris *See* Henry

Harrish *See* Harish

Harrison/Harrisson Old English: son of Henry (shifted from surname usage)

Harry A diminutive form of Henry

Harsh Hindi: cheerful, happy

Harshil From the river Harshil, Sanskrit (from Hari and zila): Vishnu's rock

Hartley Old English (from heort and leah): hart clearing, deer clearing (shifted from surname usage)

Harun/Haruun An Arabic variant of Aaron

Harveer Punjabi: courage of god (Sikh name)

Harvey/Harvi/Harvie Old Breton

(from haer and vy): battle-ready. Also possibly Old Breton (from hoiarn and viu): blazing iron

Harvin Unknown (shifted from surname usage)

Harvinder Punjabi: realisation of god (Sikh name)

Harvir *See* Harveer

Hasaan/Hasan Arabic (from hasuna): good, handsome

Hasanain A blend of Hasan and Hussein

Haseeb *See* Hasib

Hasham Arabic: servant, attendant, follower

Hashim Arabic: crusher, breaker, destroyer of evil. The title given to Hashim ibn 'Abd Manaf, the great grandfather of prophet Muhammad

Hashir Arabic: collector. The title given to prophet Muhammad

Hasib Arabic: noble, respected, esteemed. Al-Hasib is one of Allah's 99 names, meaning the Noble, and reciting it is believed to help be rid of jealousy

Hasnaat Arabic: good deeds

Hasnain A diminutive form of Hasan

Hasnat *See* Hasnaat

Hassaan/Hassan *See* Hasan

Hassnain A diminutive form of Hasan

Hatim Arabic: determined, decisive

Hayan *See* Hayyan

Haydan *See* Hayden

Haydar *See* Haidar

Hayden Old English (from heg and dun): hedge hill, enclosure hill (shifted from surname usage)

Hayder *See* Haidar

Haydn The surname of the composer Joseph Haydn. *See also* Hayden

Haydon/Haydyn *See* Hayden

Haytham *See* Haitham

Hayyaan/Hayyan Arabic: alive, energetic

Heath Old English: someone who lives near a heath (shifted from surname usage)

Hector Greek (from hekhein): to hold. The Trojan prince who was the brother of Paris

Hedley *See* Hadleigh

Hefin Welsh (from haf): summer

Hejran Arabic (from hijran): departing, separation

Hendrik A Dutch variant of Henry

Hendrix (shifted from surname usage). *See* Henry

Henley/Henlie Unknown, possibly Old English: high clearing (shifted from surname usage)

Henock/Henok *See* Enoch

Henri A French variant of Henry

Henrik A Scandinavian variant of Henry

Henrikas A Lithuanian variant of Henry

Henrique A Portuguese variant of

Henry

Henry Old German (heim and rihhi): home ruler

Henson Old English: son of Henry (shifted from surname usage)

Herbert Old German (from hari and beraht): bright army

Herbie A diminutive form of Herbert

Herkus A diminutive form of Henrikas

Hersh Yiddish: deer

Hershel Unknown, possibly from Hersh. Also possibly from Herschel, which is from the same root as Hersh (shifted from surname usage)

Hershy *See* Hersh

Heston Old English (hes and tun): enclosed town (shifted from surname usage)

Het Sanskrit (from hetu): justification, purpose

Hezekiah Hebrew: strengthened by god. A king of Judah

Hilmi A Turkish variant of Halim

Himesh Hindi (from hamesha): forever, always. Also possibly Sanskrit (from hima and iz): snow king

Himmat Arabic: ambition

Hinesh *See* Himesh

Hiren Hindi (from hiran): deer

Hiro Japanese: various, including broad, wide and expansive

Hiroki Japanese: various, including large tree and broad happiness

Hishaam/Hisham Arabic: generosity. The name of Hisham ibn Abd al-Malik, an Umayyad caliph. Also the name of Hisham ibn Urwah, a narrator of hadith

Hiten/Hitesh Sanskrit (from hitecha): well-wishing, good will

Ho Vietnamese: lake

Holden Unknown (shifted from surname usage)

Hong Chinese: various, including wide, vast and flood

Horace/Horatio Unknown, possibly Latin (from hōrus): hours, time

Howard Old Norse (from hár and varðr): high guard. Also possibly from Old German (hug and ward): guardian of the heart and mind

Howie A diminutive form of Howard

Hrithik Sanskrit (from hrttas): from the heart

Hubert Old German (from hug and berht): bright heart, famous mind

Hudayfa/Hudhaifa The name of Hudhayfah ibn al-Yaman, a companion of prophet Muhammad

Hudson Old English: son of Hugh (shifted from surname usage)

Huey A diminutive form of Hugh

Hugh Old German (from hug): heart, mind

Hughie A diminutive form of Hugh

Hugo *See* Hugh

Humaid *See* Ahmad

Humayl The name of one of prophet Muhammad's companions

Humayun Arabic: auspicious, fortunate. The name of Nasir ud-din Muhammad Humayun, the second Mughal Emperor

Humphrey Old German (from hūn and frid): bear cub of peace

Humza/Humzah *See* Hamza

Hunter Old English (from hunta): to hunt (shifted from surname usage)

Husaam *See* Husam

Husain A diminutive of Hasan

Husam Arabic: sword

Husayn/Huseyin Arabic: safety, protection. Also a diminutive form of Hasan

Husnain/Hussain Also a diminutive form of Hasan

Hussam *See* Husam

Hussan *See* Hasan

Hussein/Hussnain A diminutive form of Hasan

Huw A Welsh variant of Hugh

Huxley Unknown (shifted from surname usage)

Huzaifa/Huzaifah/Huzayfah Arabic: short

Hywel Old Welsh: eminent

i

Iago *See* Jacob. This variant is used for the name of the main antagonist in Shakespeare's *Othello*

Iain/Ian *See* John

Ianis A Romanian variant of John

Ianto A Welsh variant of John

Ibaad Arabic (from ibada): worship

Ibraaheem/Ibraheem/Ibrahim *See* Abraham

Ibrar Arabic (from ebrar): justification

Iden *See* Edan

Idrees/Idris/Idriss An Islamic prophet, possibly Enoch

Iesa *See* Eesa

Iestyn A Welsh variant of Justin

Ieuan/Ifan A Welsh variant of John

Iftikhar Arabic: honour, grace, pride

Ignacio A Spanish variant of Ignatius

Ignacy A Polish variant of Ignatius

Ignas A Lithuanian variant of Ignatius

Ignatius Latin (from ignis): fire

Igor Old Norse, from Yngvi, a name for the god Freyr

Ihsaan *See* Ahsan. *See also* Girls and Boys: Ihsan

Ihtishaam/Ihtisham Arabic: magnificence, having many people relying on you

Ijaz Arabic: the nature of the Qur'an that makes it inimitable

Ike A diminutive form of Ikechukwu, Isaac and Ivan

Ikechukwu Igbo: power of god

Ikenna Igbo: strength of god

Iker Basque: to inquire

Ikraam Arabic: honour, respect. *See also* Girls and Boys: Ikram

Ilan Hebrew: tree

Ilias A Greek variant of Elias

Ilya A Russian variant of Elias

Ilyaas/Ilyas An Arabic variant of Elias

Ilyes A French variant of Elias

Imaad/Imad *See* Emad

Imam Arabic: leader

Immanuel *See* Emanuel

Imraan/Imran *See* Emran

Imtiaz/Imtyaz Arabic: distinction

Inaam Arabic: kindness

Inayat Arabic: care, concern

Inder Punjabi: god (Sikh name)

Inderjit Punjabi: victory of god (Sikh name)

Inderpal Punjabi: protected by god (Sikh name)

Inderveer Punjabi: bravery of god (Sikh name)

Indiana A state in the US (geographical name). Also the adventure hero, Indiana Jones

Inigo A Welsh variant of Eneko, unknown, possibly Latin (from ignotus): forgiven, unknown

Innes/Innis Irish Gaelic (from inis): island (shifted from surname usage)

Ioan A Romanian and Welsh variant of John

Ioannis A Greek variant of John

Iolo A diminutive form of Iorwerth

Ionatan A Romanian variant of Jonathan

Ionut A Romanian variant of John/ Johnny

Iori A diminutive form of Iorwerth. Also Japanese: various, including weave

Iorwerth Old Welsh (from iôr and berth/prydferth): beautiful lord, handsome lord

Iosif A Turkish variant of Joseph

Iqbal Arabic (from eghbal): fortunate, prosperous, thriving

Irfaan/Irfan Arabic: knowledge, learning, insight

Irvine Welsh (from ir and afon): green river (shifted from surname usage). Also several place names, including a town and a river in Scotland (geographical name)

Isaa *See* Eesa

Isaac/Isaak Hebrew: he will laugh. A son of Abraham and Sarah

Isaam *See* Isam

Isaaq/Isac/Isacc *See* Isaac

Isah *See* Eesa

Isaiah Hebrew: Jehova is salvation. A prophet who lived in the Kingdom of Judah, most notably connected to the Book of Isaiah

Isak *See* Isaac

Isam Arabic: security, safeguard

Ishaan Sanskrit (from izana): ruling, lord. One of the names of the Hindu god Shiva

Ishaaq/Is'haaq/Ishak *See* Isaac

Ishan *See* Ishaan

Ishaq *See* Isaac

Ishmael/Ishmail Hebrew: god has listened. The first son of Abraham, from Hagar

Ishraq Arabic: radiance

Isiah *See* Isaiah

Islam Arabic (from salam): submission to god

Ismaaeel/Ismaeel/Isma'eel/Ismael/Ismail/Isma'il *See* Ishmael

Israar *See* Israr

Israel Hebrew: wrestle with god. The place in the Middle East (geographical name)

Israr Arabic (from esrar): mystery, secret

Issa *See* Eesa

Issac *See* Isaac

Issam *See* Isam

Iustin *See* Justin

Ivan *See* John

Ivo/Ivor Old German (from iv): yew (name from flowers and trees)

Iwan A Welsh variant of John

Iwo A Polish variant of Ivo

I'yad/Iyad Arabic (from yad): power, authority

Iyaz Arabic (from yaz): distinguished

Izaac/Izaak *See* Isaac

Izaan Arabic: obediance

Izac *See* Isaac

Izaiah *See* Isaiah

Izak *See* Isaac

Iziah *See* Isaiah

j

Jaabir *See* Jabir

Jaan An Estonian variant of John

Jabari Swahili: brave, fearless, proud

Jabez Hebrew: sorrow. An ancestor to Judah's kings, whose prayers were answered by God

Jabir Arabic (from jaber): force, constrain

Jabril An Arabic variant of Gabrielius

Jac A diminutive form of John

Jace A diminutive form of Jason

Jacek A Polish variant of Jack

Jack A diminutive form of John

Jackson Old English: son of Jack. *See also* Jack

Jacky A diminutive form of Jack

Jacob/Jacoby Hebrew: on the heel, to follow behind. The son of Isaac and Rebekah, who was born holding onto the heel of his twin Esau

Jacque/Jacques A French variant of James, derrived from Jacob. *See also* Jacob

Jacub *See* Jacob

Jad An Arabic variant of Gad, Hebrew: luck. A son of Jacob who formed the Tribe of Gad

Jadan Persian (from jadin): chrysolite, green like chrysolite. *See also* Jadon

Jadon Hebrew: thankful

Jaeden/Jaedon *See* Jaydon

Jafar Arabic (from ja'far): small river, stream

Jagdeep Punjabi: lamp of the world (Sikh name)

Jagjeet/Jagjit Punjabi: victory of the world (Sikh name)

Jago *See* Jacob

Jagraj Punjabi: king of the world (Sikh name)

Jagroop Punjabi: form of the world, embodiment of the world (Sikh name)

Jagveer Punjabi: bravery of the world (Sikh name)

Jahaan/Jahan Persian: the world

Jahangir Persian (from jahan and geer): world conqueror. The name of Salim Nuruddin Jahangir, a Mughal Emperor

Jahanzeb Persian (from jahan and zeeb): world's ornament, world's beauty

Jahari Swahili (from johari): essence, jewel

Jahed Arabic: diligent, industrious

Jaheem/Jaheim The name of the singer Jaheim Hoagland, whose name is thought to mean 'god's wisdom'. Also Arabic: hell's fire

Jahid *See* Jahed

Jahiem *See* Jaheem

Jahmai Hebrew: he who Jehovah guards. A son of Adam and Eve

Jahmal *See* Jamal

Jahmar/Jahmari *See* Jamar

Jahsiah/Jahziah *See* Josiah

Jaidan *See* Jaydon

Jaideep Punjabi: lamp of victory (Sikh name)

Jaidev Punjabi: god's victory (Sikh name)

Jaidon/Jaidyn *See* Jaydon

Jaimin Gujarati: victory. A variant of Jaimini, the name of an Indian sage

Jaipal Punjabi: protector of victory (Sikh name)

Jairaj Punjabi: king of victory (Sikh name)

Jaison *See* Jason

Jaiveer Punjabi: bravery of victory (Sikh name)

Jak/Jake *See* Jack

Jakir *See* Zakir

Jakob/Jakobi *See* Jacob

Jakson *See* Jackson

Jakub *See* Jacob

Jalal Arabic: glory, dignity, majesty

Jaleel Arabic: greatest, most glorious

Jalen Unknown, possibly from a Slovenian surname, for example, of the writer Janez Jalen (shifted from surname usage)

Jalil *See* Jaleel

Jamaal/Jamahl *See* Jamal

Jamaine *See* Jermain

Jamal Arabic: rare beauty

Jamar/Jamari A modernised and shifted variant of Jamal

Jameel/Jamel *See* Jamil

James A variant of Jacob from Old French. *See* Jacob

Jameson Old English: son of James (shifted from surname usage)

Jamiah Arabic: union, gathering

Jamiel *See* Jamil

Jamieson *See* Jameson

Jamil Arabic: beautiful

Janaid *See* Junaid

Jansen Old English: son of Jan (shifted from surname usage)

Japheth Hebrew: enlarged. One of the sons of Noah

Jarad *See* Jared

Jardel The surname of the Brazilian striker Mário Jardel (footballer name)

Jared Hebrew: descended from above. The father of Enoch

Jarell *See* Jarrell

Jareth The character played by David Bowie in the film *Labyrinth*

Jarlath Irish Gaelic (from iar and flaith): dark lord

Jarod *See* Jared

Jaron Unknown, possibly a modernised and shifted variant of Jared or Jason

Jaroslav Slavic (from Jarilo and slav): glory of spring, glory of harvest, glory of the sun

Jarrad/Jarred *See* Jared

Jarrell Unknown, possibly from Gerville in France (shifted from surname usage)

Jarrod/Jarryd *See* Jared

Jarvis Old German (from geri and vaulx): spear valley (shifted from surname usage)

Jase A diminutive form of Jason

Jashan Punjabi: celebrating together (Sikh name)

Jashandeep Punjabi: lamp of celebration (Sikh name)

Jasiah *See* Josiah

Jasim A town in Syria (geographical name)

Jaskaran Punjabi: singing praises of god's glory (Sikh name)

Jason Greek (from iason): healer. The leader of the Argonauts in Greek mythology

Jaspal Punjabi: protector of god's glory (Sikh name)

Jasper *See* Caspar

Jasraj Punjabi: king of god's glory (Sikh name)

Jatin Sanskrit: ascetic, restraint A name of the Hindu god Shiva

Jatinder Punjabi: conquered the five evils (Sikh name)

Javan Hebrew: Greece, Greek. One of Noah's grandsons

Javed Persian (from javeed): eternal, everlasting

Javen *See* Javan

Javier A Spanish variant of Xavier

Javon *See* Javan

Jawaad/Jawad Arabic: generous

Jax A diminutive form of Jackson

Jaxen/Jaxon/Jaxson/Jaxxon *See* Jackson

Jayan Sanskrit (from jayin): victorious

Jaycob *See* Jacob

Jaydan *See* Jaydon

Jaydeep *See* Jaideep

Jaydn/Jaydon/Jaydyn A blend of Jay and Aiden/Hayden. *See also* Jadan and Jadon. *See also* Girls and Boys: Jayden

Jayen *See* Jayan

Jayesh Sanskrit (from jayin and iz): lord of victory

Jayjay A blend of two letters of the alphabet. Also a diminutive form of double names such as Jason-James

Jayke *See* Jack

Jaylan/Jaylen/Jaylon A modernised and shifted variant of Jalen

Jayme/Jaymes *See* James

Jaymie A diminutive form of James

Jayon *See* Jayan

Jayson *See* Jason

Jayveer *See* Jaiveer

Jazz (name from an English word)

Jed/Jedd A diminutive form of Jedidiah

Jedidiah Hebrew: friend of Jehovah, beloved of Jehovah. The blessed name given to Solomon

Jeet Hindi (from jit): conquest, victory

Jeff A diminutive form of Jeffrey

Jefferson Old English: son of Jeffrey Also Old English: son of Godfrey

Jeffery/Jeffrey *See* Geoffrey

Jelani Swahili: mighty, great

Jem A diminutive form of Jeremy. *See also* Cem

Jens A Danish, German and Norwegian variant of John

Jensen/Jenson Old English: son of Jens

Jeremi A Hungarian variant of Jeremiah

Jeremiah Hebrew: exalted by Jehovah. The name of a major prophet

Jeremie A French variant of Jeremiah

Jeremy *See* Jeremiah

Jeriah Hebrew: *See*n by Jehovah. A son of Hebron, and a cousin of Moses

Jericho Unknown, possibly Hebrew: fragrant. Also possibly Hebrew: moon. The city of palm trees from the Old Testament, in present day Palestine (geographical name)

Jermain/Jermaine Latin (from germanus): brother, sibling

Jerome Ancient Greek (from hieros and onoma): holy name. The name of Saint Jerome, also known as Hieronymus

Jeron From Jeroen, a Dutch variant

of Jeremiah, Jerome or John

Jerrard *See* Gerard

Jerry A diminutive form of Gerald and Jeremy

Jeshua *See* Joshua

Jesiah From Isshiah, Hebrew: Jehovah will lend. *See also* Josiah

Jesper A Danish variant of Caspar

Jet *See* Jett

Jethro Hebrew: his excellence. The father of Zipporah, therefore the father-in-law of Moses

Jett Unknown, possible from a French variant of Judah (shifted from surname usage)

Jevan/Jevon Latin (from juvenis): young (shifted from surname usage)

Jez A diminutive form of Jeremy

Jian Arabic: life. Also Chinese: various, including strong and healthy

Jibraeel An Arabic variant of Gabrielius

Jibran Arabic (from jobran): to repair, to make amends

Jibreel/Jibril An Arabic variant of Gabrielius

Jim/Jimi/Jimmi/Jimmie/Jimmy A diminutive form of James

Jin Japanese: various, including kindness. Also Chinese: various, including gold

Jiyan Kurdish: life

JJ *See* Jayjay

Joab Hebrew: Jehovah

A nephew of King David

Joachim Hebrew: Jehovah has raised. The father of Mary and the grandfather of Jesus

Joakim A Danish, Norwegian and Swedish variant of Joachim

Joao A Portuguese variant of John

Joaquim A Portuguese variant of Joachim

Joaquin A Spanish variant of Joachim

Joash Hebrew: Jehovah has given. The name of a king of Judah and a king of Israel

Job Hebrew: hated, persecuted. The man who resists the temptations of Satan in the Book of Job

Joban Punjabi: youth (Sikh name)

Jobe/Jobi/Jobie/Joby A diminutive form of Job

Joe A diminutive form of Joseph

Joel Hebrew: Jehova is god

Joeseph *See* Joseph

Johan/Johann/Johannes/John/Johnathan/Johnathon Hebrew: Jehova is gracious

Johnnie/Johnny A diminutive form of John and Jonathan

Johnpaul A blend of John and Paul. Two popes have had this combination

Johnson Old English: son of John (shifted from surname usage)

Jokubas A Lithuanian variant of Jacob

Jolyon *See* Julian

Jon An Albanian, Basque, Swedish and Scandinavian variant of John

Jonah/Jonas Hebrew: dove. A prophet who was swallowed by a whale in the Book of Jonah

Jonatan A Scandinavian variant of Jonathan

Jonathan/Jonathon Hebrew: Jehovah has given. A friend of King David

Jonjo An Irish diminutive form of John

Jonnie/Jonny/Jonty A diminutive form of John

Jools A diminutive form of Julius

Jorawar From Zorawar, Punjabi: brave (Sikh name)

Jordi A Catalan variant of George

Jordie/Jordy A diminutive form of Jordan, Hebrew (from yarden): flowing down. See Girls and Boys: Jordan. See also Jordi

Jorge A Spanish and Portuguese variant of George

Joris A Dutch variant of George

Jos A diminutive form of Joseph

Jose A French, Portuguese and Spanish variant of Joseph

Josef A Czech, Danish, German, Norwegian and Swedish variant of Joseph

Joseff A Welsh variant of Joseph

Joseph Hebrew: Jehova will increase. The husband of the Virgin Mary

Josh A diminutive form of Joshua

Joshan Unknown, an Albanian name, possibly meaning 'eagle' from an unknown root. Also possibly Persian (from jooshan): boiling

Joshua/Joshuah Hebrew: Jehova is salvation. The central figure from the Book of Joshua

Josiah/Josias Hebrew: healed by Jehovah. A king of Judah who came to the throne at a young age

Josue A French and Spanish variant of Joshua

Jotham Hebrew: Jehovah is perfect A king of Judah

Jourdan Hebrew (from yarden): flowing down. See also Girls and Boys: Jordan

Jovan A Serbian variant of John

Jovi Latin (from Jove): the Roman god Jupiter

Jowan See John

Jozef A Polish, Slovak and Slovenian variant of Joseph

Juan A Manx and Spanish variant of John

Judah Hebrew: praised. The fourth son of Jacob and Leah who formed the Tribe of Judah

Judd A diminutive form of Jordan, Hebrew (from yarden): flowing down. See Girls and Boys: Jordan

Jujhar Punjabi: brave warrior (Sikh name)

Jules See Julius

Julian/Juliano/Julien Latin: of Julius. See Julius

Julio/Julius/Juliusz Latin: devoted

to Jove. Possibly also Greek: with a
downy beard

Jun Japanese: various, including pure,
fresh and orderly

Junaid/Junayd/Juned Arabic (from
jund): small army, soldier

Junior (name from an English word)

Justas/Justin/Justinas/Justyn
Latin: just

k

Kaamil *See* Kamil

Kaan Turkish: khan, king

Kabeer/Kabir Arabic: great, elder
Al-Kabir is one of Allah's 99
names, meaning the Greatest, and
reciting it is believed to help gain
esteem

Kacper A Polish variant of Casper

Kadan The grandson of Genghis
Khan. *See also* Cadan

Kade *See* Cade

Kadeem Arabic (from khadam):
servant, beadle

Kaden *See* Cadan. *See also* Girls and
Boys: Kayden

Kadir Arabic: powerful, able
Al-Qadir is one of Allah's 99
names, meaning the Powerful, and
reciting it is believed to help fulfil
desires

Kadyn *See* Cadan

Kaeden/Kaedon *See* Cadan

Kael Unknown, possibly from Gael,
from the word 'gale'

Kaelan/Kaelen/Kaelin *See* Cailan

Kaelum *See* Caelum

Kahlil *See* Khalil

Kaian *See* Caian

Kaid Arabic (from gha-ed): leader,
general

Kaidan *See* Cadan

Kaide *See* Kaid

Kaiden/Kaidon/Kaidyn *See*
Cadan

Kaie From Kaja, unknown, possibly
Estonian: echo. *See also* Girls and
Boys: Kaja

Kaif Arabic (from keyf): enjoyment

Kaihan Persian (from geyhan/
keyhan): the world

Kailan *See* Cailan

Kaileb *See* Caleb

Kailem *See* Kalam

Kailen *See* Cailan

Kailum *See* Kalam

Kain *See* Cain

Kainan *See* Kenan

Kaine *See* Cain

Kairan *See* Ciaran

Kairo *See* Cairo

Kairon *See* Ciaran

Kais *See* Gaius

Kaisan *See* Kaison

Kaiser Old German (from keisar):
Caesar, emperor

Kaison From Kaysone, the name
of the first Prime Minister of Lao,
Vietnamese (from cai and song):

river Cai (geographical name)

Kaito Japanese: various, including man from the sea

Kaius See Gaius

Kaiyan See Keyan. See also Girls and Boys: Kaiya

Kaizer See Kaiser

Kajetan A German variant of Gaetano, Latin: from the Italian city of Gaeta (shifted from surname usage)

Kajus A Lithuanian variant of Kajetan

Kal Persian: buffalo, male animal. Also a diminutive form of Kaleem

Kalam Hindi (from kalam): pen, quill. See also Cailan

Kalan See Cailan and Kale

Kale A Hawaiian variant of Charles

Kaleb See Caleb

Kaleem Arabic: interlocutor, speaker

Kalel/Kal-el See Khalil

Kalem See Kalam

Kalen See also Cailan and Kale

Kalib See Caleb

Kalil See Khalil

Kalim See Kaleem

Kallai Unknown (shifted from surname usage). Also possibly from Kala'i, Hawaiian: peace

Kallam See Kalam

Kallan See Cailan

Kallem See Kalam

Kallen See Cailan

Kallum See Kalam

Kalon Greek: good, virtuous

Kalub See Caleb

Kalum See Kalam

Kalvin See Calvin and Kelvin

Kamaal/Kamal Arabic: perfect, learned, accomplished. Also Hindi: lotus (name from flowers and trees)

Kamani See Khamani

Kamar See Qamar

Kamari/Kamarni Arabic (from ghamaree): lunar

Kameel See Kamil

Kamen Polish (from kamień): stone (shifted from surname usage)

Kamil Arabic: perfect, complete, genuine

Kamran/Kamren/Kamron Persian: successful, fortunate, blessed. See also Camaron

Kamrul A Bengali variant of Qamar

Kamsiyochukwu Igbo: god has answered the prayer

Kane A Welsh variant of Cathan. See also Cain

Kanye Unknown, possibly from Kaniye, from Serê Kaniyê, a variant of Ras al-Ayn, a city in Syria, near Turkey. The name of Kanye West

Kapil Sanskrit (from kapila): yellow, brown. Kapila is an incarnation of the Hindu god Vishnu

Karamveer Punjabi: bravery in god's grace (Sikh name)

Karan Persian: border, shore, coast

Karandeep From Karamdeep, Punjabi: lamp of god's grace (Sikh name)

Karanveer/Karanvir *See* Karamveer

Kareem/Karim Arabic: king, generous, noble. Al-Karim is one of Allah's 99 names, meaning Most Generous, and reciting it is believed to help gain esteem

Karl A German and Scandinavian variant of Charles

Karlton *See* Charlton

Karol A Polish variant of Charles

Karson *See* Carlson

Karsten A Danish, German and Norwegian variant of Christian

Kartar Hindi (from karatarth): grateful

Karter *See* Carter and Kartar

Karthik/Kartik Sanskrit (from karttika): the month in the Hindu calendar that falls around October and November. Also from Kartikeya, son of Krttika, a name of the Hindu god Murugan

Karun A major river in Iran (geographical name)

Kasam Arabic (from ghasam): oath

Kash Persian (from ghash): sincere

Kashan A city in Iran, famous for producing tiles. Also possibly Persian (from ghashang): handsome

Kashif Arabic (from kashef): discoverer

Kasim *See* Qasim

Kason *See* Carlson

Kaspar A German and Scandinavian variant of Caspar

Kasparas A Lithuanian variant of Caspar

Kasper *See* Caspar

Kaspian *See* Caspian

Kasra Arabic (from kesra): king, the title for kings from the Persian Sassanian Dynasty

Kassim *See* Qasim

Kassius *See* Cassius

Kavan/Kavana/Kavanagh *See* Cavan

Kavi Sanskrit: wise, intelligent

Kavin *See* Cavan

Kavish Sanskrit (from kaviza): chief of poets

Kayaan/Kayan *See* Keyaan

Kaydan/Kaydn/Kaydon *See* Cadan

Kayhan *See* Kaihan

Kaylam *See* Cailan

Kayle *See* Kyle

Kayleb *See* Caleb

Kaylem *See* Cailan

Kaylib *See* Caleb

Kaylon/Kaylum *See* Cailan. *See also* Girls and Boys: Kaylan

Kayne *See* Cain

Kaynen *See* Cianan

Kayon *See* Cianan

Kaysan/Kayson Unknown (shifted from surname usage)

Kazim *See* Qasim

Kazuki Japanese: various, including tree and noble

Keagan From Mac Aodhagáin, Old Gaelic: fire. *See* Girls and Boys:

Keegan

Kealan *See* Caelan

Kean/Keanan/Keane *See* Cianan

Keano A diminutive form of Kean

Keanu Hawaiian (from ke and anu): the cool, cool breeze

Kearan/Kearon *See* Ciaran

Keaton Unknown, possibly from an ancient town (shifted from surname usage)

Keean *See* Cianan

Keelan *See* Caelan

Keenan/Keenen *See* Cianan

Keeran *See* Ciaran

Keeyan *See* Keyan

Kegan *See* Keagan

Kei Japanese: various, including blessed and wise

Keian *See* Cianan

Keigan *See* Keagan

Keilan *See* Caelan

Keion *See* Cianan

Keir A diminutive form of Keiran

Keiran/Keiren/Keiron *See* Ciaran and Kiron

Keith From Baile Cheith, a Scottish town (geographical name, shifted from surname usage)

Keiton *See* Keaton

Kelan/Kellan *See* Caelan. *See also* Girls and Boys: Kellen

Kelson Old English: son of Ketill, Old Norse: cauldron (shifted from surname usage)

Kelton Old English (ketill and tun): town of Ketill, Old Norse: cauldron (shifted from surname usage)

Kelvin Unknown (shifted from surname usage). A river in Scotland Also from Lord Kelvin, who named the Kelvin scale

Kemal A Turkish variant of Kamal

Kemar *See* Qamar

Kemari *See* Kamarni

Ken Japanese: various, including healthy. Also a diminutive form of Kenneth

Kenan Hebrew: smith A grandson of Seth

Kendrick Old English (from cyne and ric): king's power. Also possibly Welsh (from cyngwr): chief (shifted from surname usage)

Kenechukwu Igbo: thank god

Kenji Japanese: various, including healthy child

Kenley A village in England (geographical name)

Kennedy From Ó Ceannéidigh, Irish Gaelic (from ceann and éidigh): ugly head (shifted from surname usage)

Kenneth An anglicised variant of Cinaed, Irish Gaelic: born of fire. Also an anglicised variant of Cainnech, Irish Gaelic: handsome

Kenny A diminutive form of Kenneth

Kent The county in England (geographical name, shifted from surname usage)

Kenton Old English (from cyne and tun): king's town (shifted from surname usage)

Kenzo Japanese: various, including healthy and building

Keo Cambodian: jewel

Keon An Irish variant of John

Keown Mac Eoghan (shifted from surname usage). *See also* Eoghan

Kerem A Turkish variant of Kareem

Kerim *See* Kareem

Kern Old German (from gern): desired. Also possibly Irish Gaelic (from cíar): dark, murky, black (shifted from surname usage)

Kerr Unknown, possibly Irish Gaelic (from cíar): dark, murky, black (shifted from surname usage)

Keshav Sanskrit (from kezava): with beautiful hair. A name of the Hindu god Vishnu

Keshawn A modernised and shifted variant of Shawn. *See* John

Kester A Scottish variant of Christopher

Ketan Sanskrit (from ketana): house, home, banner, symbol

Keval Sanskrit (from kevala): entire, absolute, pure, sole

Kevan/Keven/Kevin An anglicised variant of Caoimhin. *See also* Calvin

Kevinas A Lithuanian variant of Kevin

Kevins/Kevon *See* Kevin

Kewell Old English: from Keevil, a village in Wiltshire (shifted from surname usage)

Keyaan/Keyan/Keyon Persian: king, great kings. The second dynasty of Persian kings

Khaalid *See* Khalid

Khai Vietnamese: various, including victory

Khaled *See* Khalid

Khaleel *See* Khalil

Khaleem *See* Kaleem

Khalid Arabic (from khalada): eternal, lasting forever

Khalifa Arabic: successor, caliph, the head of a Caliphate

Khalil Arabic: good friend

Khalis Arabic: pure, clear, real

Khamani Persian (from khaman): bow. The name of the child actor Khamani Griffin

Khan Persian: king

Khari Unknown, possibly Sanskrit (from kari): artist, singer of praises

Khateeb Arabic: religious minister for Friday and Eid prayers

Khawaja Persian: lord, master

Khian *See* Keyan

Khizar/Khizer The Arabic name of the prophet Elijah. *See also* Girls and Boys: Elijah

Khubaib The name of Khubayb ibn Adiy, a companion of prophet Muhammad. *See also* Adiy

Khuram/Khurram Persian (from khorram): fresh, blooming, delightful, cheerful

Khush Persian (from khosh): happy, healthy, gentle, fair

Khushal A Pashto variant of Khush

Khy A modernised and shifted variant of Caius. *See* Gaius Khyan *See* Keyan

Khye *See* Khy

Ki Unknown, possibly Japanese: various, including tree and spirit

Kiaan *See* Keyan

Kial *See* Kyle

Kiam Unknown (shifted from surname usage). Also possibly Arabic (from ghaim): alive, standing, existing

Kian *See* Keyan

Kiaran/Kiaron *See* Ciaran

Kidus An Ethiopian variant of Kudus, Arabic (from ghodos): holy

Kie *See* Khy

Kiean *See* Cianan

Kiefer Old German (from kuofa): barrel repairer, cooper (shifted from surname usage). Also possibly German: pine trees (name from flowers and trees)

Kiegan *See* Keagan

Kiel *See* Kyle

Kielan *See* Caelan

Kien Vietnamese: various, including understanding, perception

Kienan *See* Cianan

Kier A diminutive form of Keiran *See also* Kerr

Kieren *See* Ciaran and Kiron

Kiernan *See* Cianan

Kieron/Kierran *See* Ciaran and Kiron

Kile *See* Kyle

Kilian/Killian *See* Cillian

Kimani *See* Khamani

King (name from an English word)

Kingsley Old English: king's clearing (shifted from surname usage)

Kingston Old English: king's town. Various place names (geographical name)

Kinsley *See* Kingsley

Kion *See* Keyan

Kip A diminutive form of Kipling, Old English: from Cyppel (shifted from surname usage)

Kirill A Greek variant of Cyril

Kirk Old Norse (from kirkja): church

Kiron Hindi: beam, ray, light, spark. *See also* Girls and Boys: Kiran

Kishan/Kishen *See* Krishnan

Kitt From a surname form of Christopher (shifted from surname usage). *See also* Christopher

Kiyaan/Kiyan *See* Keyan

Klaidas A Lithuanian variant of Clyde

Klay *See* Clay

Klayton *See* Clayton

Klein Old German (from kleyne): small (shifted from surname usage)

Klevis Albanian (from klevas): maple (name from flowers and trees)

Knox Scottish Gaelic (from cnoc): hill (shifted from surname usage)

Kobe A city in Japan (geographical name). Also a diminutive form of Cobain

Kobey/Kobi/Kobie/Koby A diminutive form of Cobain

Kodey Irish: a descendant of Cuidightheach (shifted from surname usage). *See also* Girls and Boys: Codey

Koen *See* Coen

Kofi Akan: born on a Friday

Kohen *See* Coen

Kojo Akan: born on a Monday

Kolby *See* Coleby

Kole *See* Cole

Konna/Konner/Konnor *See* Connor

Konrad A German variant of Conrad

Konstantin A Czech, Croatian, German and Scandinavian variant of Constantine

Konstantinos A Greek variant of Constantine

Koray Turkish (from kor and ay): red moon. *See also* Corey

Korban/Korben/Korbin/Korbyn *See* Corban

Kordian The central character from the Polish writer Juliusz Słowacki's Kordian trilogy

Korey/Korie *See* Corey

Kornel A Hungarian variant of Cornelius

Kory *See* Corey

Kourosh A Persian variant of Cyrus

Kraig *See* Craig

Kray Russian (from kraj): border, edge, province, land

Kris A diminutive form of Kristofer

Krish A diminutive form of Krishna/Krishnan

Krishan The name of Guru Har Krishan, the eighth Sikh Guru. *See* Krishnan

Krishiv Unknown, possibly from the Hindu gods Krishna and Shiva

Krishnan Hindi (from karashn): black, dark blue. From the name of the blue-skinned Hindu god Krishna. *See also* Girls and Boys: Krishna

Kristan *See* Christian. *See also* Girls and Boys: Kristen

Kristers A Latvian variant of Christian

Kristian/Kristians *See* Christian

Kristofer/Kristofers/Kristoffer/Kristopher/Kristupas *See* Christopher

Krrish The superhero name of Krishna Mehra from the Krrish film series. *See also* Girls and Boys: Krishna

Kruz *See* Cruz

Kryspin *See* Crispin

Krystian A Polish variant of Christian

Krzysztof A Polish variant of Christopher

Ksawery/Ksawier A Polish variant of Xavier

Kuba A Polish diminutive form of Jacob

Kudakwashe Shona: god's will

Kumail *See* Kamal

Kunal Sanskrit (from kunala): a type of bird with beautiful eyes

Kurran Unknown, possibly from Curran, Irish Gaelic (from corradh): spear (shifted from surname usage)

Kurt A diminutive form of Conrad

Kurtis *See* Curtis

Kush An ancient kingdom, now modern day Sudan

Kushal Hindu: masterful, skillful

Kuzey Turkish: north, northern

Kwabena Akan: born on a Tuesday

Kwadwo Akan: born on a Monday

Kwaku Akan: born on a Wednesday

Kwame Akan: born on a Saturday

Kwasi Akan: born on a Sunday

Kweku *See* Kwaku

Kwesi *See* Kwasi

Ky Vietnamese: various, including flag

Kyal *See* Kyle

Kyan *See* Keyan

Kyden *See* Cadan

Kye Korean: various, including honest and sincere

Kyeran/Kyeron A modernised and shifted variant of Ciaran

Kyi A name for the Lhasa river (geographical name)

Kylan A modernised and shifted variant of Caelan

Kyle Scottish Gaelic: narrow, strait (shifted from surname usage)

Kylen A modernised and shifted variant of Caelan

Kyler A modernised and shifted variant of Tylor

Kymani/Kymarni *See* Kamari

Kynan A modernised and shifted variant of Cianan

Kyon Korean: various, including healthy and strong

Kyran A modernised and shifted variant of Ciaran

Kyreece A modernised and shifted variant of Rhys

Kyrell A modernised and shifted variant of Tyrrell

Kyren A modernised and shifted variant of Ciaran

Kyrese A modernised and shifted variant of Rhys

Kyriacos Greek (from kyrios): the lord

Kyro *See* Kyros

Kyron/Kyrone A modernised and shifted variant of Ciaran

Kyros A Greek variant of Cyrus

Kyson Unknown (shifted from surname usage)

L

Labeeb/Labib Arabic: intelligent, wise, prudent

Lachlan *See* Lochlann

Laighton *See* Layton

Laith Arabic: brave

Laiton *See* Layton

Lake (name from an English word)

Laksh Sanskrit (from laks): observe, understand, aim

Lamarr Arabic: liquid gold. Also Old French: from the sea. *See also* Girls and Boys: Lamar

Lamin A Gambian variant of Al-Amin

Lance (name from an English word). Also a diminutive form of Lancelot, a knight of King Arthur's Round Table

Landen/Landon Old English (from lang and don): long hill (shifted from surname usage)

Larry A diminutive form of Lawrence

Lars A Scandinavian variant of Lawrence

Laszlo A Hungarian variant of Vladislav

Latham Old Norse (from hlatha): barn (shifted from surname usage)

Lathan *See* Layton

Latif Arabic: gentle, kind, charming, sweet

Latrell Unknown, possibly from Luttrell, from Luttrellstown in Ireland (geographical name, shifted from surname usage)

Lauchlan *See* Lochlann

Laurence/Laurent Latin: from Laurentum, an ancient Roman city, or crowned with laurel

Lawand Unknown (shifted from surname usage)

Lawi Unknown, possibly from Lavi, Hebrew: lion. Also possibly from Levi, Minaean (from lawi'u): priest. *See also* Girls and Boys: Levi

Lawrence Latin: from Laurentum, an ancient Roman city, or crowned with laurel

Lawrie A diminutive form of Lawrence

Lawson Old English: son of Lawrence (shifted from surname usage)

Lawy Polish: lava. *See also* Lawi

Layden Unknown, possibly Old English (from leac and dun): vegetable hill (shifted from surname usage). *See also* Layton

Laylan Arabic: of the night

Layne Old English (from lanu): lane, passage (shifted from surname usage)

Layth *See* Laith

Layton Old English (from lad and tun): conduit town (shifted from surname usage). Also Old English (from leac and tun): vegetable town (shifted from surname usage). *See also* Girls and Boys: Leighton

Lealand *See* Leyland

Leam Old English: to shine. The name of a river in England (geographical name)

Leander/Leandro Greek: lion of a man

Leart Unknown, possibly an Albanian variant of Leonard

Lebron Old French (from le brun): the brown (shifted from surname usage). Used as a first name by the basketball player LeBron James

Ledion Unknown, possibly Albanian (from ledhatoj): caress

Leejay A blend of Lee and Jay

Leelan/Leeland *See* Leyland

Leeroy *See* Leroy

Leeson Old English: son of Lece, son of Laetitia (shifted from surname usage)

Leevi An Estonian variant of Levi, Minaean (from lawi'u): priest. *See also* Girls and Boys: Levi

Legend (name from an English word)

Leif Old Norse (from leifr): inheritor

Leiland *See* Leyland

Leith A district north of Edinburgh (geographical name, shifted from surname usage)

Lelan/Leland *See* Leyland

Lemar Unknown, possibly Old French (from le mare): the pond,

the pool (shifted from surname usage)

Lemuel Hebrew: devoted to god

Lennard *See* Leonard

Lenni/Lennie A diminutive form of Leonard

Lennon From Leannán, Irish Gaelic (from lennán): lover, sweatheart (shifted from surname usage). Also possibly Irish Gaelic (from lonán): blackbird (shifted from surname usage). Associated with The Beatles' member John Lennon

Lennox Old Gaelic (from leamhan and ach): elm field (shifted from surname usage)

Lenny A diminutive form of Leonard

Leo/Leon Greek: lion. *See also* Girls and Boys: Leone

Leonard/Leonardo Old German: brave lion

Leonel *See* Leon

Leonidas *See* Leonard

Leopold Old German: bold people

Leroy Old French (from le roi): the king (shifted from surname usage)

Leslie Scottish Gaelic (from leas and celyn): garden of holly (shifted from surname usage)

Lester From Leicester (geographical name, shifted from surname usage)

Lev A Czech variant of Leo

Levan Old French (from le vanier): the winnower (shifted from surname usage)

Levent/Levente Hungarian (from levente): knight

Levin Old English (from leof and wine): beloved friend (shifted from surname usage). Also possibly from the Levi line (shifted from surname usage). *See also* Girls and Boys: Levi

Levon An Armenian variant of Leo, used for many Armenian kings

Lewes Old English (from hlaews): hills (shifted from surname usage). A district in Sussex (geographical name)

Lewi/Lewie Minaean (from lawi'u): priest. *See also* Girls and Boys: Levi. *See also* Louis

Lewin *See* Levin

Lewis/Lewys An anglicised variant of Llywelyn. *See also* Louis

Lex A diminutive form of Alexander

Leylan/Leyland Old English (from laegeland): uncultivated land, untilled land (shifted from surname usage)

Leyton *See* Layton

Liam A diminutive form of Uilliam, which is an Irish variant of William

Liban Unknown, possibly from Lebanon. A Somalian name

Lincoln/Lincon Old English (from llyn and colonia): lake settlement (shifted from surname usage). A town in Lincolnshire (geographical name). Also associated with Abraham Lincoln

Linden/Lindon Old English: linden trees, lime trees (name from flowers and trees, shifted from surname usage)

Linkoln *See* Lincoln

Linton Old English (from lin and tun): flax town (shifted from surname usage)

Linus A son of the Greek god Apollo. Also the name of the second Pope

Lionel *See* Leo

Llewellyn/Llewelyn *See* Llywelyn

Lleyton *See* Layton

Llion A Welsh variant of Leon

Lloyd Welsh (from llwyd): grey (shifted from surname usage)

Llyr The father of Bran, the Welsh king who became the king of Britain. Also possibly from Lir, the Irish sea god

Llywelyn Celtic (from Lugus and Belinos): the Celtic Lugus and the Celtic sun god Belinos. The name of Llywelyn the Great

Lochlan/Lochlann Scottish Gaelic (from lochlann): land of lochs, usually referring to Scandinavia

Logen/Loghan/Logun Scottish Gaelic: little hollow. *See also* Girls and Boys: Logan

Loic A French variant of Louis

Loki The Norse trickster god

Lonnie A diminutive form of Alfonso

Lorcan Irish Gaelic (from lorc): land. From the Laigin group, descended from Lóegaire Lorc, a High King of Ireland

Lord (name from an English word)

Lorenzo An Italian and Spanish variant of Laurence

Lorik Armenian: quail

Loris An Italian variant of Laurence or Louis

Lorne From Lorraine, Old English: the Kingdom of Lothar, the kingdom of the famous army (shifted from surname usage). A district of Scotland (geographical name). Associated in Canada with Marquess of Lorne, who was the fourth British governer of Canada

Louey/Loui/Louie A diminutive form of Louis

Louis/Louix From Ludwig, Old German (from hlūd and wīg): famed warrior

Loukas A Greek variant of Luke

Lovell Old French (from lou): wolf, little wolf (shifted from surname usage)

Lowan From O'Luain (shifted from surname usage)

Lowell See Lovell

Luan An Albanian variant of Leo

Luay Pashto (from loy): great

Luc See Luke

Lucan Latin: from the Lucanus family, where the best known member is the poet Marcus Annaeus Lucanus

Lucas/Lucca See Luke

Lucian/Luciano/Lucien/Lucio/Lucius Latin: light

Lucus See Luke

Ludo A diminutive form of Ludovic

Ludovic A French variant of Louis

Lui A Hawaiian variant of Louis

Luigi An Italian variant of Louis

Luis A Portuguese and Spanish variant of Louis

Lukas See Luke

Lukasz A Belgium variant of Lukas

Luke Latin: from Lucania, a place in Italy

Luke the Evangelist was a disciple of Paul, and is symbolised by the winged ox. Also the name of Luke Skywalker, making it possible to use the line, 'I am your father'

Lukman/Luqmaan/Luqman The name of the sage Luqman The Wise who features in the 31st chapter of the Qur'an

Luther Old French (from lutier): lute player (shifted from surname usage). Associated with Martin Luther

Lyall Unknown, possibly from Old Norse (from li ulfr): wolf. See also Leo and Lyle

Lyam See Liam

Lydon Old English (from hlyde and dun): loud hill (shifted from surname usage)

Lyle Old French (from l'isle): isle (shifted from surname usage)

Lynden/Lyndon *See* Linden

Lyon Old French: lion. Also a city in France (geographical name)

Lysander Unknown, possibly Greek (from lysis and andros): loosening, release, freeing a man. A Spartan general. Also a character from Shakespeare's *A Midsummer Night's Dream*

m

Maahir *See* Maher

Maalik *See* Malik

Maaz Persian (from maz): twist, maze
Also from Maas, the Dutch name for the river Meuse (geographical name, shifted from surname usage)
Also possibly Arabic (from maz-hab): faith, religion

Mabon The name of Mabon ap Modron, a Welsh warrior who fought with King Arthur
Also possibly from the Celtic god Maponos, Gaulish (from mapos): young boy, divine son

Mac Irish and Scottish Gaelic: son of
Also a diminutive form of Max

Macaulay/Macaulee/Macauley/Macaulley/Macaully/Macauly
From Mac Amhalghaidh, Scottish

Gaelic (from amhach and gad/ghaidh): part of a twig (shifted from surname usage)

Mace (name from an English word)

Maciej A Polish variant of Matthew/Matthias

Mack *See* Mac

MacKai From Mac Aodha, Old Gaelic: fire (shifted from surname usage)

Mackinley From Mac Fhionnlaigh, Scottish Gaelic (from fionn and laoch): fair warrior (shifted from surname usage)

Macorley *See* Macaulay

Macsen A Welsh variant of Maximus

Maddox Welsh: son of Madoc

Madhav Sanskrit (from madhava): sweetness, spring
A name for the Hindu god Krishna

Madoc Welsh: fortunate
The name of a legendary Welsh prince who sailed all the way to America

Mael Breton: prince

Maeson *See* Mason

Magnus Latin: great

Mahad Sanskrit (from mahada): leading to greatness

Mahamad/Mahamed/Mahammad/Mahammed *See* Muhammad

Mahbub Arabic (from mahboob): beloved, darling, friend

Mahd Arabic: praising
See also Mahmood and
Muhammad

Mahdi A redeemer in Islam
who will rule before the Day of
Judgment
See also Mahd

Mahee Sanskrit (from mahi): heaven
and earth
Also possibly from the name
of Mahé de La Bourdonnais, a
French naval officer who named
the town Mahé in India
See also Girls and Boys: Maahi

Maher Arabic: skillful, expert

Mahesh Sanskrit (from maheza):
great lord
A name for the Hindu god Shiva

Mahfuz An Ethiopian and Somalian
variant of Muhammed, from a
ruler in historical Ethiopia

Mahid See Mahd

Mahin Sanskrit: might, great

Mahir See Maher

**Mahmood/Mahmoud/Mahmud/
Mahomed**
Arabic (from madh and hamd):
praising
See also Madh and Muhammad

Maison French: house, home
(shifted from surname usage)

Majd/Majed/Majid Arabic (from
majd): greatness, glory

Makai Hawaiian: towards the sea,
side of the ocean

Maks A diminutive form of Maksim

Maksim A Russian variant of
Maximus

Maksims A Latvian variant of
Maximus

Maksym A Ukranian variant of
Maximus

Maksymilian A Polish variant of
Maximilian

**Malachai/Malachi/Malachy/
Malakai/Malakhi/Malaki/
Malakie/Malakye** Hebrew: my
messenger
A Jewish prophet

Malcolm From Mael Coluim,
Scottish Gaelic: devotee of Saint
Columba, Latin: dove

Maleek/Malick/Malik Arabic:
master, angel, king
Al-Malik is one of Allah's 99
names, meaning King, and reciting
it helps to gain wealth and esteem
See also Girls and Boys: Malek

Malikai/Maliki A follower of the
scholar Malik ibn Anas
See also Malachai and Malik

Malin From Mallinson, Old
English: son of Mary (shifted from
surname usage)

Maliq/Malique See Malik

Malkit Punjabi: master (Sikh name)

Malvin See Melvin

Mamadou A West African variant
of Muhammad

Man Arabic: benefit
Also Punjabi: mind (Sikh name)

Manas Punjabi: human (Sikh name)

Also Sanskrit: intelligence, thought, desire

Manav Hindi: man, person

Mani Sanskrit: precious stone, jewel
Also Old Norse: moon
Also the name of an Iranian prophet who founded Manichaeism

Maninder *See* Manvinder

Manish Sanskrit (from manisa): idea, thought, wisdom

Manjinder *See* Manvinder

Mannan A Manx sea god who can protect the Isle of Man from invaders

Manni/Manny A diminutive form of Emanuel

Manraj Punjabi: king of the mind (Sikh name)

Mansoor/Mansour/Mansur Arabic (from nasr): victory, helping to victory

Mantas Lithuanian (from manta): property, belonging

Manu Sanskrit: wise, intelligent, prayer, mankind
The Hindu title for the king who saved mankind from the flood
Also a diminutive form of Emanuel

Manuel *See* Emanuel

Manus An Irish variant of Magnus

Manveer Punjabi: bravery of the mind (Sikh name)

Manvinder Punjabi: lord of the mind (Sikh name)

Manvir *See* Manveer

Marc A French variant of Mark

Marcel/Marcell A French variant of Marcellus

Marcello An Italian variant of Marcellus

Marcellus Latin: of Mars
The name of several Roman generals and a saint

Marcelo A Portuguese and Spanish variant of Marcellus

Marcin A Polish variant of Martin

Marco An Italian variant of Mark

Marcos A Spanish variant of Mark

Marcus *See* Mark

Marek A Czech, Estonian and Polish variant of Mark

Mario An Italian and Spanish variant of Mark

Marios A Greek variant of Marius

Marius Unknown, possibly Latin: of Mars, the Roman god of war
See also Mark

Mariusz A Polish variant of Marius

Mark Latin: of Mars, the Roman god of war

Markas An Irish variant of Mark
See also Marius

Marko An Estonian, Finnish, German and Serbian variant of Mark

Markus A Danish, German and Scandinavian variant of Mark

Markuss A Latvian variant of Mark

Marlo *See* Marlow

Marlon Old English (from mor and

land): marsh land (shifted from surname usage)

Marlow/Marlowe Old English (from merr and lafe): remains of a lake (shifted from surname usage)

Marques Old French: marquis (shifted from surname usage)

Marshal/Marshall Old German (from marah and scalc): horse servant (shifted from surname usage)

Martell Old French (from martel): war hammer (shifted from surname usage)

Marti An Estonian variant of Martin
Also a diminutive form of Martin

Martim A place in Portugual (geographical name)
See also Martin

Martin Latin: warlike

Martins Old English: son of Martin (shifted from surname usage)

Marty A diminutive form of Martin

Martyn A Manx variant of Martin

Martynas A Lithuanian variant of Martin

Maruf Arabic (from ma'ruf): known, accepted, acknowledged

Marvin An anglicised variant of Mervyn

Marwan Arabic (from marmar): marble

Masen/Mason Old French (from masson): stone mason (shifted from surname usage)

Massimiliano An Italian variant of Maximilian

Massimo An Italian variant of Maximus

Masud Arabic (from mas-ood): happy, prosperous, fortunate

Matas A Lithuanian variant of Matthew/Matthias

Mateen Arabic: firm, strong, cool

Matei A Romanian variant of Matthew/Matthias

Matej A Bulgarian, Czech and Slovakian variant of Matthew/Matthias

Mateo A Spanish variant of Matthew/Matthias

Mateus A Portuguese variant of Matthew/Matthias

Mateusz A Polish variant of Matthew/Matthias

Matheo A Spanish variant of Matthew/Matthias

Matheus A Portuguese variant of Matthew/Matthias

Mathew A Welsh variant of Matthew

Mathias A French and German variant of Matthew/Matthias

Mathieu/Mathis A French variant of Matthew/Matthias

Matias A Spanish and Portuguese variant of Matthew/Matthias

Matin *See* Mateen

Matt A diminutive form of Matthew/Matthias

Matteo An Italian variant of

Matthew/Matthias

Matthew Hebrew: gift of god
A saint who was one of the
original twelve apostles
See also Matthias

Matthias Hebrew: gift of god
A saint and an apostle chosen to
be the twelfth after the betrayal of
Judas
See also Matthew

Matthieu A French variant of
Matthew/Matthias

Matti A Finnish variant of
Matthew/Matthias

Mattia An Italian variant of
Matthew/Matthias

Mattias A Scandinavian variant of
Matthew/Matthias

Matty A diminutive form of
Matthew and Matthias. *See also*
Girls and Boys: Mattie

Matus A Slovakian variant of
Matthew/Matthias

Matvey A Russian variant of
Matthew/Matthias

Matyas A Czech and Hungarian
variant of Matthew/Matthias

Maurice Latin (from mauros): dark,
Moorish (shifted from surname
usage)

Mauricio A Spanish variant of
Maurice

Mauro An Italian, Portuguese and
Spanish variant of Maurice

Maverick (name from an English
word). From Samuel Maverick,
who refused to brand his cattle,
giving rise to the English word
'maverick' (shifted from surname
usage)

Mawgan The name of a Cornish and
Welsh saint

Max A diminutive form of Maximus
and Maximilian

Maxen A Welsh variant of Maximus

Maxi A diminutive form of
Maximus and Maximilian

Maxim A Czech variant of
Maximus

Maximilian The name of several
Roman emperors and Bavarian
kings. *See* Maximus

Maximiliano A Spanish variant of
Maximilian

Maximilien A French variant of
Maximilian

Maximillian/Maximillion *See*
Maximillian

Maximo A Spanish variant of
Maximus

Maximos A Greek variant of
Maximus

Maximus Latin: the greatest. *See
also* Girls and Boys: Maxime

Maxton Unknown, possibly Old
English: town of Mark/Max.
The name of a Scottish clan
(shifted from surname usage)

Maxwell Old English: well of
Magnus (shifted from surname
usage)

Maxx A diminutive form of

Maximus and Maximilian

Maxymilian *See* Maximillian

Mayan From the Maya civilisation.
Also several place names in Iran
(geographical name)

Mayank Hindi (from mayanak):
moon

Mayson *See* Maison and Mason

Mayur Hindi: peacock

Mazen *See* Mazin

Mazhar Arabic (from maz-har):
manifestation, apparition

Mazin Arabic: rain clouds

Mcauley/Mccauley/Mccawley *See*
Macaulay

Mckenzi Unknown, possibly from
Mac Coinnich, Irish Gaelic (from
cáennach): mildrew (shifted from
surname usage). *See also* Girls and
Boys: MacKenzie

Mckinley *See* Mackinley

Mckye *See* MacKai

Meer Arabic: chief, prince. Also
Dutch: late (shifted from surname
usage). *See also* Girls and Boys:
Mir

Mehdi *See* Mahdi

Mehmet A Turkish variant of
Muhammad

Mehrab Arabic: santuary, altar, a
niche in a mosque

Mehran Persian (from mehr):
kindness. Also from the Persian
god Mithra

Mehtab Persian (from mahtab):
moonlight

Mehul Hindi (from madhu/
madhur): honey, sweet

Meir Hebrew: light, illuminating

Mekhi Georgian (from mekhis):
thunderbolt. Also possibly from
Mekki, an Arabic surname (shifted
from surname usage)

Melchior Persian: king's city. The
name of one of the Three Wise
Men. *See also* Balthazar and
Caspar

Melvin/Melvyn From Malleville
(Latin and Old French, from mala
and ville: bad town; shifted from
surname usage)

Menachem Hebrew: comforter
A king of Israel

Mendel Old German (from mann):
man, grown man (shifted from
surname usage)

Mendy A diminutive form of
Mendel

Menelik The first emperor of
Ethiopia, known as Ibn Al-Hakim,
Son of the Wise One, in Arabic

Mergim Albanian: exile, emigration

Merlin The wizard from Arthurian
legends. *See also* Marlon

Merrick A Welsh variant of Maurice

Mert Turkish: brave, manly,
trustworthy, dependable

Mervyn Unknown, possibly Welsh
(from mor and gwyn): fair sea

Meshach Unknown, possibly a
Hebrew variant of a Babylonian
name. A man saved from a furnice

by god, along with Shadrach and Abednego. *See also* Shadrach

Messi The surname of Lionel Messi (footballer name)

Mete A Turkish variant of Modu, the name of Modu Chanyu, an emperor of the Hunnus Empire, based around modern day Mongolia

Metin Turkish: strong, dependable

Mian Persian: with a slender waist A historical title of nobility among Pakistani Muslims

Micaiah Hebrew: who is like Jehovah. A prophet who warns king Ahab not to go into battle

Miceal An Irish and Scottish variant of Michael

Michael Hebrew: who is like god. *See also* Girls and Boys: Michele

Micheal An Irish and Scottish variant of Michael

Michee A French variant of Micah, Hebrew: who is like Jehovah. *See also* Micaiah

Michel A Dutch and French variant of Michael

Mickey/Mickie/Micky A diminutive form of Michael

Mieszko Polish (from miecz): sword

Miguel A Portuguese and Spanish variant of Michael

Mihai A Romanian variant of Michael

Mihail A Greek variant of Michael

Mihir Sanskrit (from mihira): sun

Mihran *See* Mehran

Mikaeel An Arabic variant of Michael

Mikael A Danish, Finnish and Swedish variant of Michael

Mikail/Mika'il A Turkish variant of Michael

Mikayeel An Arabic variant of Michael

Mike A diminutive form of Michael

Mikel A Basque variant of Michael

Mikey A diminutive form of Michael

Mikhael A Greek and Turkish variant of Michael

Mikhail A Russian variant of Michael

Mikie A diminutive form of Michael

Mikkel A Danish and Norwegian variant of Michael

Mikolaj A Polish variant of Nicholas

Miks A Latvian diminutive form of Michael

Mikyle A blend of Kyle and Michael

Milad Arabic (from mee-lad): birth, nativity

Miles Unknown, possibly Latin: soldier. Also possibly an Old English variant of Michael. *See also* Milos and Milosz

Millan From Mac Maolain, Scottish Gaelic (from maol): bare, blunt (shifted from surname usage). *See also* Miller

Millar *See* Miller

Millen *See* Millan

Miller Latin (from molere): to grind (shifted from surname usage)

Milo A French variant of Miles

Milos A Czech and Hungarian variant of Milosz. Also the name of the Greek island with a famous statue of Aphrodite, so also associated with love (geographical name)

Milosz Polish (from miłość): love

Milton From Middeltone, Old English (middel and tun): middle town (shifted from surname usage) Associated with the poet John Milton

Min Chinese: various, including peaceful and quick-witted

Minesh Sanskrit (from manasi): spiritual devotion

Minh Vietnamese: various, including bright

Minhaj/Minhaz Arabic: way, method

Miraj The place where prophet Muhammad ascends heaven

Miran The name of Miran Shah, son of the ruler Timur

Miro A diminutive form of Miroslav. Also Spanish (from mirar): to look (shifted from surname usage). Associated with the artist Joan Miró

Miron Unknown (shifted from surname usage). *See also* Miran

Miroslav Slavic (from mir and slava): glory of peace

Mirza Persian: noble, prince

Mitch A diminutive form of Mitchell

Mitchel/Mitchell From Michael (shifted from surname usage)

Mitesh Unknown, possibly Sanskrit (from matsya): king

Mitul Sanskrit (from matula): thorn-apple (name from flowers and trees). Also possibly Sanskrit (from madhula): sweet, honey

Mkenzie *See* McKenzi

Mobeen Arabic (from mobin): clear, doubtless, true

Modou A Gambian diminutive form of Muhammad

Moeez *See* Muiz

Mohamad/Mohamed *See* Muhammad

Mohamedamin A blend of Muhammad and Amin

Mohammad/Mohammed/ Mohammod/Mohamod/ Mohamoud/Mohamud *See* Muhammad

Mohan Sanskrit (from mohana): handsome. A name for the Hindu god Krishna

Mohanad Arabic: sword

Mohd *See* Mahd

Mohib/Mohid Arabic (from moheeb): formidable, revered

Mohit Hindi: entranced

Mohmed/Mohmmad/Mohmmed *See* Mahmood

Mohsan/Mohsen/Mohsin Arabic (from mohsen): kind, beneficent

Moin Arabic (from moeen): helper, supported

Moise A French variant of Moses

Moishe A Yiddish variant of Moses

Moiz See Muiz

Momin Arabic (from mo'men): believer, faithful

Momodou A Gambian variant of Muhammad

Moneeb Arabic: repenter

Montague Old French (from mont and agu): steep and pointed hill (shifted from surname usage). Associated with the House of Montague from Shakespeare's *Romeo and Juliet*

Montel/Montell Old French (from mont): hill (shifted from surname usage)

Montgomery From Mont Gomery, where Gomery is from Old German (from guma and ric): power of man (shifted from surname usage)

Monty A diminutive form of Montague and Montgomery

Moosa An Arabic variant of Moses

Moray A council in Scotland (geographical name). *See also* Murray

Mordechai A man from the Israeli Tribe of Benjamin

Moritz A German variant of Maurice

Morley Old English (from mor and leah): marsh clearing (shifted from surname usage)

Morris See Maurice

Morten Old English (from mor and tun): marsh town (shifted from surname usage)

Mortimer Unknown, possibly Old French: dead sea. Also possibly from a Norman place name (shifted from surname usage)

Moses/Moshe Hebrew: to draw, draw out of the water. The leader of the Exodus and the one who received the Ten Commandments

Mostafa See Mustafa

Mouhamed See Muhammad

Mousa/Moussa An Arabic variant of Moses

Muaad See Muadh

Muaaz See Muaz

Muad/Muadh/Mu'adh Arabic: protected

Muaz Arabic: powerful, strong

Mubarak/Mubarik Arabic (from barakat): blessed one

Mubashir Arabic (from basheer): one who bears good news

Mubeen See Mobeen

Mudassar Arabic: covered, wrapped, enveloped

Mueez See Muiz

Mufaro Shona: happy, joyful man

Muhaimin A blend of Muhammad and Amin

Muhamad/Muhamed/

Muhammad/Muhammed/ Muhammet/Muhammod Arabic: praiseworthy. The name of prophet Muhammad, the last prophet in Islam. *See also* Madh and Mahmood

Muhanad *See* Mohanad

Muhibur *See* Mohib

Muhmmad *See* Muhammad

Muhsin *See* Mohsan

Muir Scottish Gaelic: sea (shifted from surname usage)

Muiz/Muizz Arabic (from moeez): glorifying, giving honour. Al-Mu'izz is one of Allah's 99 names, meaning Giver of Honour, and reciting it is believed to help increase dignity

Mujahid Arabic (from jahd): struggling ones, those who struggle in the path to god

Mujtaba *See* Mustafa

Mukhtar Arabic (from mokh-tar): free, independent, chosen

Mumin *See* Momin

Munachimso Igbo: god is always with me

Munasar Arabic: friendly

Munashe From Manasseh, Hebrew: make forget. A king of Judah

Muneeb *See* Moneeb

Mungo A saint associated with Glasgow

Munib *See* Moneeb

Munir Arabic (from moneer): shining, bright.

Munro Unknown, possibly from Maolruadh, Scottish Gaelic (from maol): bare, blunt. Also the name for very high mountains in Scotland (geographical name)

Munyaradzi Shona: comforter

Murad Arabic (from morad): desire, wish, idea, purpose

Murat A Turkish variant of Murad

Murdo Also a type of very high mountain in Scotland, associated with Munros (geographical name)

Murphy From Murchadha, Irish Gaelic (from muir and cathar): sea warrior

Murray Unknown, possibly Old English: merry. Also possibly Old English: son of Mary (shifted from surname usage)

Murtaza Arabic: chosen one. A name for the prophet Muhammad. *See also* Mustafa

Musa An Arabic variant of Moses

Musab/Mus'ab The name of Mus'ab ibn Umair, one of prophet Muhammad's companions

Mussa An Arabic variant of Moses

Mustaf/Mustafa/Mustafaa/ Mustafe/Mustapha Arabic: chosen one. A name for the prophet Muhammad. *See also* Murtaza

Mutasim Arabic: abstaining from sin

Muzamil/Muzammil/Muzzammil Arabic: the mantled one. The 73rd

chapter of the Qur'an

Myles *See* Miles

Mylo *See* Milo

Myron *See* Miron

n

Nabeel/Nabil Arabic: noble

Nadeem Arabic: companion, close friend

Nader Arabic: rare, unusual

Nadim *See* Nadeem

Nadir *See* Nader

Naeem Arabic: blessing, happiness, peace, bliss

Nael *See* Niall

Nafees/Nafis Arabic: precious, exquisite, fine

Naftali/Naftoli Hebrew: my struggle. A son of Jacob

Naglis The name of a dragon in Lithuanian mythology who was in love with the giantess Neringa

Naheem *See* Naim

Nahid Persian (from na-heed): from Venus

Nahim *See* Naim

Nahom *See* Nahum

Nahshon Hebrew: snake-bird. A descendent of Judah who was the first to brave the Red Sea during Exodus

Nahum Hebrew: comforting. A prophet who foretold the fall of the Assyrian Empire

Naim Arabic (from na-eem): delight, pleasure

Nairn The name of a Scottish town (geographical name, shifted from surname usage)

Naitik Sanskrit (from naitika): moral

Najeeb/Najib Arabic: noble, gentle, chaste, pure

Nali The pen name of a famous Kurdish poet, taken from the name of a traditional flute

Nam Vietnamese: various, including boy, man

Naman Sanskrit: name, true nature

Nandan Sanskrit (from nandana): rejoicing, son. The name of the garden owned by the Hindu god Indra

Naod The name of Dil Na'od, an Ethiopian king

Naqeeb Arabic (from nagheeb): chief, leader

Narayan/Naryan A name for the Hindu god Vishnu, representing the first man

Nasar Persian: in the shade (shifted from surname usage). Also Arabic (from nasr): eagle. *See also* Nasir

Naseem Arabic: breeze, zephyr

Nash Old English (from aesc): ash tree (name from flowers and trees, shifted from surname usage)

Nashaun A blend of Nathan and Shaun

Nasif Arabic (from nazeef): clean,

pure

Nasim *See* Naseem

Nasir Arabic (from naser): assister, defender. An-Nasir is an additional name to Allah's 99 names, meaning Helper

Nasri Arabic (from nasr): helping to victory

Nasser *See* Nasar and Nasir

Nassim *See* Naseem

Nassir *See* Nasir

Natan A Yiddish variant of Nathan

Natanael/Nataniel *See* Nathaniel

Nate A diminutive form of Nathan and Nathaniel

Nathan Hebrew: gift, given

Nathanael/Nathanial/Nathaniel Hebrew (from nathan and el): gift of god

Nathen A diminutive form of Nathaniel

Natnael An Arabic variant of Nathaniel

Nauman From Neumann, Old German: new man (shifted from surname usage)

Navdeep Punjabi: lamp of the new (Sikh name)

Naveed Persian (from noveed): good news

Naveen Punjabi: ever new (Sikh name)

Navid *See* Naveed

Navin *See* Naveen

Navjot Punjabi: light of the new (Sikh name)

Navraj Punjabi: king of the new (Sikh name)

Nawaf Arabic: high, elevated

Nayan Sanskrit (from nayana): guiding, leading, eye

Nayeem/Nayim *See* Naim

Nazam Arabic (from nazm): orderly

Nazim *See* Naseem and Nazam

Nazir Arabic (from nazeer): parallel, alike. *See also* Nasir

Nazmul Arabic (from najm): star

Neal An anglicised variant of Niall

Ned A diminutive form of Edward

Nedas Unknown (shifted from surname usage). Also possibly Arabic (from neda): calling, proclamation

Neeko A diminutive form of Nicholas

Neel Sanskrit (from nil): dark, indigo, blue. *See also* Niall

Neeraj *See* Niraj

Nehan Persian: secret

Nehemiah Hebrew: comfort of Jehovah. The cup-bearer for a Persian king who led the rebuilding of the walls of Jerusalem

Neil An anglicised variant of Niall

Nelson Old English: son of Niall (shifted from surname usage)

Neo Greek (from neos): new, young

Nestor Unknown, possibly Ancient Greek (from nostos): coming home. A Greek king who appears in *The Iliad* as an old and wise warrior

Netanel A Yiddish variant of Nathaniel

Nevan Irish Gaelic (from noíbán): saint

Neville Old French (from neuf and ville): new settlement (shifted from surname usage)

Nevin *See* Nevan

Newton Old English (from neowa and tun): new town (shifted from surname usage). Associated with Isaac Newton

Neyo The stage name of the musician Shaffer Smith, known as Ne-Yo, from the name Neo, as a reference to *The Matrix*

Nial/Niall Unknown, possibly Irish Gaelic (from nia): warrior. Also possibly Irish Gaelic (from nel): cloud

Niam Unknown, possibly from Niamh, Irish Gaelic: bright, radiant

Niaz Persian: prayer, gift, dedication

Niccolo/Nicholas Greek: victory of the people

Nick A diminutive form of Nicholas

Nickolas/Nicolae/Nicolai/ Nicolas/Nicolo *See* Nicholas

Nidal Arabic: fight, struggle, effort

Niels A Danish variant of Nicholas

Nigel An anglicised variant of Niall

Nii Ga: king

Nik Persian (from neek): good, positive. Also a diminutive form of Nicholas

Nikesh Unknown, possibly from Nilesh, Sanskrit (from nil and iz): dark, indigo, blue lord. A name for the Hindu god Krishna

Nikhil Sanskrit (from nikhila): entire, complete, whole

Niklas A Danish, German, Finnish and Swedish variant of Nicholas

Niko A German diminutive form of Nicholas

Nikodem A German variant of Nicodemus, Ancient Greek (from niko and demos): victorious people. A saint mentioned in the Gospel of John

Nikolai A Danish, Finnish and Norwegian variant of Nicholas

Nikolaos/Nikolas A Greek variant of Nicholas

Nikolay A Russian variant of Nicholas

Nikos A diminutive form of Nikolaos

Nile The name of the African river (geographical name). *See also* Niall

Niles From Niall (shifted from surname usage)

Nils A diminutive form of Niklas and Nikolai

Nino Spanish (from niño): boy. Also a diminutive form of Giovanni

Niraj Sanskrit: shine, illuminate. Also Sanskrit (from niraja): lotus, pearl

Nirav Sanskrit (from nirava): quiet, tranquil

Nishaan/Nishan Hindi: mark,

token, flag, trace

Nishant Hindi (from nishanat): dawn, daybreak, sunrise

Nishil *See* Nikhil

Nitesh Sanskrit (from nita and iz): lord of the guided, lord of the right

Niyam Sanskrit (from niyama): law, rule, vow

Niyaz *See* Niaz

Nizar Unknown, possibly Persian (from nezar): lean, thin

Nnamdi Igbo: my father is living

Noah Unknown, possibly Hebrew: rest. Also possibly Hebrew: comfort. The one instructed by God to build the ark before the Flood

Noam Hebrew: pleasant, gracious

Noble (name from an English word)

Noe A French, Italian and Spanish variant of Noah

Noel French: Christmas

Nojus A Lithuanian variant of Noah

Nokutenda Shona: with thanks

Nolan From O'Nuallain, Irish Gaelic (from núallán): loud cryer, loud roarer (shifted from surname usage). Also possibly Irish Gaelic (from núall): famous, noble, champion

Nomaan/Noman *See* Numan

Norbert Old German (from nord and berht): brightness of the north

Norman Old English: men of the North (shifted from surname usage). Also possibly Old French:

men from Normandy

Norton Old English: northern town (shifted from surname usage)

Nu An Arabic variant of Noah

Numaan *See* Numan

Numair Arabic: panther

Numan Al-Nu'man is the family name of several kings of Hirah, in modern day Iraq. Also Al-Nu'man ibn Muqrin was one of prophet Muhammad's companions

Nuno Unknown, possibly Latin (from nonnus): monk, squire, tutor

Nyal/Nyall *See* Niall

Nye From Atteneye, Old English (from aet and thaem and ea): at the river (shifted from surname usage)

Nyle *See* Niall

O

Oak (name from flowers and trees, name from an English word)

Obaid Arabic: small slave

Oban Scottish Gaelic: little bay. Also a town in Scotland (geographical name)

Obed Hebrew: servant, worshipper

Obi/Obie Igbo: heart

Obinna Igbo: father's heart, god's heart

Octavian Latin: eight, from the Octavius family, most notably of Gaius Octavius, emperor Augustus

Odhran Irish Gaelic: pale green.

Also Scottish Gaelic (from odhar):
pale

Odin Old Norse: fury, frenzy, poetry,
mind, inspiration. One of the
major gods in Norse mythology,
associated with war, wisdom,
prophecy and poetry

Oguzhan Turkish (from oğuz and
han): khan of the Oguz Turks,
king of the young bull, king of the
honest man

Oisin Irish Gaelic: little deer

Ojas Sanskrit: vigour, strength,
power, lustre

Okan Turkish: insightful,
understanding

Oladimeji Yoruba: two riches
combined

Olaf Old Norse: descendent of the
ancestors

Olamilekan Yoruba: my wealth has
been increased

Olanrewaju Yoruba: my wealth is
moving forward

Olaoluwa Yoruba: god's wealth

Ole *See* Olaf

Oli A diminutive form of Oliver

**Oliver/Olivers/Olivier/Oliwer/
Oliwier** Old French: olive tree
(name from flowers and trees).
See also Olaf

Olley/Olli A diminutive form of
Oliver

Olliver *See* Oliver

Olly A diminutive form of Oliver

Olufemi *See* Oluwaferanmi

Olumide Yoruba: god has come

Oluwadamilare Yoruba: god has
vindicated me

Oluwafemi *See* Oluwaferanmi

Oluwaferanmi Yoruba: god loves
me

Oluwakorede Yoruba: god has
brought me goodness

Oluwamayowa Yoruba: god has
brought us joy

Oluwatimilehin/Oluwatimileyin
Yoruba: god is supporting me

Oluwatomiwa Yoruba: god searched
for me

Oluwatosin Yoruba: god is worthy
to be served

Om Sanskrit: a syllable that is sacred
in Buddism and Hinduism

Omair/Omar Hebrew: sheaf of
wheat

Omari/Omario/Omarion *See*
Umar

Omed/Omeed Persian: hope

Omer *See* Umar

Omid *See* Omed

Ondrej *See* Andrew

Oneil From O'Neil/O'Niall, son of
Niall (shifted from surname usage)
See also Niall

Onkar Punjabi: one supreme reality,
god's name (Sikh name)

Onur Turkish: honour

Oran An anglicised variant of
Odhran. *See also* Oren

Oren Hebrew: pine tree

Orestas Greek (from orestias):

from the mountain, conquerer of mountains. A variant of Orestes, the son of Agamemnon in Greek mythology who killed his mother to avenge his father

Orhan Turkish: judge

Orin An anglicised variant of Odhran. *See also* Oran

Orion Ancient Greek: heaven's light A hunter who was killed by Artemis in Greek mythology, then turned into the constellation

Orlando A city in Florida (geographical name). *See also* Roland

Orrin An anglicised variant of Odhran. *See also* Oran

Orry From Wulfric, Old English: power of a wolf (shifted from surname usage)

Orson Unknown, possible Latin (from ursus): bear

Osama/Osamah *See* Usama

Osayande Edo: god owns the world, god owns the day

Osca/Oscar Irish Gaelic (from os and cara): friend of deer

O'Shea Unknown, possibly Old English (from sceaga): wood (shifted from surname usage). *See also* Girls and Boys: Shea

Osher Hebrew: happy, blessing. *See also* Girls and Boys: Asher

Osian *See* Oisin

Oska/Oskar/Oskaras *See* Oscar

Osman/Ossama *See* Usama

Ossian *See* Oisin

Oswald Old English (from ōs and weald): god's power

Othman *See* Usama

Othniel Hebrew: lion of god

Otis/Otto Old German: riches, wealth

Ousman/Oussama *See* Usama

Owain A Welsh variant of Eoghan

Owais *See* Uwais

Owen/Owyn An anglicised variant of Owain

Oz A diminutive form of Osborne, Oscar and Oswald

Ozair *See* Uzair

Ozan Turkish: poet, minstrel

Ozzie/Ozzy A diminutive form of Osborne, Oscar and Oswald

P

Pa A diminutive form of Papa

Pablo A Spanish variant of Paul

Pacey Unknown, possibly from Pacey in Normandy (shifted from surname usage)

Paddy A diminutive form of Padraic and Patrick

Padraic/Padraig An Irish variant of Patrick

Panagiotis Greek (from panagia): all holy

Panayiotis *See* Panagiotis

Paolo An Italian variant of Paul

Papa Latin: bishop, pope (shifted from surname usage)

Param Punjabi: supreme (Sikh name)

Paramveer/Paramvir Punjabi: supremely brave, supreme warrior (Sikh name)

Paras Sanskrit: beyond, in the future

Pardeep Punjabi: mystical light (Sikh name)

Parker Old English: park-keeper (shifted from surname usage)

Parmeet Punjabi: mystical friend, friend of the mystic (Sikh name)

Parmveer *See* Paramveer

Parsa Persian: pious

Parth Sanskrit (from partha): prince. One of the names of the Hindu hunter and hero Arjuna

Pascal Latin (from pascha): Easter

Pasha Turkish: lord

Patric/Patrick/Patrik/Patryk Latin (from patricius): patrician, noble

Paul From Paulus, Latin: few, little, small. The name of the saint, Paul the Apostle

Paulius A Lithuanian variant of Paul

Paulo A Portuguese variant of Paul

Pauric *See* Padraig

Pavan Punjabi: sacred, pure, holy (Sikh name)

Pavandeep Punjabi: sacred light (Sikh name)

Pavel A Czech, Estonian and Russian variant of Paul

Pavlos A Greek variant of Paul

Pawan *See* Pavan

Pawel A Polish variant of Paul

Peadar An Irish and Scottish variant of Peter

Pearce/Pearse A variant of Peter, initially used as a surname (shifted from surname usage)

Pedro A Portuguese and Spanish variant of Peter

Pele The nickname of the legendary footballer Edison Arantes do Nascimento (footballer name)

Peniel Hebrew: face of god. A place east of Jordan where Jacob visited (geographical name)

Percival The name of a knight from King Arthur's round table who went on the quest for the Holy Grail

Percy A diminutive form of Percival

Perez Spanish: son of Pedro (shifted from surname usage)

Perran *See* Piran

Petar A Croatian variant of Peter

Peter Latin (from petrus): rock

Petr A Czech variant of Peter

Petros A Greek variant of Peter

Pharell/Pharrell *See* Farrell

Phelan From Ó Faoláin, Irish Gaelic (from fáel): wolf (shifted from surname usage)

Phelim The name of an Irish saint

Phil A diminutive form of Philip

Philip/Philipp/Philippe/Phillip Greek: friend of horses

Phineas Unknown, possibly Ancient Egyptian: bronze-coloured. The name of a king of Thrace in Greek mythology. Also the name of a priest who is the grandson of Aaron

Piaras An Irish variant of Pearce

Pierce *See* Pearce

Pierre A French variant of Peter

Piers *See* Pearce

Pieter A Dutch variant of Peter

Pietro An Italian variant of Peter

Pijus Lithuanian: pious

Pinchas/Pinchos *See* Phineas

Piotr A Polish variant of Peter

Pip A diminutive form of Philip

Piran The name of a Cornish saint whose day falls on 5th March

Piyush Hindi: nectar, holy water

Pol A Catalan and Dutch variant of Paul

Pranav Sanskrit (from pranava): the sound of 'om'. A sacred sound in Hinduism and Buddhism

Pranay Hindi: love

Prashant Hindi (from prashanat): tranquil, calm

Pratham Hindi: first

Pratik Sanskrit (from pratika): symbol, token

Praveen/Pravin Sanskrit (from pravini): be skillful

Prem Hindi: love

Prentice Old English: apprentice (shifted from surname usage)

Preston Old English (from preost and tun): town with a priest (shifted from surname usage). Also various place names (geographical name)

Prince (name from an English word)

Pritesh Sanskrit (from priti and iza): loved by the lord, loved by god. *See also* Priyesh

Prithvi Sanskrit: earth. A wife of the Hindu god Vishnu

Pritpal Punjabi: loving caretaker, god (Sikh name)

Priyan Sanskrit (from priya): beloved

Priyesh Sanskrit (from priya and iz): loved by the lord, loved by god. *See also* Pritesh

Prosper (name from an English word)

Przemyslaw Polish (from pomysłowy): clever, ingenious

Ptolemy Greek: warlike

q

Qaasim *See* Qasim

Qais Arabic: example, firm, measurement

Qamar Arabic (from ghamar): moon Al-Qamar is the name of the 54th chapter of the Qu'ran, referring to the splitting of the moon

Qasim Arabic: distributor, divider

Qays *See* Qais

Qazi Arabic: judge, justice

Qi Chinese: various, including extraordinary and equal

Quade/Quaid Urdu: leader

Quentin Latin: fifth child

Quillan Unknown, possibly Irish Gaelic: descendent of Cole (shifted from surname usage). Also a territory in author D. J. MacHale's Pendragon series

Quin Irish Gaelic: descendent of Conn (shifted from surname usage)

Quincy *See* Quentin

Quinlan Irish Gaelic: from the Caoinleain family, and a variation of Quinlivan (shifted from surname usage)

Quinten/Quintin/Quinton *See* Quentin

Quoc Vietnamese: country, nation

r

Raahil *See* Raheel

Rabbi Hebrew: master. The teacher of Torah in Judaism

Radley Old English (from reade and leah): red clearing (shifted from surname usage). Also a village in Oxfordshire (geographical name)

Radoslaw Slavic (from rado and slava): happiness and glory

Radwan Polish (from ród): clan of knights (shifted from surname usage). A Polish coat of arms awarded to noble families

Raees *See* Rais

Raef A diminutive form of Raphael. *See also* Raif

Raekwon The stage name of the rapper Corey Woods from the Wu-Tang Clan

Rafael *See* Raphael

Rafal A Polish variant of Raphael

Rafan Unknown, possibly from Ralph (shifted from surname usage)

Rafay/Rafe/Rafee *See* Raffi

Raffael/Raffaele *See* Raphael

Rafferty From O'Raithbheartaigh, Irish Gaelic (from rath and beartaigh): wielding prosperity (shifted from surname usage)

Raffi/Rafi Arabic: exalting. Also a diminutive form of Raphael

Rafiq Arabic (from rafeegh): companion, friend

Raghav Sanskrit (from raghava): ocean, sea

Rahand Kurdish: dimensions

Rahat Arabic: rest, comfort, tranquility

Raheel Arabic (from rahel): traveller

Raheem/Raheim/Rahiem *See* Rahim

Rahil *See* Raheel

Rahim Arabic: kind, compassionate Ar-Rahim is one of Allah's 99 names, meaning Most Merciful, and reciting it is believed to help to prevent misfortune and encourage the doing of good deeds

Rahman Arabic: compassionate, merciful. Ar-Rahman is one of Allah's 99 names, meaning Most Beneficent and More Gracious, and reciting it more than 100 times it is believed to help in becoming more mindful and attentive

Rahul The name of Buddha's son

Rai Japanese: various, including thunder. Also a title of honour in India, usually incorporated into surnames

Raiden Japanese: thunder and lightning. A name for Raijin, the Japanese god of thunder, seldom used as a name in Japan

Raif Arabic (from raoof): kind, merciful

Raife *See* Raif and Ralph

Raihaan/Raihan *See* Rehan

Rais Arabic: captain, leader

Raiyan *See* Rayyaan

Raj/Raja Sanskrit: radiant, king, chief

Rajab Arabic: to respect, the seventh month of the Arabic calendar

Rajan Sanskrit: king, chief. *See also* Raj

Rajeev *See* Rajiv

Rajesh Sanskrit (from raj and iz): lord of kings

Rajinder Punjabi: god of kings (Sikh name)

Rajiv Sanskrit (from rajiva): blue lotus flowers, striped, streaked

Rajpal Punjabi: protector of kings (Sikh name)

Rajveer/Rajvir Punjabi: bravery of kings (Sikh name)

Rakan Unknown, possibly Arabic (from rekan): friend, companion

Rakeem Persian (from rakheem): melodious

Rakesh Sanskrit (from raka and iz): lord of the sun, lord of the full moon

Rakib Arabic (from rakeeb): fellow traveller, fellow passenger

Rakim Arabic (from ragheem): letter

Ralf A German and Swedish variant of Ralph

Ralfie A diminutive form of Ralph

Ralfs A Latvian variant of Ralph

Ralph Old German (from reda and wulfaz): counsel of wolves (shifted from surname usage). Also diminutive form of Raphael

Ralphie/Ralphy A diminutive form of Ralph

Ram Hebrew: exalted. Also from Rama, a form of the Hindu god Vishnu

Ramadan Arabic: ninth month of the Arabic calendar, associated with fasting

Ramazan A Turkish variant of Ramadan

Rameez Arabic (from ramz): mystery, symbol

Ramel Old French (from raim and el): small branch (shifted from surname usage)

Rami Persian (from ramee): gentle, mild. Also Arabic (from ram): honoured, revered. *See also* Ram

Ramin Avestan: tamer. Also the lover of Vis in an epic Persian poem by Asad Gorgani

Ramiro Old German (from ragin and mer): counsel and fame

Ramiz *See* Rameez

Ramon A Spanish variant of Raymond

Ramone Unknown, possibly from Raymond (shifted from surname usage)

Ramsay/Ramsey Old English (from harmsa and ieg): garlic island (shifted from surname usage)

Ramy *See* Rami

Ramzan *See* Ramazan

Ramzi Arabic (from ramzee): mysterious, secretive

Ranbir *See* Ranvir

Randy A diminutive form of Randall and Randolph, Old Norse (from rond and ulfr): shield wolf. *See also* Ranulph

Ranjit Punjabi: victory of the battle (Sikh name)

Ranulph Old Norse (from regin and ulfr): coucil of wolves

Ranveer/Ranvir Punjabi: bravery of the battle (Sikh name)

Raoul A French variant of Ralph

Raphael Hebrew: god is healer. The name of an archangel

Raqeeb Arabic (from ragheeb): rival, guardian, keeper

Rares The nickname of Peter IV Rares, a famous ruler of Moldavia, in present day Eastern Europe, so named due to his thin hair

Rashaan *See* Roshan

Rashad Arabic: directed to the right path

Rashan/Rasharn/Rashaun *See* Roshan

Rashed/Rasheed/Rashid Arabic: rightly guided

Ratu Fijian: chief. Also Hindi: seasons

Rauf Arabic (from raoof): kind, merciful

Raul A Spanish variant of Ralph

Raunak *See* Ronak

Raven (colour and bird name, name from an English word)

Ravi Sanskrit: sun, Sunday

Rawa Martu: forever

Rawand *See* Roland and Rowland

Ray A diminutive form of Raymond

Rayaan/Rayane *See* Rayyaan and Rehan. *See also* Girls and Boys: Rayana

Rayhaan/Rayhan *See* Rehan

Raymond Old German (from ragin and mund): protector, advice

Rayn Arabic: river Rhine (geographical name). Also possibly from the word 'rain' or 'reign'.

See also Girls and Boys: Rayne

Rayon (name from an English word). *See also* Rayyaan

Rayyaan Arabic: sated, no longer thirsting. *See also* Girls and Boys: Rayyan

Raza Sanskrit (from rasa): legend

Razvan/Razwan *See* Redwan

Reace *See* Reis and Rhys

Red (colour name, name from an English word)

Reda *See* Redd and Reza

Redd Old English: red (shifted from surname usage)

Redford Old English: red ford (shifted from surname usage)

Redmond From Raymond (shifted from surname usage)

Redwan Arabic (from rez-van): satisfaction, blessing, paradise, angel guarding the gates of paradise

Reed *See* Redd

Reef Old English (from rap): rope, roper (shifted from surname usage)

Reehan *See* Rehan

Rees/Reese *See* Rhys

Reeve Old English (from gerefa): steward, reeve (shifted from surname usage)

Reggie A diminutive form of Reginald

Reginald Old Norse (from rogn and valdr): power of council

Rehaan/Rehan Arabic: sweet basil. *See also* Girls and Boys: Reyhan

Rehman *See* Rahman

Reice *See* Reis and Rhys

Reid *See* Redd

Reiley/Reilly/Reily From O'Raghallaigh, unknown (shifted from surname usage). *See also* Rilee

Reis/Reiss Turkish: leader. Also Old German: rice (shifted from surname usage). *See also* Rhys

Remel/Remell Hungarian: to hope. Also possibly from Remmel (shifted from surname usage)

Remi From Remigius, Latin (from remex): quill, feathers, rower

Remigiusz A Polish varaint of Remi

Remus One of the twin founders of Rome along with Romulus, who was suckled by a wolf

Remy *See* Remi

Ren Japanese: various, including lotus

Renato Latin (from renatus): reborn

Reno Italian: the river Rhine (geographical name, shifted from surname usage)

Renzo A diminutive form of Lorenzo

Reo Italian, Portuguese and Spanish (from rio): river. *See also* Girls and Boys: Rio

Reon Unknown, possibly a modernised and shifted variant of Leon

Reuban/Reuben Hebrew (from reu and ven): look at the son, look to the son of god. The first son of

Jacob

Reuel Hebrew: friend of god. Another name for Jethro, the father-in-law of Moses

Rex Latin: king

Reyaan/Reyan *See* Rehan

Reyansh Unknown, possibly Sanskrit (from amz): part of, the aspect of a Hindu god. The main character from *Dil Dosti Dance*, Reyansh Singhania

Reza Arabic (from rezz): content

Rezwan *See* Ridwan

Rhett Unknown (shifted from surname usage). Associated with Rhett Butler from *Gone with the Wind*

Rhidian *See* Rhydian

Rhiley *See* Rilee

Rhodri Unknown, possibly Welsh (from rhodres): graces, airs. The name of the Welsh king Rhodri the Great

Rhuari/Rhuaridh *See* Ruaraidh

Rhuben *See* Reuben

Rhun Irish Gaelic (from rún): mystery, secret, resolution, affection, friend

Rhyan *See* Ryaan

Rhyce *See* Rhys

Rhydian From Rhydwyn, unknown, possibly Welsh (from rhyd and gwyn): white ford

Rhylan *See* Rylan

Rhylee/Rhyley/Rhylie *See* Rilee

Rhys/Rhyse Old Welsh (from rīs):

ardour

Riaan *See* Ryaan

Riad *See* Riyad

Riaz *See* Riyaz

Ricardo A Portuguese and Spanish variant of Richard

Ricards A French variant of Richard

Riccardo An Italian variant of Richard

Ricco A diminutive form of Riccardo

Richard Old German (from riko and harduz): strong, brave king

Richie A diminutive form of Richard

Richmond Old French (from riche and mont): rich, splendid hill (shifted from surname usage)

Rick/Rickie/Ricky A diminutive form of Richard

Rico A diminutive form of Enrico and Ricardo

Ridhwaan/Ridhwan *See* Ridwan

Ridley Old English (from rydde and leah): clearing (shifted from surname usage)

Ridwaan/Ridwan Arabic: satisfaction, the name of an angel at the gates of paradise

Rielly/Riely *See* Reilly

Rikesh *See* Rakesh

Riki Japanese: various, including power, strength. Also a diminutive form of Richard

Rilee/Rileigh Old English (from rygh and leah): rye meadow. *See*

also Reilly. *See also* Girls and Boys: Rylee

Rion *See* Ryaan

Riordan From O'Rioghbhardain, Irish Gaelic (from rígrach and bard): royal bard (shifted from surname usage)

Rishaan *See* Rishan

Rishab/Rishabh Sanskrit (from rsabha): the best, the greatest. Also an avatar of the Hindu god Vishnu

Rishan *See* Rishi and Rishon

Rishi Sanskrit (from rsi): inspired poet, seer

Rishikesh Sanskrit (from hrsika and iz): lord of the senses. A name for the Hindu god Vishnu. Also a district in India near the Himalayas (geographical name)

Rishit Sanskrit (from rsti): spear, lance, sword

Rishon Hebrew: the first. Also from the Israeli city Rishon LeZion (geographical name)

Ritchie From Richard (shifted from surname usage). Also a diminutive form of Richard

Rithik/Rithvik/Ritik/Ritvik Sanskrit (from rtvik): priest

Rivaldo The name of the Brazilian midfielder Rivaldo Vítor Borba Ferreira (footballer name)

Rivers From La Rivière, a village in Normandy, Old French: river (shifted from surname usage)

Riyad/Riyadh Arabic: gardens, meadows. The capital city of Saudi Arabia (geographical name)

Riyaz Hindi: practise, especially practising music. *See also* Riyad

Rizwaan/Rizwan *See* Ridwan

Roan (colour name). *See also* Rowan

Roary *See* Rory

Rob/Robbie/Robby A diminutive form of Robert

Robel An Arabic variant of Reuben

Robert Old German (from hrod and berhtaz): bright fame

Robertas A Lithuanian variant of Robert

Roberto An Italian and Spanish variant of Robert

Roberts From Robert (shifted from surname usage)

Robinson Old English: son of Robin (shifted from surname usage)

Robson Old English: son of Rob (shifted from surname usage)

Rocco The Italian name for the French saint, Saint Roch, who died in Italy

Rocky A diminutive form of Rocco

Roddy A diminutive form of Roderick

Roderick Old German (from hrod and ric): fame and power

Rodi A diminutive form of Roderick

Rodin Unknown (shifted from surname usage). Associated with the sculptor Auguste Rodin

Rodney Old English: Hrod's island, famous island (shifted from surname usage)

Rodrigo A Portuguese and Spanish variant of Roderick

Rogan An anglicised variant of Ruadhan (shifted from surname usage)

Roger Old German (from hrod and gar): famous spear

Rohaan *See* Rohan

Rohail Arabic (from raheel): traveller

Rohan An anglicised variant of Ruadhan (shifted from surname usage). Also Sanskrit (from rohana): healing, ascending

Rohat Sanskrit: rising, ascending, growing

Rohin Sanskrit: rising, ascending, growing, tall

Rohit/Rohith Sanskrit (from rohita): red. A name for the Hindu god Vishnu

Rojus Lithuanian: heaven, paradise

Rokas Lithuanian: rock

Roland Old German (from hrod and land): renowned land (shifted from surname usage). *See also* Rowland

Rollo An Old French variant of Rolf. Also a diminutive form of Roland and Rowland

Romaan A Dutch variant of Roman

Romain/Romaine A French variant of Roman

Roman Latin (from romanus): from Rome

Romano An Italian variant of Roman

Romario The name of the Brazilian footballer Romário de Souza Faria (footballer name). *See also* Romero

Rome The city in Italy (geographical name)

Romeo The main character from Shakespeare's *Romeo and Juliet*

Romero Spanish: rosemary (name from flowers and trees, shifted from surname usage)

Ron Hebrew: joyful singing. Also a diminutive form of Ronald

Ronak Persian: shining

Ronald *See* Reginald

Ronaldinho A diminutive form of Ronaldo. The nickname of the Brazilian footballer Ronaldo de Assis Moreira, given to him to differentiate him from Ronaldo Luís Nazário de Lima (footballer name)

Ronaldo The name of the Brazilian footballer Ronaldo Luís Nazário de Lima (footballer name)

Ronan Irish Gaelic (from rón and án): little seal

Ronel Hebrew (from ron and el): joyful singing of god

Roni Hebrew (from ron): joyful singing. Also Kurdish: rising sun. Also a Finnish diminutive form of Aaron and Ronald

Ronin Japanese: a samurai who belongs to no master, now used to describe students who are unable to get into a high school or university, so must repeat a year outside of school. It is not used as a name in Japan. *See also* Ronan

Ronit Hebrew (from ron): joyful singing. Also an anglicised form of Rathnait, Irish Gaelic (from rathach): fortunate, prosperous, or Irish Gaelic (from rathmar): gracious. Also possibly Sanskrit (from ranat): ringing, sounding

Ronny A diminutive form of Ronald

Rooney From O' Ruanaidh, Irish Gaelic (from rúanaidhecht): champion (shifted from surname usage)

Rorey/Rorie/Rory An anglicised variant of Ruairidh

Roscoe Old Norse (from ra and scogr): roe deer thicket (shifted from surname usage)

Roshaan/Roshan/Roshane/Roshaun Hindi: lighted, illuminated

Ross Irish Gaelic (from ros): a wood (shifted from surname usage)

Rossa/Rossi Latin (from rous): red (shifted from surname usage)

Rourke From O'Ruairc, possibly Irish Gaelic (from rúarc): storm (shifted from surname usage)

Roux French: redhead (shifted from surname usage)

Rowland Unknown, possibly Old Norse (from ra and lundr): roe deer wood (shifted from surname usage). *See also* Roland

Roy An anglicised variant of Raj and Ruadhan. Also possibly French (from roi): king

Royce Unknown, possibly Old German: rose (shifted from surname usage)

Royston From Croyroys, Old French: Royce's cross (shifted from surname usage)

Ruadhan Scottish Gaelic (from ruadh): red

Ruairi/Ruairidh Irish and Scottish Gaelic: red king

Ruan Chinese: various, including a white gem

Ruaraidh/Ruari/Ruaridh *See* Ruairidh

Ruban/Ruben *See* Reuben

Rubens From Robert and Rupert (shifted from surname usage)

Rubin *See* Reuben

Rudra Sanskrit: howling, roaring. A Hindu god of wind, storm and hunting

Rudy A diminutive form of Rudolph, Old Norse (from hrod and olf): famous wolf, glorious wolf

Rudyard Old English (from rudd and yard): fish lake (shifted from surname usage)

Rueben *See* Reuben

Rufus Latin: red

Ruhan Turkish (from ruh): heart, soul. *See also* Rohan

Ruhel/Ruhul Arabic (from roohol): essence of spirits. *See also* Rahul

Rui A Portuguese variant of Roderick

Ruman Unknown (shifted from surname usage). Also Arabic (from romman): pomegranate (name from flowers and trees)

Rupert An Old German variant of Robert

Rushil Hindi: charming

Ruslan A Russian variant of Aslan

Russell Old French (from rossel): with red hair

Ruzgar Turkish (from rüzgar): wind, breeze

Ryaan From O'Riain, Irish Gaelic (from rí and an): little king (shifted from surname usage). *See also* Girls and Boys: Ryan

Ryandeep From Randeep, Punjabi: lamp of the battle (Sikh name)

Ryann *See* Ryaan

Ryden Old English (from rygen and dun): rye hill (shifted from surname usage)

Ryder Old English (from ridan): rider, mounted warrior (shifted from surname usage)

Ryhan *See* Rehan

Ryker Old German (from reich): empire (shifted from surname usage)

Rylan/Ryland/Rylen Old English (from rygen and land): rye land (shifted from surname usage)

Ryo Japanese: various, including bright and good

Ryu Japanese: various, including dragon

S

Saabir *See* Sabir

Saad/Sa'ad Hebrew: help, aid

Saagar Sanskrit (from sagara): of the sea

Saahil *See* Sahil

Saahir *See* Sahir

Saaim *See* Saim

Saajan *See* Sajan

Saami *See* Samih

Sabbir *See* Sabir

Sabeel Arabic: way, path, road

Sabian Worshippers of a monotheist religious, mentioned in the Qur'an along with Christians and Jews

Sabir Arabic (from saber): patient

Sabri A Turkish variant of Sabir

Sacha A French diminutive form of Alexander

Sachin From Shachindra, Shachi's Indra, a name of the Hindu god Indra

Sadiq Arabic (from sadegh): truthful, honest

Saeed Arabic (from sa-eed): happy

Safal Hindi (from saphal): successful

Safeer Arabic: ambassador, mediator

Safi Arabic: pure

Safian *See* Sofian

Safraz Arabic (from saraf-raz): distinguished, exalted, honourable

Safwaan/Safwan Arabic: rocks

Safyaan/Safyan *See* Sofian

Sagar *See* Saagar

Sahaj Sanskrit (from sahaja): natural, innate

Sahal Arabic (from sahl): easy

Sahand A volcano in Iran (geographical name)

Sahel *See* Sahil

Sahibdeep Punjabi: lamp of the master (Sikh name)

Sahibjot Punjabi: light of the master (Sikh name)

Sahil Arabic (from sahel): beach, shore. Also Hindi: shore

Sahir/Sahr Sanskrit (from sahira): mountain

Said Arabic: happy, lucky

Saif/Saifan/Saiful *See* Seif

Saifullah Arabic (from seyf and allah): sword of god

Saifur *See* Seif

Saihaan Arabic (from sayalan): flowing

Saim Arabic (from sa-em): fasting, one who fasts

Sajad *See* Sajjad

Sajan Sanskrit (from sajana): kinsman

Sajid Arabic (from sajed): prostrating before god, bowing down to god

Sajjad Arabic: adorer, worshipper, one who repeatedly prostrates before god

Sakariya/Sakariye A province in Turkey (geographical name)

Sakib A town in Jordan (geographical name)

Saksham Hindi: capable

Salah Arabic: righteousness, virtue

Salahuddin/Salahudeen From Salah ad-Din, Arabic: righteousness of faith, virtue of faith

Saleem *See* Salim

Saleh Arabic: good, right

Salem *See* Salim and Sholom

Salih *See* Saleh

Salim Arabic: safe

Salmaan/Salman Arabic: peaceful

Salvador Spanish: Saviour, Christ

Salvatore Italian: Saviour, Christ

Samad Arabic: eternal, elevated, lord, chief, elder. As-Samad is one of Allah's 99 names, meaning the Eternal, and reciting it repeatedly when in need is believed to help

Samarth Sanskrit: comfort, encourage. The name of Samarth Ramdas, a Hindu religious poet

Samay Sanskrit (from samaya): time, the unit of time in Hindu mythology. Also possibly Sanskrit (from another form of samaya): pact, vow

Samee A diminutive form of

Samuel. *See also* Samih

Sameer *See* Samir

Samer *See* Samir

Samet Yiddish: velvet. Also a Turkish variant of Samad

Samih Arabic: high, exalted, supreme. *See also* Girls and Boys: Sami

Samim Arabic (from samin): precious, valuable

Samir Arabic: companion, entertaining companion in nightly conversations

Samiul A diminutive form of Samiullah. *See also* Samuel

Samiullah Arabic (from sam-anand allah): listening to god

Sampson *See* Samson

Samraj Punjabi: supreme king (Sikh name)

Samson Hebrew (from shemesh): sun. A judge of the Israelites granted great strength by god and who was betrayed by Delilah

Samual/Samuel/Samuele Hebrew: god has listened

Samy A diminutive form of Samuel

San Turkish: fame

Sanchez Spanish (from Sancho and ez): Sancho's son (shifted from surname usage)

Sancho, Latin (from sanctius): holy

Sander A diminutive form of Alexander

Sanjay Hindi (from sanajay): victory

Sanjeev Sanskrit (from samjiv): revive, maintain, live, flourish

Santhosh Sanskrit (from samtosa): satisfaction, pleasure, joy, delight

Santiago The capital of Chile, from Saint Diego. *See also* Diego

Santino Italian: saint

Saqib Arabic (from sahv): brightness, clarity

Saqlain Arabic: two worlds

Sarbjit Punjabi: victory of all, victory of patience (Sikh name)

Sardar Persian (from sar-dar): commander, leader

Sarim Arabic (from sarem): sharp, stern

Sartaj Hindi (from satej): powerful

Sarthak Sanskrit (from sarthaka): meaningful, significant

Sarvesh Sanskrit (from sarveza): lord of all, supreme being

Satnam Punjabi: accepting god is true, accepting the one god (Sikh name)

Saud From the House of Saud, the ruling h Dionysus ouse of Saudi Arabia

Saul Hebrew: prayed for. The first king of Israel

Savan Sanskrit (from sahvan): powerful

Savas Turkish: fighting, thriving

Savio Italian: wise. The name of the Brazilian footballer Sávio Bortolini Pimentel (footballer name)

Sawan *See* Savan

Sawyer Old English (from saghe):

sawer of wood (shifted from surname usage. Associated with Tom Sawyer, the character from Mark Twain's novels

Sayam/Sayan Sanskrit (from saya): of the evening. Also Turkish (from şayan): worthy, remarkable

Sayed/Sayeed *See* Saeed

Sayhan *See* Saihaan

Scot/Scott A Scottish person (shifted from surname usage)

Se Portuguese: See. From Santa Sé, the Holy See of the Vatican Also an area of São Paulo (geographical name)

Seamus An Irish variant of James

Sean An Irish variant of John

Seb A diminutive form of Sebastian

Sebastian Latin: from Sebaste, the venerable lands, which is modern day Sivas in Turkey

Sebastiano An Italian variant of Sebastian

Sebastien A French variant of Sebastian

Seif Arabic (from seyf/seyfon): sword

Sekou Guinean French: learned

Selim *See* Salim

Semih Turkish: bounteous, generous

Senan Unknown, possibly Old Gaelic: wise man. The name of Senán mac Geirrcinn, an Irish saint. *See also* Sinan. *See also* Girls and Boys: Sennen

Sepehr Persian: sky, heaven

Serge A French variant of Sergius, a Roman saint after whom several popes are named

Sergio A Italian and Spanish variant of Sergius, a Roman saint after whom several popes are named

Serhan Turkish (from şah): king. Also Arabic: wolf

Serhat Turkish: border, frontier

Serkan Turkish: noble

Seth Hebrew: chosen. Also Cornish: arrow. The third son of Adam and Eve

Seumas A Scottish variant of James

Seve A Spanish diminutive form of Severinus, Latin (from severus): serious, stern

Seweryn A Polish variant of Severinus, Latin (from severus): serious, stern

Seyed *See* Saeed

Seyon A variant of Zion, used in Amda Seyon, the name of several Ethiopian kings, meaning 'pillar of Zion'. *See also* Sion

Shabaan Arabic: eighth month

Shabaaz *See* Shahbaz

Shaban *See* Shabaan

Shabaz *See* Shahbaz

Shad A diminutive form of Shadrach. *See also* Chad

Shadab Persian: fresh

Shadrach Unknown, possibly a Hebrew variant of a Babylonian name. A man saved from a furnice by god, along with Meshach and

Abednego. *See also* Meshach

Shafi/Shafiq Arabic: mercy, compassion

Shahab Arabic: meteor, shooting star

Shahan Persian: king, usually used in the context of shahan-shah, king of kings

Shahbaz Hindi (from shah and baj): royal falcon

Shaheem Arabic: pudgy, rounded

Shaheer Arabic: famous, celebrated

Shahid Arabic (from shahed): witness, proof. Also possibly Arabic (from shahd): honey

Shahir *See* Shahir

Shahmeer Persian (from shah and ameer): king of princes, king of commanders

Shahriar/Shahriyar Persian (from shah-riar): monach, king. A city and a county in Tehran (geographical name)

Shahrukh Persian (from shah and rokh): king's face, king's cheeks

Shahzad Persian (from shah and rokh): born from a king

Shahzaib/Shahzain/Shahzeb Persian (from shah and zeeb): king of beauty

Shaikh Arabic (from sheykh): elder, wise man, chief. A title for learned men and tribal leaders. *See also* Girls and Boys: Sheik

Shaine An Irish variant of John

Shakai Hebrew: almighty

Shakeal/Shakeel *See* Shakil

Shakib Persian (from shakeeb): patient

Shakiel/Shakil Arabic: beautiful, handsome

Shakir/Shakur Arabic (from shaker): thankful, grateful, content

Shamar/Shamari From the historical Shammar tribe in Saudi Arabia

Shamas Arabic: candle, light, kind, good

Shamil Arabic: complete, united, joint

Shamir Hebrew: flint, thorn

Shamus From Seamus, an Irish variant of James

Shane From Sean, an Irish variant of John

Shanil Unknown

Shaquille *See* Shakil

Sharan Punjabi: guru's shelter (Sikh name)

Sharaz *See* Shiraz

Sharif Arabic: noble, protector

Sharif was used as a tribal title

Shariq Unknown

Shaun An Irish variant of John

Shaurya Hindi (from shaury): power, valour

Shaw Old English (from sceaga): small wood (shifted from surname usage)

Shawn An Irish variant of John

Shayaan/Shayan Persian: worthy, deserving

Shayden/Shaydon Unknown, possibly a modernised and shifted variant of Hayden

Shayen *See* Shayan

Shaylan/Shaylen Unknown, possibly a masculine variant of Shayla, Latin: way of the blind, or Latin (from caelum): heaven

Shayne An Irish variant of John

Shayon *See* Shayan

Shazad *See* Shahzad

Shazaib/Shazeb *See* Shahzaib

Shazil Unknown

She Chinese: various, including dwelling

Shehryar *See* Shahriar

Shelton Old English (from scylf and tun): ledge town (shifted from surname usage)

Shem Hebrew: essence, fame. A son of Noah

Shemar *See* Shahmeer

Sheng Chinese: various, including rise and victory

Sheraz *See* Shiraz

Sherif *See* Sharif and Sheriff

Sheriff (name from an English word). Old English (from scir andý gerefa): shire official, usually applicable for Scotland

Shezad *See* Shahzad

Shimon A Hebrew variant of Simon and Simeon

Shiraz The city in Iran (geographical name)

Shiv (name from an English word) Romani (from chiv): knife. *See also* Shiva

Shiva/Shivam Sanskrit (from ziva): favourable, gracious. The name of the Hindu god

Shivan/Shiven Sanskrit (from zivan): resting

Shloime A Yiddish variant of Solomon

Shlok Sanskrit (from zlok): compose, compose music

Shlomo A Hebrew variant of Solomon

Shmuel A Hebrew variant of Samuel

Shoaib/Shohaib *See* Shuaib

Sholom Hebrew: peace. *See also* Girls and Boys: Shalom

Sholto From Sioltach, Scottish Gaelic: sower

Shomari Swahili: forceful

Shrey/Shreyan Sanskrit (from zraya/zrayana): shelter, protection

Shreyas Sanskrit (from zreyas): fortunate, superior, bliss

Shuaib/Shuayb Arabic: showing the right path. A prophet mentioned in the Qur'an

Shubh Sanskrit (from zubh): beauty, splendour

Shubham Sanskrit (from zubha): auspicious

Shulem *See* Sholom

Shyam/Shyheim Hindi (from shyam): black (colour name)

Siam The name for Thailand

(geographical name)

Sid *See* Syd

Sidar A Kurdish and Turkish variant of Sardar

Siddhant Sanskrit (from siddhanta): theory, doctrine

Siddharth/Siddhartha Sanskrit (from siddhartha): successful, prosperous, achieving the goal. The name of Buddha

Sikandar/Sikander The Hindi variant of Alexander

Silas A diminutive form of Silvanus, Latin (from silva): forest, wood. A saint who was a companion to Saint Paul

Simao A Portuguese variant of Simon

Simas A Lithuanian variant of Simon

Simbarashe Shona: god's power, god's strength

Simcha Hebrew (from sameyach): happy

Simeon/Simon Hebrew: one who hears. *See also* Girls and Boys: Simone

Sinan Arabic (from senan): spear

Sion Hebrew (from Zion): Jerusalem (geographical name). *See also* Girls and Boys: Zion

Siraaj/Siraj Arabic (from seraj): lamp, light, candle

Sivakumar Sanskrit (from Siva and kumara): prince of the auspicious one, prince of the Hindu god Shiva

Siyam Arabic: fasting

Siyar Arabic: conduct, behaviour

Sofian/Sofiane Arabic: devoted

Sohaib *See* Suhaib

Sohail *See* Suhail

Soham/Sohan The name of Sa'sa'a bin Sohan, one of Ali's companions. *See also* Suhan

Sol The Roman sun god. Also a diminutive form of Solomon

Soloman/Solomon Hebrew (from shalom): peace. A king of Israel known for his wisdom and his large number of wives

Somtochukwu Igbo: join me in praising god

Soner Turkish (from son): last one, last man

Sonni/Sonnie/Sonny From the word 'son' (a term of endearment)

Soren A Danish and Swedish variant of Severinus, Latin (from severus): serious, stern

Sorley From Somerled, Old Norse: summer traveller

Soul (name from an English word)

Spencer From Dispencier, Old French: despenser (shifted from surname usage)

Spike (name from an English word)

Stan A diminutive form of Stanley

Stanislav Slavic: become glorious

Stanislaw A Polish variant of Stanislav

Stanlee/Stanley Old English (from stan and leah): stone clearing

(shifted from surname usage)

Stanton Old English (from stan and tun): stone town (shifted from surname usage)

Stavros Greek: cross

Stefan A Danish, German, Norwegian and Swedish variant of Stephen

Stefano An Italian variant of Stephen

Stefanos A Finnish and Swedish variant of Stephen

Steffan A Welsh variant of Stephen

Steffen A Danish, German and Norwegian variant of Stephen

Stelios Greek (from stulos): pole, firmness

Stephan A Danish and German variant of Stephen

Stephane A French variant of Stephen

Stephanos A Greek variant of Stephen Stephen

Ancient Greek (from stephanos): crown

Sterling *See* Stirling

Steve A diminutive form of Steven

Steven *See* Stephen

Stevie A diminutive form of Steven

Stewart Old English: steward (shifted from surname usage)

Stirling The ancient capital of Scotland (geographical name, shifted from surname usage)

Struan Scottish Gaelic (from sruthan): stream. A village in Skye (geographical name)

Stuart *See* Stewart

Subhaan/Subhan Arabic (from sobh): morning

Success (name from an English word)

Sudais Arabic (from sodos): sixth

Sufian/Sufiyaan/Sufiyan/Sufyaan/Sufyan *See* Sofian

Suhaan *See* Suhan

Suhaib Arabic: red haired

Suhail Arabic: gentle

Suhan Hindi (from suhānā): pleasant. Also the name of Zayd ibn Suhan, one of prophet Muhammad's companions

Suhayb *See* Suhaib

Suhayl *See* Suhail

Sujal Sanskrit (from sujala): water, sweet water

Sukhbir *See* Sukhveer

Sukhdev Punjabi: god of peace (Sikh name)

Sukhman Punjabi: bring the mind to peace (Sikh name)

Sukhraj Punjabi: king of peace (Sikh name)

Sukhveer/Sukhvir Punjabi: bravery of peace (Sikh name)

Sulaimaan/Sulaiman/Sulaymaan/Sulayman/Suleiman/Sulemaan/Suleman/Suleyman/Suliman An Arabic variant of Soloman

Sullivan Irish Gaelic (from súil and dubh): dark eyed (shifted from surname usage)

Sully A diminutive form of Sullivan

Sulman *See* Soloman (shifted from surname usage)

Sultan Arabic: strength, authority A noble title of certain rulers. *See also* Zoltan

Sundeep Punjabi: lamp of beauty (Sikh name)

Sunil Sanskrit (from sunila): blackish blue, pomegranate tree (colour name, name from flowers and trees)

Sunni Arabic (from sunnah): habit A term that describes Sunni muslims. *See also* Girls and Boys: Sunny

Suraj Hindi: sun

Sven Old Norse (from sveinn): boy, servant

Syan *See* John and Sayan

Syd A diminutive form of Sydney, Old English: wide island (shifted from surname usage). *See also* Girls and Boys: Sydney

Syed *See* Saeed

Sylvester Latin (from silva): forest, woods

Syon Sanskrit (from syona): tender, pleasant, gentle. *See also* Sion

Syrus *See* Cyrus

Szymon A Polish variant of Simon

t

Taaha *See* Taha

Taariq *See* Tariq

Tadas A Lithuanian variant of Thaddeus

Tadhg Irish Gaelic (from tadg): poet

Tadiwanashe Shona: we are greatly loved by god

Tae Korean: various, including big, great

Tafara Shona: we are happy, we are rejoicing

Tafari Amharic: one who inspires awe

Taha The name of the 20th chapter of the Qur'an

Taheem Arabic: pure

Taher/Tahir Arabic (from taher): pure, chaste

Tahmeed/Tahmid/Tahmidur Arabic (from tahmeed): repeatedly praising god

Tailor (name from an English word, shifted from surname usage). *See also* Girls and Boys: Taylor

Taimoor Unknown, possibly Sanskrit (from tamori): sun

Taine From Tain, a town in Scotland (geographical name, shifted from surname usage)

Taio A diminutive form of Taiyewo, Yoruba: the first to taste the world (given to the elder twin)

Tait/Taite Old Norse (from teitr): happy, joyful (shifted from surname usage)

Taiyon *See* Tayon

Taj Persian: crown

Tajus Unknown

Takudzwa Shona: we are honoured

Takunda Shona: we have overcome

Tal Arabic: disciple

Talal Arabic: remains. The name of a king of Jordan

Talan *See* Talon

Talha/Talhah The name of Talha ibn Ubaydullah, a companion of prophet Muhammad

Talib Arabic (from taleb): *See*ker, searcher

Taliesin A bard who served several kings, whose work is preserved in the *Book of Taliesin*

Talon (Name from an English word)

Talvin Unknown, possibly a modernised and shifted variant of Alvin or Calvin. Also possibly Estonian (from talv): winter

Tam A Scottish diminutive form of Thomas

Tameem Arabic: strong

Tamer Persian (from taham): brave man

Tamim *See* Tameem

Tamir *See* Tamer

Tamjid Arabic (from tamjeed): praise, glorify

Tanay Sanskrit (from tanaya): son

Tanbir *See* Tanvir

Tane A Maori god of the forest

Tanish Sanskrit (from tanas): offspring

Tanmay Sanskrit (from tanmaya): absorbed

Tanner (Name from an English word, shifted from surname usage)

Tanush Sanskrit (from tanus): body. Also possibly from Dhanush, a name for the Hindu god Shiva

Tanveer/Tanvir Punjabi: brave body (Sikh name)

Tanzeel/Tanzil Arabic (from enzil): descent

Tao Chinese: various, including waves

Tapiwa Shona: given

Taran Punjabi: freedom, salvation (Sikh name). *See also* Tarran and Tarun

Tarandeep Punjabi: lamp of freedom, lamp of salvation (Sikh name)

Taranveer/Taranvir Punjabi: bravery of freedom, bravery of salvation (Sikh name)

Tarek Persian (from tarak): crown, summit

Tarell Unknown, possibly Old Welsh (from tarddu): bubbling. The name of a river in Wales (geographical name)

Tareq/Tarik/Tariq/Tarique *See* Tarek

Taro Japanese: various, usually person, man

Taron A region in historical Armenia (geographical name)

Tarran/Tarrin From Taranis, the Celtic god of thunder

Tarun Hindi: young

Taryll *See* Tarell

Taryn *See* Tarran

Taseen Arabic: decoration, praise. *See also* Girls and Boys: Tahseen

Tashan Hindi: style

Tashinga Shona: we have won through adversity

Tauheed *See* Tawheed

Tauqeer Arabic: honour

Tauseef Arabic: praise

Tavis/Tavish A Scottish variant of Thomas

Tawanda Shona: we are many

Tawheed/Tawhid Arabic: one god, unique god

Tay A river in Scotland (geographical name). Also a diminutive form of Taylor

Tayab *See* Tayyab

Tayan Unknown, possibly from an aboriginal Taiwanese tribe

Tayden A modernised and shifted variant of Aiden/Hayden

Taye *See* Tay

Taylan/Taylen/Taylon Unknown, possibly a modernised and shifted variant of Taylor

Tayo *See* Taio

Tayon From Taius, unknown

Tayyab/Tayyeb/Tayyib Arabic (from tayyeb): kind, good-natured

Teagan A diminutive form of Tadhg

Teal (colour name, name from an English word)

Ted/Teddie/Teddy A diminutive form of Theodore

Teegan A diminutive form of Tadhg

Teejay A blend of two letters of the alphabet

Tegan A diminutive form of Tadhg

Teilo The name of a British saint who was a bishop of Llandaff

Tej Amharic: honey, mead

Tejan Sanskrit (from tejana): shaft of an arrow. *See also* Tegan

Tejas Sanskrit: bright flame, fierceness, glory, majesty

Tejay A blend of two letters of the alphabet

Tendai Shona: thankful

Tenzin Tibetan: upholder of teachings. A name commonly given to the Dalai Lama

Teo A diminutive form of Teodor

Teodor A Romanian and Scandinavian variant of Theodore

Teoman Turkish (from duman): smole

Teon *See* Theon

Tequan A modernised and shifted variant of Teagan

Terell *See* Tyrrell

Terence/Terrance *See* Terrence

Terrel/Terrell *See* Tyrrell

Terrence Unknown, from the Roman name Terentius

Terry A diminutive form of

Terrence. Also an anglicised variant of Thiery

Tevez The surname of the footballer Carlos Tévez (footballer name)

Tevin *See* Devin

Thabo Tswana: joy, happiness

Thaddeus One of the apostles of Christ

Thai From Thailand

Thando Ndebele: love

Thane A historical title given to Scottish leaders

Thanh Vietnamese: various, including blue and pure

Thanushan Unknown

Tharun *See* Tarun

Theo A diminutive form of Theodore

Theodor/Theodore/Theodoros Greek: god's gift

Theon Greek (from theos): god-like

Theophilus Greek (from theos and philos): friend of god. Also historically used as a title for academics among Romans and Jews

Theron Greek (from theerin): hunter

Thiago A Portugese variant of Diego

Thibault A French variant of Theobald, Old German (from theo and bald): bold people, brave people

Thierry A French variant of Derek

Thom A diminutive form of Thomas

Thomas Aramaic: twin. The name of the apostle Doubting Thomas

Thor Old Norse: thunder. The Norse god of thunder

Thorfinn Scottish Gaelic (from Thor and finn): fair thunderer. The name of Thorfinn the Mighty, an Earl of Orkney

Thurston Old Norse (from Thor and steinn): Thor's stone (shifted from surname usage)

Tiago A Portugese variant of Diego

Tian Chinese: various, including sky, heaven

Tiarnan Irish Gaelic (from tigerna): lord, superior

Tibor From Tibur, an ancient town near Rome (geographical name). Also possibly from the Tiber River (geographical name)

Tien Vietnamese: fairy, gods

Tiernan *See* Tiarnan

Tiger (name from an English word)

Tim A diminutive form of Timothy

Timileyin Yoruba: supporting me, with me. *See also* Oluwatimileyin

Timmy A diminutive form of Timothy

Timo A German form of Timothy

Timon Ancient Greek (from timi): honour. The name of Timon of Athens, a legendary figure who inspired Shakespeare's play of the same name

Timotei A Bulgarian and Romanian variant of Timothy

Timothee A French variant of Timothy

Timothy Ancient Greek (from timao and theos): honouring god

Timur Turkish (from demir/teemoor): iron. The name of a Turkish ruler

Tino Spanish: good aim. The nickname of the footballer Alberto Costa due to his skill and accuracy (footballer name)

Tirth Sanskrit (from tirtha): water, sacred place. Tirtha also refers to Jain pilgrimage sites

Tishan *See* Tejan

Titas A river in Bangladesh and India (geographical name). *See also* Titus

Titus The name of a Roman emperor

TJ/Tjay A blend of two letters of the alphabet

Tobechi Igbo: praise be to god

Tobenna Igbo: praise god

Tobey/Tobi A diminutive form of Tobias. *See also* Girls and Boys: Toby

Tobias/Tobiasz Hebrew: god is good

Tobie A diminutive form of Tobias. *See also* Girls and Boys: Toby

Tobiloba Yoruba: mighty king

Tobin/Tobyn Old French: from St Aubyn (shifted from surname usage)

Tochukwu Igbo: praising god

Todd Old English (from todde): fox (shifted from surname usage)

Tolga Turkish: war helmet

Toluwanimi Yoruba: I belong to god

Tom A diminutive form of Thomas

Toma A Hawaiian variant of Thomas

Tomas A Danish, Norwegian and Swedish variant of Thomas

Tomass A Latvian variant of Thomas

Tomasz A Polish variant of Thomas

Tomi A diminutive form of Thomas

Tommaso An Italian variant of Thomas

Tommee/Tommi/Tommie/Tommy A diminutive form of Thomas

Tommylee A blend of Tommy and Lee

Tomos A Welsh variant of Thomas

Toms A Latvian variant of Thomas

Tony A diminutive form of Anthony

Toprak Turkish: earth

Tor A Scandinavian variant of Thor

Torben From Thorbjorn, Old Norse (from Thor and bjorn): Thor's bear

Torin/Torran Unknown, possibly Scottish Gaelic (from tòrr): hill, from the hills. Also possibly Scottish Gaelic (from torranach): thunderous

Torres Latin (from turris): towers (shifted from surname usage)

Torrin *See* Torin

Torsten Old Norse (from Thor and

sten): Thor's stone

Toure Unknown (shifted from surname usage)

Trae *See* Trey

Trafford Old English (from trog and ford): valley river crossing (geographical name, shifted from surname usage)

Trai Vietnamese: oyster, pearl

Travis Old French: traverse (shifted from surname usage)

Trayvon *See* Trevon

Tre *See* Trey

Tremaine/Tremayne Cornish (from tre and man): stone settlement (shifted from surname usage)

Trent Celtic (from tros and hyn): flowing over. A river in England (geographical name)

Trenton Old English: by River Trent (shifted from surname usage)

Trevon Cornish (from tre and avon): water settlement (shifted from surname usage)

Trevor Unknown, possibly Cornish or Welsh (from tre and mor/mawr): large settlement (shifted from surname usage)

Trey French (from treis): three

Treyvon *See* Trevon

Tristan/Tristen/Tristian/Triston/Tristyn Unknown, possibly Welsh (from trystau): thunder. One of King Arthur's knights of the Round Table, known for his love story with Iseult

Troi/Troy A city in modern day Turkey, where the legendary Trojan War took place (geographical name)

Trystan *See* Tristan

Tuan The name of Tuan mac Cairill, a hermit from Irish mythology

Tudor From Tewdwr, a Welsh variant of Theodore (shifted from surname usage)

Turlough A type of lake that dries up in the summer, from Irish Gaelic (from tuar and lach): dry place

Turner Unknown, possibly Old French (from tornei): tournament worker (shifted from surname usage)

Tushar Sanskrit (from tusarartu): winter

Twm A Welsh diminutive form of Thomas

Ty/Tye/Tyee A diminutive form of Tylor

Tylan Unknown, possibly a modernised and shifted variant of Tylor

Tylor English: tiler (shifted from surname usage). *See also* Girls and Boys: Tyler

Tymon *See* Timon

Tymoteusz A Polish variant of Timothy

Tyran *See* Tyrone

Tyrece *See* Tyrese

Tyree Unknown, possibly from Tiree

in Scotland (geographical name, shifted from surname usage)

Tyreece *See* Tyrese

Tyreek *See* Tarek

Tyreese *See* Tyrese

Tyreke *See* Tarek

Tyrel/Tyrell/Tyrelle *See* Tyrrell

Tyren *See* Tyrone

Tyrese/Tyresse/Tyrhys A blend of Ty and Reese/Rhys. The name of the singer and rapper Tyrese Darnell Gibson

Tyrik/Tyriq/Tyrique *See* Tarek

Tyron/Tyrone/Tyronne Irish Gaelic: land of Eoghan. A county in Ireland (geographical name)

Tyrrell Unknown, possibly from Thorold, Old English: Thor's wolf (shifted from surname usage)

Tyrus From Tyre, a city in Lebanon (geographical name)

Tyson Unknown, possibly Old French (from tison): fiery (shifted from surname usage)

Tzvi *See* Zvi

u

Ubaid *See* Abd

Ubaidullah *See* Abdullah

Ubayd *See* Abd

Ubaydullah *See* Abdullah

Uchechukwu Igbo: god's will

Uchenna Igbo: god's thoughts

Uday Arabic: ascend

Ugnius Lithuanian: fire, flames

Ugochukwu Igbo: god's eagle, god's crown

Ugur/Uğur Turkish: luck

Ultan Irish Gaelic: Ulster (geographical name)

Umair Arabic: intelligent

Umar The name of Farooq the Great, one the prophet Muhammad's companions. *See also* Amr

Umayr *See* Umair

Umer *See* Umar

Umut Turkish: hope

Unais Arabic: love, affection

Uriah Hebrew: my light is god

Uriel Hebrew: god is my light. The archangel who carries a flaming sword

Usaamah *See* Usama

Usaid Arabic: small lion

Usama/Usamah Arabic: lion

Usayd *See* Usaid

Usmaan/Usman/Uthmaan/ Uthman *See* Usama

Uwais Arabic: small wolf

Uzair/Uzayr A figure in the Qu'ran identified with Ezra the Scribe. *See* Ezra

v

Vadim Old Norse: ruler

Vakaris Unknown, possibly Latvian: evening

Valentin/Valentine/Valentino Latin: strong, healthy. The name of Saint Valentine, now associated with love

Vansh Hindi (from vanash): ancestry, blood

Varun From Varuna, the Hindu god of the celestial ocean

Vasco From the name Velasco (Basque: crow)

Vasile *See* Basil

Vaughan/Vaughn Welsh (from bychan): small (shifted from surname usage). Also various place names, including a city in Canada (geographical name)

Ved A diminutive form of Vedant

Vedant From the Hindu philosophy Vedanta, which aims to understand the ultimate reality

Veer A diminutive form of Veeran

Veeran Tamil: warrior

Vernon Gaulish: place of alders (shifted from surname usage). Also various place names (geographical name)

Victor Latin: victor

Viet From Vietnam

Viggo Old Norse: war

Vihaan Bhojpuri (from bihaan): tomorrow

Vijay Sanskrit (from vijaya): victory. A name for Arjuna, a hero in Hindu scripture

Vikas Sanskrit: beam, shine, be bright

Vikash/Vikesh Sanskrit (from vikaz): to appear, to make clear

Vikram Sanskrit (from vikrama): prowess, power, step, stride, implying the stride of the Hindu god Vishnu

Viktor *See* Victor

Vinay Sanskrit (from vinaya): guidance

Vince A diminutive form of Vincent

Vincent/Vincenzo Latin: conquer

Vinesh From Vighnesha, a name of the Hindu elephant-headed god, Ganesha

Vinicius Latin: wine (shifted from surname usage)

Vinni/Vinnie/Vinny A diminutive form of Vincent

Vir Punjabi: brave

Viraaj/Viraj Sanskrit: king, warrior

Viren Unknown, possibly Sanskrit (from vira): brave, hero

Vishal Hindi: large

Vishnu The name of the Hindu god who is the preserver of the universe

Vito Latin: life **Vittorio** *See* Victor

Vivaan Hindi: spirit of life

Vivek Hindi: conscience

Vlad Slavic: rule, command. Also a diminutive form of Vladimir and Vladislav

Vladimir Slavic: commanding great power

Vladislav Slavic: one who commands fame

Volkan Turkish: volcano

Vraj *See* Viraj

Wade Old English: ford (shifted from surname usage)

Wael Arabic: return for shelter

Wafi Arabic: true, trustworthy

Wahab Arabic: to grant. Al-Wahab is one of Allah's 99 names, meaning Gifter and Bestower, and reciting it repeatedly, it is believed, can alleviate the effects of poverty and grant fulfilment

Waheed/Wahid Arabic: unique

Wajahat Arabic: dignity, elevate

Wajid Arabic: finder, lover

Waleed *See* Walid

Wali Arabic: prince, protector, saint, symbolised by the crown. Also short for Waliullah, meaning friend of god

Walid Arabic: newborn child

Wallace Old French: foreigner, Welshman (shifted from surname usage)

Walter Old German: ruler of the army

Waqar Arabic: majesty, dignity, grace

Waqas Arabic: companion

Waris Arabic: heir, successor

Warren Old German: enclosure

Warrick/Warwick Old English: dwelling by the weir (shifted from surname usage). Also the name of the town in Warwickshire (geographical name)

Waseem Arabic: beautiful, graceful

Wasif Arabic: one who praises

Wasim/Wassim Arabic: handsome, graceful

Wayne Old English: wagon (shifted from surname usage)

Wei Chinese: various, including mighty and power

Wesley/Westley Old English: west meadow (shifted from surname usage)

Weston Old English: west town (shifted from surname usage)

Wezley *See* Wesley

Wiktor *See* Victor

Wil A diminutive form of William

Wilbur Old English: wild boar

Wilf A diminutive form of Wilfred

Wilfred/Wilfrid Old English: desire for peace

Wiliam *See* William

Will A diminutive form of William

Willem/William Old German: will, desire and helmet, protection

Willis *See* William (shifted from surname usage)

Willoughby Old English: willow town (shifted from surname usage)

Wilson Old English: son of William (shifted from surname usage)

Winston Old English: joy stone (shifted from surname usage)

Wisdom (name from an English word)

Witold The Polish form of Vytautas (Lithuanian: pursuer of the people). Vytautas the Great was a famous ruler of Lithuania

Wojciech Slavic: the happy warrior, the joy of war

Wolfgang Old German: wolf path

Woodrow Old English: row of houses by the wood (shifted from surname usage). Also used as a first name by former president of the USA Woodrow Wilson

Woody A diminutive form of Woodrow

Wyatt Old English: war hardy (shifted from surname usage)

Wyn Welsh (from gwyn): fair

Xander A diminutive form of Alexander

Xavi A diminutive form of Xavier

Xavier The name of the Catholic saint Francis Xavier, who took his surname from the town where he was born (shifted from surname usage)

Yaakov *See* Jacob

Yaaseen *See* Yasin

Yaasir *See* Yasir

Yacine *See* Yasin

Yacob/Yacoub/Yacqub *See* Jacob

Yad Hebrew: hand. The name of the Torah pointer

Yafet *See* Japheth

Yahia/Yahya/Yahyaa/Yahye Arabic: the name of John the Baptist, son of Zechariah. *See also* John

Yakov/Yakub *See* Jacob

Yameen/Yamin Arabic: right side

Yan Chinese: various, including severe and grey geese. *See also* John

Yanis/Yann/Yannick/Yannis *See* John

Yaqoob/Yaqub *See* Jacob

Yasar *See* Yaser

Yaseen *See* Yasin

Yaser Arabic: prosperity, wealth

Yash Hindi: success

Yasin From Ya Sin, the 36th chapter of the Qur'an, known as the heart of the Qur'an

Yasir Arabic: prosperous, wealthy

Yasser *See* Yaser

Yassin/Yassine *See* Yasin

Yassir *See* Yasir

Yaw Akan: born on a Thursday

Yazan Persian: determined

Yechiel Hebrew: may god live

Yehoshua *See* Joshua

Yehuda/Yehudah *See* Judah

Yiannis *See* John

Yigit/Yiğit Turkish: brave

Yilmaz Turkish: undaunted

Yishai *See* Jesse

Yisroel *See* Israel

Yitzchok *See* Isaac

Yoan *See* John

Yoel *See* Joel

Yohan *See* John

Yona *See* Jonah

Yonatan *See* Jonathan

Yong Chinese: various, including brave and everlasting

Yoni A diminutive form of Yonis

Yonis *See* Jonah

Yosef *See* Joseph

Yossi A diminutive form of Yusuf

Youcef *See* Joseph

Younes/Younis/Younus *See* Jonah

Yousaf/Yousef/Yousif/Youssef/ Yousuf *See* Joseph

Yuan Chinese: various, including fated connection, meadow and river source

Yug Hindi: a measurement of time

Yunis/Yunus *See* Jonah

Yuri *See* George. (This is also a Japanese girls' name meaning lily)

Yusaf/Yusef *See* Joseph

Yusha Japanese: hero (not usually used as a name in this form). *See also* Joshua

Yusif/Yussuf/Yusuf *See* Joseph

Yusuke Japanese: various, often including the particle that means masculine

Yuta Japanese: various, including many friends, very brave and very abundant

Yuusuf *See* Joseph

Yuvan Sanskrit: strong, beautiful, healthy

Yuvraaj/Yuvraj Sanskrit (from yuvaraja): kumar, crown prince (Sikh name)

Yves A French variant of Ivo

Z

Zaakir *See* Zakir

Zac A diminutive form of Zachary

Zacary *See* Zachary

Zacchaeus Hebrew: pure and righteous. The name of a tax collector from the Gospel of Luke

Zach A diminutive form of Zachary

Zachari/Zacharia/Zachariah/ Zacharias/Zacharie/Zachariya/ Zachary/Zachery Hebrew: god has remembered. The name of various biblical characters

Zack A diminutive form of Zachary

Zackaria/Zackariah/Zackariya/ Zackary/Zackery *See* Zachary

Zade *See* Zaid

Zaeem Arabic: rich, healthy, ruler

Zafar Arabic: victory

Zafir Arabic: victorious

Zaheer Arabic: blooming, shining, helper, supporter

Zahi Arabic: beautiful, glowing

Zahid Arabic: devout

Zahir Arabic: apparent, evident

Zaid/Zaidan/Zaiden Arabic: abundance, growth

Zaim Arabic: leader

Zain/Zaine Arabic: beauty

Zainul Arabic: ornament

Zaiyan *See* Zayyan

Zak A diminutive form of Zachary

Zakai *See* Zakiah

Zakari/Zakaria/Zakariah/ Zakariya/Zakariyah/Zakariye/ Zakariyya/Zakariyyah/Zakary/ Zakarya/Zakeriya/Zakery *See* Zachary

Zaki/Zakiah Hebrew: pure

Zakir Arabic: remembering, grateful

Zakk A diminutive form of Zachary

Zaman Arabic: time, era

Zameer Arabic: conscience

Zander A diminutive form of Alexander

Zane Unknown, shifted from surname usage

Zarif Arabic: elegant, witty

Zavier *See* Xavier

Zayaan/Zayan Arabic: beauty

Zayd *See* Zaid

Zaydan/Zayden Arabic: growth and increase

Zayed *See* Zaid

Zayn/Zayne *See* Zane

Zayyan *See* Zayan

Ze Diminutive form of Jose

Zeb Persian: beauty, decoration

Zebedee Hebrew: gift of god. The father of James and John in the New Testament

Zechariah *See* Zachary

Zed A diminutive form of Zedekiah (Hebrew: justice of god), the name of the last king of Judah

Zeeshaan/Zeeshan Arabic: pompous

Zein *See* Zain

Zeke A diminutive form of Ezekiel

Zeki Turkish: intelligent

Zen Japanese: the Buddist word for the meditative state

Zeno/Zenon The name of several philosophers from antiquity. *See also* Zeus

Zeph/Zephan A diminutive form of Zephaniah

Zephaniah Hebrew: god has hidden The name of the prophet. Zephaniah and several others from the Old Testament

Zephyr (name from an English word). Derived from Zephyrus, the Greek god of the west wind

Zeshaan/Zeshan *See* Zeehaan

Zeus The father of gods and men, and the ruler of the Olympians from Greek mythology

Zev Hebrew: wolf

Zeyad *See* Ziyaad

Zhen Chinese: various, including true and treasure

Zheng Chinese, various, including proper and conquer

Zhir *See* Zahir

Zia Arabic: light, glowing

Ziad *See* Ziyaad

Zico The nickname of Arthur Antunes Coimbra, the Brazilian former footballer, who was called Arthurzico by his sister (footballer name)

Zidaan/Zidan/Zidane *See* Zaid. Also the surname of Zinedine Zidane (footballer name)

Ziggy A diminutive form of Sigmund

Zinedine A form of the name Zayn ad-Din (Arabic: ornament of religion). This form became more well-known for being the one used by the footballer Zinedine Zidane (footballer name)

Zishaan/Zishan *See* Zeehaan

Ziyaad/Ziyad Arabic: increasing, abundant

Ziyan Arabic: light

Zohaib Arabic: golden

Zohair Arabic: bright, shining

Zoheb *See* Zohaib

Zoltan/Zoltán Turkish: sultan. *See also* Sultan

Zoran Slavic: dawn, daybreak

Zubair/Zubayr Arabic: small piece of iron, brave person

Zubin Persian: spear

Zuhaib *See* Zohaib

Zuhair/Zuhayr Arabic: small flower

Zuriel Hebrew: god is my rock. The son of Abihail from the Old Testament

Zvi Hebrew: dear

Girls and boys

a

Aarya *See* Arya

Abrar Arabic: faithful

Ada Hebrew: adornment. Also diminutive form of Adelaide and Adeline, Old German: noble, kind

Adan Irish Gaelic (from áed): fire. Also a Spanish variant of Adam. Also a traditional Kurdish name for girls

Addison Old English: son of Adam (shifted from surname usage)

Aiman *See* Ayman

Aimen *See* Ayman

Ainsley Old English: clearing in the wood

Akira Japanese: bright, shining, clear

Al A diminutive form of Albert and Alberta

Alaa Arabic: high rank, noble

Alexi/Alexis Greek: to help

Ally A diminutive form of various names, including Aliza and Alice

Amal Arabic: hope

Aman Arabic: safe, protected. Also Punjabi: peace

Amandeep Punjabi: lamp of peace (Sikh name)

Amani Arabic: wishes, aspiration

Amardeep Punjabi: lamp of immortality (Sikh name)

Amari Sanskrit: goddess. Also Hindi: immortal

Ameya Sanskrit: immeasurable

Amran Arabic: crown. Also Irish Gaelic (from amrae): wonderful

Amrit Sanskrit (from amrta): immortality, the nectar that grants immortality. Also the holy water used in Amrit Sanskar, a baptism ceremony in Sikhism

Amun Egyptian: the hidden one, the name of a self-created Egyptian god

Andi A diminutive form of Andrea and Andrew

Andrea Greek (from andreios): man, manly

Anesu Shona: is with us

Angel (name from an English word)

Anh Vietnamese: England (geographical name)

Anmol Arabic: precious

Areen Arabic: bird song

Aria Hebrew: lioness. Also Italian: air, a song accompanying a solo voice in the musical terms

Arian Welsh: silver

Ariel Hebrew: lion of god

Armani Persian: Armenian. Also associated with the Italian designer

Giorgio Armani (shifted from surname)

Arshia Persian: throne
Also possible Sanskrit (from arghya): honey

Arya Sanskrit: worthy, noble, wise, polite. *See also* Aria

Asha Sanskrit (from aza): hope

Asher Hebrew (from osher): happy, blessing. Also Old English: place with ash trees (shifted from surname usage)

Ashlee/Ashleigh/Ashley Old English (aesc and leah): ash clearing (shifted from surname usage)

Ashton Old English (aesc and tun): ash clearing (shifted from surname usage)

Aspen (name from flowers and trees, name from an English word)

Aubrey French: ruler of elves

August (name from an English word)

Avery From Aubri, Old German (from alb and ric): elf ruler (shifted from surname usage)

Ayman/Aymen Arabic: righteous, lucky

Ayomide Yoruba: my joy has arrived

Ayomikun Yoruba: my joy is full

Azariah Hebrew: Jehovah has helped

b

Baby (term of endearment, name from an English word)

Bailee/Baileigh/Bailey/Bailie/Baillie Old English: bailiff (shifted from surname usage)

Baran Persian: rain

Bay (name from an English word)

Baylee/Bayleigh/Bayley *See* Bailey

Beau French: beautiful

Beren Tolkien's Sindarin: brave, the name of Beren Erchamion

Billie/Billy A diminutive form of Belinda and William

Blair Scottish Gaelic (from blàr): various, including battlefield, field and moss

Blaise/Blaize French: lisping

Blake Old English: black or pale (shifted from surname usage)

Blaze (name from an English word). *See also* Blaise

Blessing (name from an English word)

Blu *See* Blue

Blue (name from an English word)

Bo Old Norse (from búa): to live
Also French (from beau): handsome. Also a diminutive form of Bonita

Bobbi/Bobbie/Bobby A diminutive form of Robert and Roberta

Boe *See* Bo

Boluwatife Yoruba: the way god wants it

Bracken (name from flowers and trees, name from an English word). From O' Breacain, Irish Gaelic (from brecc): speckled

Brodi/Brodie/Brody Unknown (shifted from surname usage)

Brogan From the O'Brogan family (shifted from surname usage)

Brook/Brooke (name from an English word) Brooklyn/Brooklynn/Brooklynne. *See* Brooke. Also an area in New York (geographical name)

C

Cally A diminutive form of Calandra, from O'Cathalain, Irish Gaelic: little Charles (shifted from surname usage). Also a diminutive form of Calista, Greek: most beautiful

Cameron Scottish Gaelic (from cam and sròn): crooked nose (shifted from surname usage)

Casey From the Irish surname Cathasach (Irish Gaelic, from cathaisech: watchful, vigilant)

Cassidy Irish Gaelic: curly haired (shifted from surname usage)

Ceejay A blend of two letters of the alphabet

Celyn Welsh: holly (name from flowers and trees)

Ceri A diminutive form of Ceridwen, Unknown, possibly Welsh (gwyn): fair. Also Turkish (from çeri): army

Chaise See Chase

Chance (name from an English word)

Charley/Charli/Charlie/Charly A diminutive form of Charles and Charlotte

Chase (name from an English word). Old English: huntsman (shifted from surname usage)

Chay A diminutive form of Charles and Chase

Che Spanish: friend. Also a diminutive form of José. Associated with Che Guevara

Chesney Old French (from ches and nai): dweller by oaks (shifted from surname usage)

Chi Chinese: various, including sustain and support. Also Japanese: earth, though not commonly used in Japan as a name

Chidera Igbo: what god has said, what god has written

Chisom From Chisholm, unknown (shifted from surname usage)

Christie A diminutive form of Christopher and Christina

Christy A diminutive form of Christopher and Christina

Cian Irish Gaelic: ancient

Codey/Codi/Codie/Cody Irish: a descendant of Cuidightheach (shifted from surname usage)

Courtney Old French: pug nose

Cy A diminutive form of Cyril and Cyrilla

d

Dakota Lakota Sioux: friendly. Also the US states of North Dakota or South Dakota (geographical name)

Dale Old English: valley (shifted from surname usage)

Dallas Scottish Gaelic (from dail and fàs): meadow growth (shifted from surname usage). Also the city in Texas (geographical name)

Damilola A diminutive form of Oluwadamilola

Dani A diminutive form of Daniel and Daniela

Dara Arabic: moon. Also Turkish: leader. *See also* Daria and Darragh

Darcey/Darcy/D'arcy Old English: from Arcy in France (shifted from surname usage)

Darragh Unknown, possibly Irish Gaelic (from dairbre): oak

Deanne Old English: valley

Dempsey From O'Diomasaigh, Irish Gaelic (from díummusach): proud (shifted from surname usage). Also possible Old English (from dembel): on the lake

Denver From Danefella, Old English (from Dena and faer): way of the Danes, path of the Danes (shifted from surname usage). The city in Colorado (geographical name)

Deon See Dion

Derry Irish Gaelic: oak grove, oak wood (shifted from surname usage). Also a diminutive form of Diarmaid. Also a city in Northern Ireland (geographical name)

Destiny (name from an English word)

Devan Persian (from divan): poetry. *See also* Devon

Deven *See* Devan and Devon

Devon Unknown, possibly French (from devin): holy, divine (shifted from surname usage). Also possibly French (from devan): before, in front. Also a county in England (geographical name). *See also* Devan

Devyn See Devan and Devon

Diamond (gemstone name, name from an English word)

Diaz Spanish: son of Diago (shifted from surname usage)

Dilan Turkish: love

Dion A diminutive form of Dionysius, from Dionysus, the god of wine from Greek mythology

Divine (name from an English word)

Drew A diminutive form of Andrew (Greek: warrior)

Dylan Welsh (from dy and llanw): tide, flow

e

Eden Possibly Aramaic: watered, fruitful. God's garden where Adam and Eve lived before their fall from grace

Ekin Turkish: harvest

Elham Old English (from alor and ham): alder village (shifted from surname usage). *See also* Ilham

Eli Hebrew: lofty and high. The name of the Jewish High Priest and last of the Israelite judges in Shiloh tradition

Elia See Elijah

Elie See Eli and Elijah

Elijah Hebrew: my god is Jehovah. A prophet from the Book of Kings

Elis A Swedish form of Elias. Also a diminutive form of Elizabeth

Elisha Hebrew: my god is salvation. The name of a prophet who could work wonders, including the ressurection of a child

Elliot/Elliott Old English: son of Elijah (shifted from surname usage)

Ellis Old English: of Elijah (shifted from surname usage). Also a Danish variant of Alice. *See also* Elis

Ellison Old English: son of Ellis (shifted from surname usage)

Emaan Sanskrit (from eman): way, course. Also possibly Persian (from eman): always, constant. *See also* Imaan

Emerson Old English: Amery's son (Amery, Old German, from amal and ric: powerful and brave; shifted from surname usage)

Eniola Yoruba: of wealth

Erin Gaelic: Ireland

Eris Greek: strife. A Greek goddess of discord who set the Trojan War in motion by making Aphrodite, Athena and Hera fight for the golden apple labelled 'to the fairest one'

Evan Hebrew: Jehova is gracious. A Welsh variant of John

Evin Turkish: kernel. See also Evan

Ezel Turkish: eternity

Ezra Hebrew: help. The name of Ezra the Scribe

f

Franki/Frankie A diminutive form of Francesca or Frank

Freddie A diminutive form of Frederica

g

Gabriel/Gabriele Hebrew: warrior of god, strength of god. The angel who acts as a messenger of god

Gurvinder Punjabi: lord, Guru (Sikh name)

h

Hadley Old English (from haeth and leah): heathland clearing (shifted from surname usage)

Hanan Arabic: tender, compassionate. Also Hebrew: gift of god. *See also* Hannan

Hani Arabic: happy, satisfied. Also possibly Arabic (from hanee): wholesome. Also a diminutive form of Hannah

Hannan From O'Hannon, Irish Gaelic: from the city Hanna (shifted from surname usage). *See also* Hanan

Hardeep Punjabi: lamp of god (Sikh name)

Harjot Punjabi: light of god (Sikh name)

Harlee *See* Harley

Harleigh/Harley/Harli/Harlie Old English (from hoer and leah): rock clearing (shifted from surname usage)

Harlow Old English: unknown, possibly temple hill (shifted from surname usage). Also a town in Essex (geographical name)

Harman Old English: grey man (shifted from surname usage)

Harmeet Punjabi: beloved friend of god (Sikh name)

Harnoor Punjabi: aura light of god (Sikh name)

Harper (shifted from surname usage, name from an English word)

Harpreet Punjabi: one who loves god (Sikh name)

Honor/Honour (name from an English word)

Hope (name from an English word)

i

Ibukunoluwa Yoruba: god's blessing

Ifeoluwa Yoruba: god's love

Ihsan Arabic: beautiful, handsome, perfection, excellence

Ikram Arabic: honour, respect

Ilham Arabic (from elham): inspiration. *See also* Elham

Ilhan Turkish: ruler of a province

Imaan/Iman/Imani Arabic: faith

Indi A diminutive form of India, Indiana and Indigo

Indie A diminutive form of India,

Indiana and Indigo

Indigo Greek: blue dye from India (colour name)

Indy A diminutive form of India, Indiana and Indigo

Inioluwa Yoruba: receiving god's treasure

Ira Hebrew: watchful. Also a diminutive form of Irene

Isa An Arabic form of Jesus. Also a diminutive form of Isabella/Isabelle

Isher Hindi (from ishara): sign

j

Jacey A blend of two letters of the alphabet. Also a diminutive form of Jack and Jacqueline

Jackie A diminutive form of Jack and Jacqueline

Jacy Native American: moon. *See also* Jacey

Jade (gemstone name, name from an English word)

Jaden/Jadyn Hebrew (from jadon): thankful. Also Persian (from jadin): chrysolite, green like chrysolite. Also a blend of Jay and Aiden/Hayden

Jae/Jai A diminutive form of Jaden and Jason

Jaiden See Jaden

Jaime A Portuguese and Spanish variant of James

Jaimie/Jamie A diminutive form of James

Jamielee A blend of Jamie and Lee

Jan Hebrew: Jehova is gracious. A Croatian, Czech, Danish, Dutch, Polish, Slovenian and Scandinavian variant of John. Also a diminutive form of Janet

Jasdeep Punjabi: lamp of god's glory (Sikh name)

Jaskirat Punjabi: dedicated to god's glory by honest and hard work (Sikh name)

Jasmeet Punjabi: beloved friend of god's glory (Sikh name)

Jaspreet Punjabi: love of god's glory (Sikh name)

Jay From the letter 'J'

Jaycee A blend of two letters of the alphabet

Jaydee A blend of two letters of the alphabet

Jayden See Jaden

Jaye A diminutive form of Jaden and Jason

Jaylee A blend of Jaye and Lee

Jaz A diminutive form of James, Janet and Jasmine

Jean Hebrew: Jehova is gracious. A feminine form of John. Also a French variant of John

Jeevan Hindi (from jivan): life, soul, existence

Jess/Jesse/Jessie/Jessy Hebrew: god

exists. The father of King David. Also diminutive form of Jessica

Jewel (name from an English word)

Jia Chinese: various, including good

Jing Chinese: various, including capital, respect and well

Jo A diminutive form of Joanna, Joseph and Josephine

Jocelyn Old French: From the tribe of the Gauts

Jodi/Jody Hebrew: praised. Also Hebrew: Jehovah will increase A variant of Judy. Also a diminutive form of Joseph

Joey/Jojo A diminutive form of Joanna, Joseph and Josephine

Jordan/Jorden/Jordon/Jordyn Hebrew (from yarden): flowing down. Named after the River Jordan (geographical name)

Jorgie A diminutive form of George and Georgina

Joss A diminutive form of Jocelyn and Joseph

Joy (name from an English word)

Jude A diminutive form of Judas, Hebrew: praised. A brother of Jesus

Justice (name from an English word)

k

Ka The vital essence of the soul from Egyptian mythology

Kacey/Kaci See Casey

Kai Unknown, possibly Hawaiian: sea. Also an Estonian diminutive form of Kaja. Also a Danish and Norwegian variant of Caius

Kaiya Old Norse: hen. Also a diminutive form of Katarina. See also Kaya

Kameron See Cameron

Karam Arabic: generous

Kasey See Casey

Kavya Sanskrit: poem, sonnet

Kaya Turkish: rock

Kayde A blend of two letters from the alphabet. Also unknown, possibly from the Cathán family (Irish Gaelic, from cathaigid: battle, fight; shifted from surname usage)

Kayden Unknown, possibly from the Cathán family (Irish Gaelic, from cathaigid: battle, fight; shifted from surname usage)

Kaylan/Kaylen Scottish Gaelic: young dog

Kayra Turkish: grace, kindness, favour

Kazi Arabic: a judge and scholar of Islamic law

Keegan From Mac Aodhagáin, Old Gaelic: fire

Keelin See Kellen

Kehinde Yoruba: the last to come (given to the younger twin). See also Taiyewo

Kelby Old English (from cild and byr): child's farm (shifted from surname usage)

Kelechi Igbo: glorifying god

Kellen Irish Gaelic: slender

Kelly Irish Gaelic (from ceallach): bright headed

Kelsey Old English (from cēol and siġe): victorious ship

Kendal/Kendall Old English (from Kent and dæl): valley of Kent shifted from surname usage)

Kenzi/Kenzie/Kenzy See Mackenzi

Kerry Irish Gaelic: Ciar's people, Irish Gaelic (from cíar): dark, murky, black

Kes Unknown, possibly from the word 'kestrel'

Kia/Kiah Persian: lord, master. Also Swedish diminutive form of Christina. *See also* Kiya and Kya

Kieran Hindi: beam, ray, light, spark. Also Scottish Gaelic (from ciaradh): darkening, twilight. Also Irish Gaelic (from cíar): dark, murky, black

Kim A diminutive form of Kimberley

Kimi A diminutive form of Joakim and Kimberley

Kiran Hindi: beam, ray, light, spark

Kirby Old English (from kirk and byr): church's farm (shifted from surname usage)

Kit A diminutive form of Christopher and Katherine

Kiya Hindi: bird's cooing. Also Oromo: mine. *See also* Kia and Kya

Kodi/Kodie/Kody See Cody

Kori Unknown (shifted from surname usage). Also Quechua: gold. Also a diminutive form of Corrina

Kosisochukwu Igbo: as it is wished by god

Krishna Hindi (from karashn): black, dark blue. From the name of the blue-skinned Hindu god Krishna

Kristen A Danish variant of Christian and a variant of Christina

Kya/Kyah Yurok: spring. *See also* Kia and Kiya

Kym *See* Kim

l

Laine Estonian and Finnish: wave (shifted from surname usage)

Lamar Arabic: liquid gold. Also Old French: from the sea

Laurie A diminutive form of Laura and Laurence

Lee/Leigh Old English (from leah): clearing (shifted from surname usage)

Leighton Old English (from lad and tun): conduit town (shifted from surname usage). Also Old English (from leac and tun): vegetable town (shifted from surname usage)

Leone Italian: the star sign Leo

Levi Minaean (from lawi'u): priest. Also possibly Hebrew: join. A son of Jacob

Lexus Created Alexis by Toyota. Also from Lexis (shifted from surname usage). *See* Alexis

Li Chinese: various, including sharp and beautiful

Lian Chinese: various, including lotus

Logan Scottish Gaelic: little hollow

London The capital of the UK (geographical name)

Lowen A German variant of Leuven, a city in Belgium (geographical name)

Luca An Italian variant of Luke

Luka A Croatian, Finnish, German and Russian variant of Luke

m

Maahi Sanskrit (from mahi): heaven and earth

Mackenzie/Makenzie Unknown, possibly from Mac Coinnich, Irish Gaelic (from cáennach): mildrew (shifted from surname usage)

Madison Old English: Madde's son, Magdalene's son

Malek Arabic: master, angel, king

Al-Malik is one of Allah's 99 names, meaning King, and reciting it is believed to help gain wealth and esteem

Mali The country in West Africa (geographical name). Also a Welsh variant of Mary. Also a diminutive form of Malachi

Mandeep Punjabi: lamp of sages, lamp of the mind (Sikh name)

Manjot Punjabi: light of sages, light of the mind (Sikh name)

Manmeet Punjabi: friend of sages, friend of the mind (Sikh name)

Manpreet Punjabi: happiness of the heart, from love of the mind (Sikh name)

Marian A blend of Maria and Anne. Also a German variant of Marius

Marlee/Marley/Marli/Marlie/ Marly Old English (from mearth and leah): pine clearing (shifted from surname usage)

Marni Hebrew: rejoice. Also unknown (shifted from surname usage)

Marvellous (name from an English word)

Mattie A diminutive form of Martha, Matthew and Matthias

Maxime Latin: the greatest

Mckenzie *See* Mackenzie

Memphis The capital city in ancient Egypt, named after a woman from Greek mythology (geographical name)

Micah Hebrew: one who is like Jehovah

Michal Hebrew: one who is like Jehovah. A daughter of Saul and wife of David. Also a Czech and Slovakian variant of Michael

Michele An Italian variant of Michael. Also an anglicised French variant of Michelle

Mika A diminutive form of Michael and Michaela. Also Native American: clever raccoon

Milan Slavic (from mil): beloved, dear. Also the name of the Italian city (geographical name)

Miley Unknown (shifted from surname usage). The nickname of Miley Cyrus, because she is smiley

Ming Chinese: various, including bright and tomorrow

Mir Arabic: chief, prince

Miracle (name from an English word)

Misha A Russian variant of Michael. Also a dimiutive form of Michelle

Morgan/Morgen Unknown, possibly from Morrígan, a goddess of war and strife from Irish mythology

Myka A dimiutive form of Michael and Michelle

n

Nana Japanese: various, including enduring plant. Also Akan: chief

Neev Irish Gaelic: bright, radiant. Also Persian: brave, heroic

Nehal Persian: shoot, twig, young

Nicky/Nico A diminutive form of Nicholas and Nicole

Nikita Greek (from aniketos): unconquerable

Nikola A Croatian and Czech variant of Nicholas and Nicole

Nima Unknown, possibly Persian: just, fair, bow. Also Burmese (from nyima): younger sister

Noa A Hawaiian variant of Noah

Noor/Nour Arabic: light

Nurul Arabic (from nur and ul): light of Nyasha
Shona: grace, mercy

o

Oakleigh/Oakley Old English: oak clearing (shifted from surname usage). Also several place names in the UK and the US (geographical name)

Ocean (name from an English word)

Olamide Yoruba: my wealth has come

Ollie A diminutive form of Olvier and Olivia

Oluwadamilola Yoruba: god has rewarded me with wealth

Oluwadarasimi Yoruba: god is good to me

Oluwademilade Yoruba: god has crowned me

Oluwajomiloju Yoruba: god has surprised me

Oluwanifemi Yoruba: god has love for me

Oluwapelumi Yoruba: god is with me

Oluwasemilore Yoruba: god has done me a favour

Oluwaseun Yoruba: thanks be to god

Oluwaseyi Yoruba: god has done this

Oluwatamilore Yoruba: god blessed me with a gift

Oluwatobi Yoruba: god is mighty

Oluwatobiloba Yoruba: god is a mighty king

Oluwatomisin Yoruba: god is enough for me to serve

Oluwatoni Yoruba: god is worth having

Oreoluwa Yoruba: gift of god

P

Paisley Unknown, possibly Greek (from basilike): church. The name of the Scottish town, for which the paisley design is named (geographical name)

Panashe French: plume of feathers, flamboyant, panache

Paris The name of the Trojan prince who eloped with Helen, and, according to Greek mythology, started the Trojan War. Also the capital city of France (geographical name)

Parminder Punjabi: highest god (Sikh name)

Payton See Peyton

Perri/Perrie/Perry Old English (from pyrige): pear tree (name from flowers and trees, shifted from surname usage). Also a diminutive form of Peregrine, Latin (from peregrinus): foreigner

Peyton Old English: from Peyton, possibly the village in Essex (shifted from surname usage)

Pheonix See Phoenix

Phoenix (name from an English word). Also various place names, including the city in the US (geographical name)

Prabhjot Punjabi: god's light (Sikh name)

Praise (name from an English word)

Precious (name from an English word)

Preet Hindi (from priti): love, affection

Presley Old English (from preost and leah): priest's clearing (shifted from surname usage). Associated with Elvis Presley

Puneet Punjabi: pure, holy (Sikh name)

q

Quinn From O'Cuinn, Irish Gaelic (from conn): counsel (shifted from surname usage)

r

Raegan See Reagan

Rajdeep Punjabi: lamp of the kingdom (Sikh name)

Raman Sanskrit (from rama): dear, beloved. A name of the Hindu god Rama

Ramandeep Punjabi: lamp of god's love (Sikh name)

Rana Arabic: gaze, eye-catching. Also Sanskrit: king, gladness, delight

Rand Old German: edge of a shield (shifted from surname usage). Also Arabic: bay laurel (name from flowers and trees)

Ravinder Punjabi: lord of the sun god (Sikh name)

Rayan See Rayyan and Reyhan

Rayne Unknown, possibly Old German (from ragin): counsel (shifted from surname usage). Also possibly Old French (from reine): queen

Rayyan Arabic: sated, no longer thirsting

Reagan From O'Riagan, Irish Gaelic (from ríodhg): impulsive (shifted from surname usage)

Reece Turkish (from reis): leader. Also Old German: rice (shifted from surname usage). Also Old Welsh (from rīs): ardour

Reegan/Regan See Reagan

Rene French (from rené): reborn

Reyhan Arabic: sweet basil

Rhian/Rian Welsh (from rhiain): maiden. *See also* Reyhan and Ryan

Ricki/Rikki A diminutive form of Richard

Riley Old English (from rygh and leah): rye meadow

Rio Portuguese: river. Also from Rio de Janeiro, the city in Brazil (geographical name)

Ripley Old English (from ripel and leah): strip of clearing (shifted from surname usage)

River (name from an English word)

Riyaan/Riyan *See* Rayyan and Reyhan

Robin/Robyn Old German (from hrod): fame

Romi Japanese: various, including beautiful. Also a diminutive form of Romeo and Rosemary

Roni/Ronnie A diminutive form of Ronald

Rowan/Rowen From Ó Ruadháin, Irish Gaelic (from ruadh): red, red-haired

Rudi A diminutive form of Rudolf

Ryan From O'Riain, Irish Gaelic (from rí and an): little king (shifted from surname usage)

Rylee/Ryleigh/Ryley/Rylie Old English (from rygh and leah): rye meadow

S

Sahib Punjabi: companion, friend, the Guru (Sikh name)

Sai Hindi: a flower. Also Chinese: various, including competition

Sam A diminutive form of Samuel and Samantha

Saman Persian: riches, welfare, strength. Also Arabic: value

Samar Arabic: result, fruit, conversation, story

Sami Arabic: high, exalted, supreme. Also a diminutive form of Samuel

Sammi/Sammy A diminutive form of Samuel and Samantha

Sandeep Punjabi: lighted lamp, symbolising always there for you (Sikh name)

Sandy A diminutive form of Alexander and Alexandra

Saran Sanskrit (from sarani): path, way. Also Persian: commander, general

Sascha/Sasha A diminutive form of Alexander and Alexandra

Saxon Unknown, possibly Old English (from seax): a type of knife carried by the Saxons

Sennen Unknown, possibly Old Gaelic: wise man. A parish and cove in Cornwall (geographical name)

Seren Welsh: star

Shaan Hindi (from shan): dignity, brilliance, joy

Shae A diminutive form of Shamus. *See also* Shai

Shah Persian: king, soverign

Shaheen Persian (from shāhīn): royal falcon

Shai Hebrew: gift, offering

Shalom Hebrew: peace

Shamim Arabic: fragrant, sweet smell, perfume

Shan Chinese: various, including coral and mountain. *See also* Shaan

Shannon Gaelic: wise one, little owl

Shay/Shaya/Shaye *See* Shai and Shea

Shea Unknown, possibly Old English (from sceaga): wood (shifted from surname usage)

Sheik/Sheikh Arabic (from sheykh): elder, wise man, chief. A title for learned men and tribal leaders

Sheldon Old English (from scylf and denu): ledge valley, steep valley

(shifted from surname usage)

Sheridan From O'Sirideain, Irish Gaelic (from siride and an): little elf (shifted from surname usage)

Shia A diminutive form of Isshiah, Hebrew: Jehovah will lend. *See also* Shea

Shiloh Hebrew: tranquil, quiet, rest. An ancient city in Israel that is mentioned as the host for the Ark of the Covenant (geographical name)

Si Chinese: various, including silk and thought. Also a diminutive form of Simon

Sidney See Sydney

Simone Hebrew: one who hears

Simran Punjabi: prayer, remembrance of god (Sikh name)

Sina An Irish and Scottish variant of Jane

Sky/Skye (name from an English word). Also named from the Isle of Skye in Scotland (geographical name)

Skyler Dutch: scholar

Sonam Tibetan: happy, virtuous. The name of the first official Dalai Lama

Sri Sanskrit: radiant, splendid. Also one of the names of the Hindu goddess Lakshmi

Storm (name from an English word)

Sukhdeep Punjabi: lamp of peace (Sikh name)

Sunny (name from an English word)

Surya Sanskrit: the sun. A Hindu sun god

Sydney Old English: wide island (shifted from surname usage). Also the name of the Australian city (geographical names)

Tadiwa Shona: we are favoured

Tafadzwa Shona: we are pleased, we are happy

Tahseen/Tahsin Arabic: decoration, praise

Tai Chinese: various, including moss

Taiwo A diminutive form of Taiyewo, Yoruba: the first to taste the world (given to the elder twin)

Tanaka Sanskrit: reward. Also Japanese: a common surname with various meanings, including middle of a ricefield

Tanatswa Shona: we have been purified

Tanzim Arabic: organisation

Tate An English surname (shifted from surname usage). Also various places, including a county in the US (geographical name)

Tatenda *See* Tinotenda

Tawana Shona: we have gained. Also Native American: tan hide

Tayla/Tayler/Taylor Old English: to cut (shifted from surname

usage)

Temiloluwa Yoruba: god is mine

Temitayo Yoruba: happiness is mine

Temitope Yoruba: enough to give thanks

Teniola Yoruba: foundation of wealth

Tinashe Shona: god is with us

Tinotenda Shona: thank you

Toby Hebrew: god is good

Tolulope Yoruba: thanks to god

Toluwalase Yoruba: let god's will be done

Toluwani Yoruba: god's own

Treasure (name from an English word term of endearment)

Tyla/Tylah/Tylar/Tyler English: tiler (shifted from surname usage)

Tyne Named from the River Tyne (shifted from surname usage)

W

Wai Cantonese: various

Wan Chinese: various, including meander

Wen Chinese: various, including literature

Wing (name from an English word). Also Cantonese: various, including honour and pride

Wren (name from an English word)

X

Xi Chinese: various, including happy, lucky and playful. *See also* Cy

Xiao Chinese: various, including smiling, dawn and respectful

Xin Chinese: various, including new, full of gold, heart, happy

y

Yi Chinese: various, including meaning, benefit and wings

Ying Chinese: various, including hero, welcoming, plentiful

Yu Chinese: various, including jade, feather and universe

Yuki Japanese: various, including snow

Z

Zhi Chinese: various, including wisdom and knowledge

Zi Chinese: various, including purple

Zion Hebrew: Jerusalem (geographical name)

Double names

Mae, Rose, Lou. Lee, Jay, James. All these make popular combinations with other familiar names to create one longer, more ususal double name. Here you will find a list of tried and tested double name combinations in the UK.

Girls

Abbie-Leigh	Amelia-Rose	Annie-Rose
Abbie-Louise	Amelie-Rose	Ann-Marie
Abbie-Mae	Amie-Leigh	Autumn-Rose
Abbie-May	Ami-Leigh	Ava-Grace
Abi-Leigh	Amy-Jane	Ava-Jane
Aimee-Lee	Amy-Jo	Ava-Leigh
Aimee-Leigh	Amy-Lea	Ava-Lilly
Aimee-Louise	Amy-Lee	Ava-Lily
Aimee-Rose	Amy-Leigh	Ava-Louise
Alana-Rose	Amy-Louise	Ava-Mae
Alicia-May	Amy-May	Ava-Mai
Alisha-May	Amy-Rose	Ava-Marie
Amber-Jade	Ana-Maria	Ava-May
Amber-Leigh	Angel-Marie	Ava-Rae
Amber-Lily	Angel-May	Ava-Rose
Amber-Louise	Angel-Rose	Bailey-Rae
Amber-Marie	Anna-Leigh	Bella-Louise
Amber-May	Anna-Louise	Bella-Mae
Amber-Rose	Anna-Mae	Bella-Mai
Amelia-Grace	Anna-Maria	Bella-Rose
Amelia-Jane	Anna-Marie	Bethany-Ann
Amelia-Jayne	Anna-May	Bethany-Jane
Amelia-Lily	Anna-Rose	Bethany-Louise
Amelia-Mae	Anna-Sophia	Bethany-Rose
Amelia-Mai	Anne-Marie	Billie-Jean
Amelia-May	Annie-May	Billie-Jo

Bobbie-Jo

Bobbie-Leigh

Bobbi-Jo

Brooke-Leigh

Brooke-Louise

Brooke-Marie

Carrie-Ann

Carrie-Anne

Casey-Lee

Casey-Leigh

Casey-Mae

Casey-May

Ceri-Ann

Charley-Ann

Charlie-Ann

Charlie-Anne

Charlie-Louise

Charlie-Mae

Charlie-Marie

Charlie-May

Charlotte-Louise

Charlotte-Rose

Chelsea-Anne

Chelsea-Leigh

Chelsea-Louise

Chelsea-Marie

Chloe-Ann

Chloe-Anne

Chloe-Jayne

Chloe-Leigh

Chloe-Louise

Chloe-Mae

Chloe-Mai

Chloe-Marie

Chloe-May

Chloe-Rose

Codie-Leigh

Connie-Mae

Courtney-Jade

Courtney-Leigh

Courtney-Louise

Daisie-Mae

Daisy-Grace

Daisy-Leigh

Daisy-Lou

Daisy-Mae

Daisy-Mai

Daisy-May

Daisy-Rae

Daisy-Rose

Darcie-Leigh

Darcie-Mae

Darci-May

Darcy-Leigh

Darcy-Mae

Demi-Jo

Demi-Lea

Demi-Lee

Demi-Leigh

Demi-Louise

Demi-Mae

Demi-Mai

Demi-Marie

Demi-May

Demi-Rae

Demi-Rose

Dolly-May

Ebony-Grace

Ebony-Rose

Eden-Rose

Eleanor-Rose

Eliza-Mae

Ella-Grace

Ella-Jade

Ella-Jane

Ella-Louise

Ella-Mae

Ella-Mai

Ella-Marie

Ella-May

Ella-Rae

Ella-Rose

Elle-Louise

Elle-Mae

Elle-Mai

Elle-May

Ellie-Ann

Ellie-Anne

Ellie-Grace

Ellie-Jade

Ellie-Jane

Ellie-Jay

Ellie-Jayne

Ellie-Jean

Ellie-Jo

Ellie-Leigh

Ellie-Louise

Ellie-Mae

Ellie-Mai

Ellie-Marie

Ellie-May

Ellie-Rae

Ellie-Rose

Elli-Mae

Elly-May

Elsie-Mae

Elsie-Mai

Elsie-May

Elsie-Rose

Emilia-Rose

Emily-Grace

Emily-Jade

Emily-Jane

Emily-Jayne

Emily-Jo

Emily-Louise

Emily-Mae

Emily-Mai

Emily-May

Emily-Rose

Emma-Jane

Emma-Jayne

Emma-Jo

Emma-Lee

Emma-Leigh

Emma-Louise

Emma-Rose

Emmie-Lou

Emmie-Mae

Emmie-Rose

Erin-Mae

Erin-May

Erin-Rose

Esme-Rose

Eva-Grace

Eva-Lily

Eva-Mae

Eva-Mai

Eva-Marie

Eva-May

Eva-Rose

Evelyn-Rose

Evie-Grace

Evie-Lea

Evie-Lee

Evie-Leigh

Evie-Louise

Evie-Mae

Evie-Mai

Evie-Marie

Evie-May

Evie-Rae

Evie-Rose

Frankie-Leigh

Frankie-Mae

Freya-Louise

Freya-Mae

Freya-Mai

Freya-May

Freya-Rose

Gemma-Louise

Georgia-Leigh

Georgia-Louise

Georgia-Mae

Georgia-May

Georgia-Rose

Gracey-May

Gracie-Jane

Gracie-Lea

Gracie-Lee

Gracie-Leigh

Gracie-Lou

Gracie-Louise

Gracie-Mae

Gracie-Mai

Gracie-May

Gracie-Rae

Gracie-Rose

Hailie-Jade

Halle-Mae

Hannah-Louise

Hannah-Marie

Hannah-May

Hannah-Rose

Hollie-Mae

Hollie-Mai

Hollie-Marie

Hollie-May

Holly-Ann

Holly-Anne

Holly-Mae

Holly-Marie

Holly-May

Honey-Rose

Imogen-Rose

India-Rose

Indi-Rose

Isabella-Grace

Isabella-Rose

Isla-Grace

Isla-Mae

Isla-Mai

Isla-May

Isla-Rose

Jade-Louise

Jade-Marie

Jaimee-Leigh

Jaime-Lee

Jaime-Leigh

Jamie-Lea

Jamie-Lee

Jamie-Leigh

Jamie-Louise

Jasmine-Rose

Jayme-Leigh

Jaymie-Leigh

Jessica-Jane

Jessica-Leigh

Jessica-Louise

Jessica-Mae

Jessica-May

Jessica-Rose

Jessie-Leigh

Jessie-Mae

Jessie-May

Jodie-Lee

Jodie-Leigh

Jordan-Leigh

Julie-Anne

Kacey-Leigh

Kacey-Mae

Kacey-Mai

Kacey-May

Kacie-Leigh

Kacie-Mae

Kacie-Mai

Kaci-Leigh

Kaci-Louise

Kadie-Leigh

Kara-Leigh

Kara-Louise

Kasey-Leigh

Katie-Ann

Katie-Anne

Katie-Jane

Katie-Jo

Katie-Lea

Katie-Lee

Katie-Leigh

Katie-Louise

Katie-Mae

Katie-Marie

Katie-May

Katie-Rose

Kaycee-Leigh

Kayla-Mae

Kayla-Mai

Kayla-May

Kayla-Rose

Kayleigh-Ann

Kayleigh-Anne

Keira-Lea

Keira-Leigh

Keira-Louise

Kelly-Ann

Kelly-Anne

Kelly-Marie

Kelsey-Leigh

Kelsey-May

Kerri-Ann

Kerri-Anne

Kerry-Ann

Kerry-Anne

Kiera-Leigh

Kitty-Rose

Kyla-Mae

Kyra-Leigh

Lacey-Jane

Lacey-Jayne

Lacey-Jo

Lacey-Leigh

Lacey-Lou

Lacey-Louise

Lacey-Mae

Lacey-Mai

Lacey-Marie

Lacey-May

Lacey-Rae

Lacey-Rose

Lacie-Leigh

Lacie-Louise

Lacie-Mae

Lacie-Mai

Lacie-May

Lacie-Rose

Laila-Mae

Laila-Mai

Laila-May

Laila-Rose

Laura-Beth

Laura-Jane

Laura-Jayne

Layla-Grace

Layla-Jane

Layla-Mae

Layla-Mai

Layla-Marie

Layla-May

Layla-Rae

Layla-Rose

Leah-Grace

Leah-Mae

Leah-Marie

Leah-May

Leah-Rose

Leigh-Ann

Leigh-Anne

Leila-Rose

Lexi-Ann

Lexie-Leigh

Lexie-Louise

Lexie-Mae

Lexie-Mai

Lexie-May

Lexi-Grace
Lexi-Jay
Lexi-Jo
Lexi-Leigh
Lexi-Lou
Lexi-Louise
Lexi-Mae
Lexi-Mai
Lexi-Marie
Lexi-May
Lexi-Rae
Lexi-Rose
Libby-Anne
Libby-Mae
Libby-Mai
Libby-May
Libby-Rose
Lila-Rose
Lili-Mae
Lili-Mai
Lili-Rose
Lilli-Ann
Lillie-Ann
Lillie-Anne
Lillie-Grace
Lillie-Jo
Lillie-Mae
Lillie-Mai
Lillie-May
Lillie-Rose
Lilli-Mae
Lilli-Mai
Lilli-May
Lilli-Rose
Lilly-Ann
Lilly-Anna

Lilly-Anne
Lilly-Ella
Lilly-Grace
Lilly-Jade
Lilly-Jane
Lilly-Jo
Lilly-Louise
Lilly-Mae
Lilly-Mai
Lilly-Marie
Lilly-May
Lilly-Rae
Lilly-Rose
Lilly-Sue
Lily-Ann
Lily-Anna
Lily-Anne
Lily-Belle
Lily-Beth
Lily-Ella
Lily-Grace
Lily-Jane
Lily-Jayne
Lily-Jo
Lily-Louise
Lily-Mae
Lily-Mai
Lily-Marie
Lily-May
Lily-Rae
Lily-Rose
Lily-Sue
Lisa-Marie
Lola-Belle
Lola-Grace
Lola-Mae

Lola-Mai
Lola-May
Lola-Rae
Lola-Rose
Lottie-Rose
Lucie-Mae
Lucie-May
Lucy-Ann
Lucy-Anne
Lucy-Jane
Lucy-Jo
Lucy-Mae
Lucy-May
Lucy-Rose
Lyla-May
Lyla-Rose
Macey-Leigh
Macie-Leigh
Macie-Mae
Madison-Leigh
Maggie-Mae
Maggie-May
Maisey-Leigh
Maisie-Grace
Maisie-Jane
Maisie-Jayne
Maisie-Lee
Maisie-Leigh
Maisie-Louise
Maisie-Mae
Maisie-May
Maisie-Rae
Maisie-Rose
Maisy-Grace
Mary-Ann
Mary-Anne

Mary-Beth
Mary-Jane
Mary-Jayne
Mary-Kate
Maya-Rose
Mckenzie-Leigh
Megan-Louise
Megan-Rose
Mia-Grace
Mia-Jade
Mia-Leigh
Mia-Louise
Mia-Rae
Mia-Rose
Miley-Mae
Miley-Rae
Miley-Rose
Millie-Ann
Millie-Anne
Millie-Grace
Millie-Jane
Millie-Jo
Millie-Louise
Millie-Mae
Millie-Mai
Millie-May
Millie-Rae
Millie-Rose
Milly-May
Mollie-Ann
Mollie-Mae
Mollie-May
Molly-Ann
Molly-Anne
Molly-Jo
Molly-Louise

Molly-Mae
Molly-Mai
Molly-May
Molly-Rose
Morgan-Leigh
Mya-Rose
Nevaeh-Rose
Noor-Fatima
Olivia-Grace
Olivia-Jane
Olivia-Leigh
Olivia-Mae
Olivia-Mai
Olivia-May
Olivia-Rose
Phoebe-Grace
Phoebe-Louise
Phoebe-Rose
Pixie-Lou
Poppy-Jane
Poppy-Leigh
Poppy-Mae
Poppy-Mai
Poppy-May
Poppy-Rae
Poppy-Rose
Rose-Marie
Rosie-Mae
Rosie-Mai
Rosie-May
Rubie-Mae
Ruby-Ann
Ruby-Anne
Ruby-Grace
Ruby-Jane
Ruby-Jean

Ruby-Jo
Ruby-Lea
Ruby-Lee
Ruby-Leigh
Ruby-Lou
Ruby-Louise
Ruby-Mae
Ruby-Mai
Ruby-Marie
Ruby-May
Ruby-Rae
Ruby-Rose
Sally-Ann
Sally-Anne
Samantha-Jayne
Sammi-Jo
Sammy-Jo
Sarah-Jane
Sarah-Jayne
Sarah-Louise
Scarlet-Rose
Scarlett-Louise
Scarlett-Mae
Scarlett-Rose
Shannon-Leigh
Shannon-Louise
Shauna-Leigh
Sienna-Leigh
Sienna-Mae
Sienna-Mai
Sienna-May
Sienna-Rae
Sienna-Rose
Skye-Louise
Skye-Marie
Skyla-Mai

Skyla-Rose
Sky-Louise
Sofia-Rose
Sophia-Louise
Sophia-May
Sophia-Rose
Sophie-Ann
Sophie-Anne
Sophie-Ella
Sophie-Leigh
Sophie-Louise
Sophie-Mae
Sophie-Mai
Sophie-Marie
Sophie-May
Sophie-Rose
Stevie-Leigh
Summer-Grace
Summer-Leigh
Summer-Lily
Summer-Louise

Summer-Mae
Summer-Marie
Summer-May
Summer-Rae
Summer-Rose
Tara-Louise
Tayla-Mae
Taylor-Leigh
Taylor-Mae
Taylor-May
Taylor-Rose
Terri-Ann
Terri-Anne
Terri-Leigh
Tia-Leigh
Tia-Louise
Tia-Mae
Tia-Mai
Tia-Marie
Tia-May
Tiana-Rose

Tia-Rose
Tiffany-Rose
Tiger-Lily
Tillie-Mae
Tillie-Mai
Tillie-May
Tillie-Rose
Tilly-Ann
Tilly-Mae
Tilly-Mai
Tilly-Marie
Tilly-May
Tilly-Rose
Toni-Ann
Toni-Leigh
Toni-Louise
Toni-Marie
Violet-May
Willow-Ros

Boys

Aiden-James
A-Jay
Alex-James
Alfie-George
Alfie-Jack
Alfie-James
Alfie-Jay
Alfie-Joe
Alfie-John
Alfie-Lee

Alfie-Ray
Archie-Lee
Ashton-James
Ashton-Jay
Ashton-Lee
Bailey-James
Bailey-Jay
Billy-Joe
Billy-Ray
Bobby-Jack

Bobby-Joe
Bobby-Lee
Brad-Lee
Brandon-Lee
Callum-James
Cameron-James
Cameron-Lee
Charlie-George
Charlie-James
Charlie-Jay

Charlie-Joe
Charlie-Ray
C-Jay
Cody-James
Cody-Jay
Cody-Lee
Connor-James
Connor-Jay
Connor-Lee
Corey-Jay
Corey-Lee
Daniel-James
Danny-Lee
Dylan-James
Ethan-James
Ethan-Lee
Frankie-Joe
Frankie-Lee
Harley-James
Harley-Jay
Harley-Joe
Harry-James
Harry-Lee
Harvey-James
Harvey-Jay
Harvey-Lee
Hayden-Lee
Jack-James
Jacob-James
Jaiden-Lee
James-Dean
James-Junior
Jamie-Lee
Jayden-James
Jayden-John
Jayden-Lee

Jay-J
Jay-Jay
Jean-Luc
Jean-Paul
Jean-Pierre
Jenson-James
Jesse-James
Jimmy-Lee
J-Jay
John-James
John-Junior
John-Luke
John-Paul
Jon-Luke
Jon-Paul
Jordan-Lee
Joshua-James
Joshua-Lee
Kaiden-Lee
Kayden-James
Kayden-Lee
Kenzie-Lee
Kian-Lee
Ky-Mani
Leo-James
Lewis-James
Logan-James
Logan-Jay
Logan-Lee
Louie-Jay
Luca-James
Lucas-James
Marley-Jay
Mason-James
Mason-Jay
Mason-Lee

Mckenzie-Lee
Michael-John
Muhammad-Ali
Muhammad-Ibrahim
Muhammad-Yusuf
Noah-James
Oliver-James
Ollie-James
Ollie-Jay
Riley-James
Riley-Jay
Riley-Joe
Riley-Scott
Ronnie-Lee
Ryan-Lee
Sean-Paul
Sonny-Lee
Taylor-James
Taylor-Jay
Taylor-Lee
Tee-Jay
Thomas-James
Thomas-Jay
Thomas-Lee
T-Jay
Tommy-Jay
Tommy-Joe
Tommy-Lee
Tyler-James
Tyler-Jay
Tyler-Joe
Tyler-John
Tyler-Lee

Less common names

Here you will find a list of names from different UK heritages that are commonly used.

Cornish, Gaelic and Manx

Girls

Aalid/Aelid: The Manx word for beauty

Aalin: The Manx word for beautiful

Achall: A princess from Irish mythology

Adwen: The Cornish Saint Adwen. It has the same connotations as Saint Valentine, and is associated with love and romance

Afina: The Cornish word for beautify

Aibell/Aoibheall: A fairy queen in Irish mythology

Ailstreena: The feminine form of Alister

Aimel: The Manx word for beloved

Aimend: A princess from Irish mythology, and possibly a sun goddess

Ainle: The Manx word for angel

Andrasta: A Celtic goddess of war worshipped by Boudica

Anta: The Cornish village of Lelanta is named after Saint Anta

Arduinna: A Celtic goddess of the moon worshipped by the Gauls

Aveta: A Celtic mother goddess worshipped by the Gauls

Banba: The patron goddess of Ireland

Berriona/Berryan: The Cornish Saint Berriona was originally from Ireland

Blae: the Manx word for flower

Bleujen: The Cornish word for flower

Breaca: The Cornish Saint Breaca enjoyed the solitary life

Briallen: The Cornish word for primrose

Canola: The woman who invented the harp from Irish mythology

Carola: The Manx word for noble

Cessair/Kesair: A granddaughter of Noah and a leader in Irish mythology who came to Ireland before the Flood

Cethlion: A prophetess in Irish mythology

Cissolt: The Manx variant of Cecilia

Creena: Wise

Damara: A fertility goddess with

associations to May

Damona: A Celtic goddess, possibly associated with cows, worshipped by the Gauls

Danu: An Irish mother goddess

Darva: The Cornish word for place of oaks

Doona: Dark maiden

Ealee: The Manx word for noble

Emblyn: A Cornish variant of Emmeline

Eseld: A Cornish variant of Isolde

Eunys: The Manx word for joy

Feena: The Manx word for fair maiden

Gilmurr: The Manx variant of Gilmore

Gweder: The Cornish word for glass, mirror

Gwennel: The Cornish word for swallow

Hedra: The Cornish word for October

Kaja: The Cornish word for daisy

Kelemmi: The Cornish word for doves

Kelynn: The Cornish word for holly

Keresen (Keres): The Cornish word for cherry (cherries)

Kesseni: The Cornish word for harmonise

Krysi: The Cornish word for belief

Lailie: The Manx variant of Elizabeth

Lasair: A spring goddess of growth, and Latiaran's sister

Latiaran: A goddess of harvest, and Lasair's sister

Malane: The Manx variant of Magdelene

Margaid: The Manx variant of Margaret

Meave: She who intoxicates (a queen of Connacht)

Mellyon: The Cornish word for violets, clovers

Morel: The Cornish word for jet black

Moren: The Cornish word for maiden

Mureal: Sea bright

Nessa: The Manx word for secret

Paaie: The Manx variant of Peggy

Ranhilda: The Manx word for god's fight

Rew: The Cornish word for ice, frost

Roseen: The Manx word for little rose

Rosmerta: A Celtic goddess of fire and wealth, worshipped by the Gauls

Sewena: The Cornish word for success

Sirona: A Celtic goddess of astronomy, worshipped by the Gauls

Tosha: The Manx word for the first

Vorana: The Manx word for great

Wenna: The Cornish Saint Wenna married Salomon of Cornwall, a warrior prince

Boys

Abarta: One of the gods belonging to the Danu race

Asmund: A Manx name meaning a gift from the gods

Austell/Austol: The Cornish Saint Austell was a friend of Saint Mewan

Avalloc: Father of the goddess Modron

Brentin/Bryntin: Grand, noble, splendid

Breward: The Cornish Saint Breward travelled widely. Some places in Brittany and the Channel Islands may be named after him

Cador: A Cornish king and duke who raised Guinevere in Arthurian legends

Carbry: The Manx word for love

Corentin: Saint Corentin is associated with a miraculous fish that would regrow itself after being eaten

Dalleth: The Cornish word for beginning

Delen: The Cornish word for leaf

Derowen/Derwen: The Cornish word for oak

Esus: A Celtic god of agriculture worshipped by the Gauls

Faragher: The Manx variant of Fergus

Gilrea: A Manx name meaning king's servant

Golan: The Cornish word for seagull

Gwelsen: The Cornish word for blade of grass

Gwenen: The Cornish word for bee

Gwener: The Cornish word for Friday

Illiam: The Manx word for defender

Kalester: The Cornish word for pebble

Karrek: The Cornish word for rock

Kasor: The Cornish word for warrior

Kesten: The Cornish word for chestnuts

Kurun: The Cornish word for crown

Loer: The Cornish word for moon

Lowender: The Cornish word for mirth

Luhesen: The Cornish word for lightning

Mabon: From King Arthur's band of warriors, also known for being a god of hunting

Massen: A Cornish variant of Maximus

Mewan: The Cornish Saint Mewan was a friend of Saint Austell

Mordonn: A Cornish name meaning sea wave

Nuadu: A god of healing, also known as the Silver Hand

Seonaidh/Shoney: A water spirit, possibly a Scottish variant of the name John

Sether: The Cornish word for archer

Stoill: A Manx name meaning with
  a will
Trumach: The Cornish word for sea
  voyage

Other names

Girls

Abeba Amharic: flower

Adey Amharic: a type of yellow daisy

Adowa Amharic: noble

Adsila Cherokee: blossom

Ailen Mapuche: hot coal

Ailin Mapuche: clear

Algoma Native American: valley of flowers

Amareche Amharic: she is beautiful

Amitola Native American: rainbow

Angeni Native American: spirit

Awendela Native American: morning

Bedelwa Amharic: with her luck

Catori Hopi: spirit

Chaska Quechua: star, Venus

Chilaili Native American: snowbird

Cholena Native American: bird

Desta Amharic: happy, joyful

Eluney Mapuche: gift

Hermona Amharic: into the palace

Hopa Lakota: beautiful

Huyana Miwok: falling rain

Illary Quechua: rainbow

Iracema Tupí: from honey

Itatí Guaraní: white stone

Jalene Oromo: we loved

Jember Amharic: horizon

Killa Quechua: moon

Kimimela Sioux: butterfly

Koko Blackfoot: night

Lalla Oromigna: tulip

Lelo Oromigna: grace

Leotie Native American: flower of the prairie

Litonia Miwok: darting hummingbirds

Magena Native American: moon

Maka Sioux: earth

Malén Mapuche: young lady

Miniya Tigrigna: I expect much of her

Mirabe Amharic: west

Nadie Algonquin: wise

Nita Choctaw: bear

Ogin Native American: wild rose

Olathe Native American: beautiful

Orenda Iroquois: magic power

Pavati Hopi: clear water

Persinna A queen of Ethiopia

Poloma Choctaw: bow

Rayen Mapuche: flower

Rozene Native American: rose

Satinka Native American: magical dancer

Sihu Hopi: flower

Silluka Quechua: beautiful fingernails

Sisika Native American: bird

Sosina/Sosinna Amharic: rose

Soyala Hopi: winter solice

Taima Native American: thunder

Tica Quechua: flower

Tiva Hopi: dance
Tizita Amharic: memory

Yana Quechua: dark, beloved
Zema Amharic: melody

Boys

Abellio A god of apples worshipped
in what is now the Garonne Valley
in France
Abera Amharic: he shines
Alem Amharic: world
Alo Hopi: spiritual guide
Altan Mongolian: gold
Baslios Amharic: a king of Ethiopia
Brehan Amharic: light
Cono Mapuche: dove
Cusi Quechua: joy
Dagim Amharic: again, a second
time
Dejen Amharic: foundation, pillar,
support
Diyami Native American: eagle
Elsu Native American: falcon
Esen Mongolian: good health
Girum Amharic: great, wonderful
Hassun Algonquin: stone
Hatun Quechua: big
Hodari Swahili: clever, strong, brave
Inti Aymara: skillful
Iskinder Amharic: defender of men
Jasiri Swahili: bold, brave
Kele Hopi: sparrow
Kitchi Algonquin: brave
Lebna Amharic: heart
Len Hopi: flute

Liben Amharic: a king of Ethiopia
Maren Amharic: spare us
Mato Lakota: bear
Mesfin Amharic: duke
Paco Native American: eagle
Senay Ge'es: gift from above
Skah Sioux: white
Songan Native American: strong
Takoda Sioux: friends with everyone
Traful Mapuche: union
Viho Cheyenne: chief
Wayra Quechua: like the wind
Wowita Lakota: glory

UK £7.99